LITTLE PLATOONS

A Defense of Family in a Competitive Age

MATT FEENEY

BASIC BOOKS
NEW YORK

Basic Books
Hachette Book Group
1290 Avenue of the Americas, New York, NY 10104
www.basicbooks.com

Printed in the United States of America
First Edition: March 2021

Published by Basic Books, an imprint of Perseus Books, LLC, a subsidiary of Hachette Book Group, Inc. The Basic Books name and logo is a trademark of the Hachette Book Group.

The Hachette Speakers Bureau provides a wide range of authors for speaking events. To find out more, go to www.hachettespeakersbureau.com or call (866) 376-6591.

The publisher is not responsible for websites (or their content) that are not owned by the publisher.

Print book interior design by Linda Mark

Library of Congress Cataloging-in-Publication Data
Names: Feeney, Matt, author.
Title: Little platoons : a defense of family in a competitive age / Matt Feeney.
Description: First edition. | New York : Basic Books, [2021] | Includes
    bibliographical references and index.
Identifiers: LCCN 2020030905 | ISBN 9781541645592 (hardcover) |
    ISBN 9781541645585 (ebook)
Subjects: LCSH: Parenting—United States. | Families—United States. |
    Competition (Psychology)—Social aspects. | Social status.
Classification: LCC HQ755.8 .F426 2021 | DDC 306.850973—dc23
LC record available at https://lccn.loc.gov/2020030905

ISBNs: 978-1-5416-4559-2 (hardcover), 978-1-5416-4558-5 (ebook)

LSC-C

Printing 1, 2021

LITTLE PLATOONS

To my parents

Contents

Introduction

M Y WIFE JULIET AND I WERE MARRIED IN A FAIRLY modern, nontraditional way, standing under a pair of California redwoods in the front yard of her parents' shambling ranch house in a humble corner of the Oakland Hills, in an unreligious ceremony officiated by a tall unclerical woman discovered, if I remember correctly, on Craigslist. I was wearing the nicest suit I've ever owned, but it was a suit, not a tux, and deep green, not black, and Juliet was in a lovely but subtle and casual vintage Valentino dress, white cotton with a faint pattern of lavender flowers, that she bought for a hundred bucks in a consignment store in Northwest DC. Of course we wrote our own vows—we had no church or tradition to pre-scribe vows to us—and I will admit that, though I am a writer, I had to look on the internet for tips, a general template, specific ceremonial beats I ought to hit.

It's been nearly twenty years since then. I can't remember the actual words I said, much less the models I used from those long-dead internet pages, but I remember being drawn to the old-fashioned, vaguely heroic formulations, the ones that set the

touchy-feeliness aside in favor of stout and straightforward dec-
larations of commitment, vows that seemed to relish in the self-
negating, do-or-die logic of vowing itself. This vowing business
struck me as, in the deepest and most dignified sense, political.
When else, I thought, does one get to found a political body, bind
oneself to a common destiny through a sovereign declaration?

Thus inspired, I took the vowing language I read and amped
it up just a little, sharpened it here and there, so that its antino-
mian political edge would be, if not over-apparent to our guests
as they heard it, palpable to me as I said it. And so, for the cli-
mactic exchange of self-written vows in our modern and secular
California wedding ceremony, Juliet pledged herself to me in
light, loving terms that made specific reference to my tender
side, my sensitivities and idiosyncrasies, while I—as it seemed
in my mind, anyway, and as it felt in my chest—pledged myself
to her like a Viking.

I won't dwell on this idea of a family as a little band or polis
founded by death-suggesting vows. I will simply begin from the
assumption, which strikes me as not just true but obviously so,
that that's what a family is. For starters, that's what a marriage
is. That's what vowing is. Not every vow summons death as its
standard or limit. Not every vow mortifies your life as such. But
every vow does mortify your interests and desires, everything
that, in defiance of its terms, you might find yourself wanting.
And a vow that explicitly mentions death, a vow that binds you
to another person "until death"? You can't deny there's a certain
fatality to that one.

This might sound morbid, like I'm arguing *against* getting
married because of its close associations with death, but most
people who consciously, ceremonially, speak serious vows don't

feel the death-dare they entail as morbid. They feel it, rather, as a sort of ecstasy. It's a beautiful thing, to release your self from itself, to offer it as a sacrifice to something bigger. Besides, getting married is a pretty luxurious version of this, if you think about it, sort of a best-of-both-worlds situation. You get to experience the ecstatic loss of self that comes with this depth of commitment, the thrilling plunge into a deeper way of being, but, unlike entering the Marines, say, the ritual summoning of death in a wedding doesn't actually summon death. You're not committing yourself to ship into war zones to fight and die for your fellow Marines. You're committing yourself to be good and faithful to a person you love and probably find physically lovely, who loves you and finds your physical person appealing, too, where enacting your heroic self-renunciation in the daily run of life involves such things as sharing meals, having conversations, making love, raising children.

But this daily run of life involves unfriendlier things too, in light of which the fighting spirit that overcame me as I wrote my wedding vows seems entirely fitting. Indeed, when I shared some initial reflections on these matters with a handful of friends and colleagues—my ideas about the heroic side of the wedding commitment, how it had made me think those odd thoughts of Vikings—their earnest reactions surprised me. These were bookish people, several of them academics and not, say, Marines or members of some other warlike clan you might expect to have a benign view of Vikings. A few of them, independently of each other, quoted a formulation back to me that I hadn't actually formulated: "The Viking Wedding."

This fighting spirit—which I entertained as a sort of poetic lark at the time, the romantic indulgence of a man not just aswim in romantic love but academically trained in Romantic philosophy—turns out to have real-world applications. The wedding vows themselves are a sort of fighting declaration, and the things to which they commit us as spouses and parents often involve a barely metaphorical kind of fighting. Couples "fight for" their kids. In hard times they "fight for" their marriage, which might involve "fighting" temptation. And they "fight for" their family, inwardly or outwardly, in myriad ways that may not even be recognizable to them, at the time, as fighting.

For example: I don't remember how I thought of my first few days of fatherhood as they happened, but in retrospect I could see that the mood I'd been in much of the time was a fighting one. Juliet had given birth to our first daughter after a frustrating two-day labor but in a fairly speedy and healthy-seeming delivery. One thing I thought odd and maybe cute but not alarming during the delivery was that the baby emerged with her head accompanied by one arm, mashed vertical against her ear, as if the little hand were pointing to a hypothetical sky. Now, newborns have flexible joints, and this was no threat to either her arm or her head, but it meant that the arm was not tucked along the rib cage when the torso emerged, which, in turn, meant her lungs received a lesser squeeze. This, anyway, is what our delivery nurse suggested could be the reason our daughter failed to empty enough amniotic fluid from her lungs to begin her life outside her mother's body as babies are supposed to, that is, crying and breathing, crying and breathing. Instead, she began her life shallowly gulping and sucking after air in what resembled desperate little hiccups.

I don't want to make too much of this, as parental trauma or whatever. That I'm using it as an example means I've been very lucky so far. Were I less lucky, a friend's story of sitting through his son's heart surgery might be mine, or a cousin's story of lovingly nursing her first daughter, also born with a faulty heart, through a single year of life, or another friend's story of the twins she gave birth to at thirty weeks, who—as one of them told my kids—were born "the size of Coke cans." This was about the size of the boy in the big incubator next to my daughter's baby-sized ventilator in the NICU. She lay there for two days, my daughter, a tiny catheter slipped through each nostril into each lung, an oxygen line taped under her nose, gaining a new margin of depth in her breathing every five or six hours, a higher decimal on her blood-oxygen monitor, while the worry the doctors put inside my head about pneumonia, about her lungs needing to clear before the microbes took over, bloomed like its own infection.

So I was in a sort of fighting state over those first days of fatherhood. This was an abstract kind of fighting, obviously. There was nothing concrete for me to take on. I'm not a physician, and, anyway, the physicians had done what they could. After the first couple hours they were just checking in. It was the catheters' job to keep those minuscule dribbles of fluid moving from her lungs, which they did slowly and haltingly, and with so little force that at times the fluid actually reversed course.

It would perhaps be melodramatic to say my daughter was "fighting for her life," but in a routine way it's the truth. She was struggling for each breath, her eight-pound body plugging along, muscling after more air than it could have, a little engine that would, if only. Looking down at her from my designated dad's spot in the NICU, I experienced a sort of confirmation, much realer and grimmer than I'd have preferred, of those poetical thoughts on family and fighting I'd had as I wrote and spoke my wedding vows.

I have not gotten into any fistfights since becoming a father, but, I have to admit, I've sort of been looking for one. When you speed past the family in the crosswalk instead of yielding to their legal and sentimental right of way, for instance, I'm the dad who glares an angry challenge onto your face through your side window, perhaps mouthing something that starts with the lower lip pinned under the upper teeth. Or at least I was when my kids were little. This may run in my family. Long before I had kids my oldest brother told me that when he brought his first child out into the world for the first time, the rush of protectiveness he felt was so strong and feral it was like he *wanted* a threat to show itself, so he'd have something to go after. I've known the feeling.

I usually regret my pugnacious moments, and civilizing this side of my disposition is continuing work, but these things have a softer and more general analog that I don't renounce. The profound meaning and distinctive pleasures of family life are inextricably tied to the feelings of loyalty and solidarity that grow within it—the deep assumption that, confronted by life's challenges, we will *stick together, as a family*. In a realm of laws, where people reasonably view social peace as a founding aim of common life, the fighting loyalty of family members to each other poses obvious problems. But its tension with larger social forces is what makes family feeling indispensable, as I see it. Our gut-level connections with our filial band, as compared with our generalized obligations to our fellow citizens and our counterparties in market exchange, are not just rewarding in themselves but a useful reminder that the modern way of ordering our sentiments isn't the only way, or necessarily the best.

To these other social forms the unique intensity of family relations stands as bracing counterpoint: siblings seeing each other as secret keepers and protectors and protégés, parents curiously, consciously willing to *die* (and, if it came to it, kill) to protect their children. Where else, besides in family life, does your connection to other selves entail such ready renunciation of your own? Where else, besides in parenthood, does your interest in other people's success and survival take the form of such total identification, where it's your job to feel risks to your kids as risks to you, where harm to them is harm to you? Where else do your human connections entail such feelings of vulnerability and exposure?

But here's where it gets tricky for families. When these deep bonds are viewed in contrast to other social relations, their suggestions of self-renunciation and total sacrifice stand out as dire and beautiful, heroic even. But when the fierce commitment of parents to their children takes the form of competition with other parents and other children, it becomes much less heroically strange, much more run-of-the-mill. The status of families as existentially different sorts of human bonds, compared to the normal systems of social life, becomes a profile of families scrabbling against each other for margins of advantage. That is, families in competition with each other form just another normal system.

And here is where it gets a little rueful and complicated for me as a writer, conservative in his intellectual past and still somewhat traditionalist in his background sentiments and philosophical instincts. At a certain scale, under certain conditions, competition among families starts to undermine a key aspect of conservative social thought. In Britain and America especially,

conservative thinkers have tended to celebrate sources of authority and identity and loyalty that exist beneath and prior
to state and nation. (Conservatism in continental Europe, by
contrast, is more explicitly religious and nationalist, generally.)
From American and British conservatives you hear such phrases
as "spontaneous order," "organic community," "civil society,"
"voluntary associations," "intermediate associations." These
expressions refer to the sort of smaller-scale human groupings
that form themselves without the help or sanction of a central
government and, also, serve as a check against the manipulative and coercive impulses of the central government. The most
basic and sturdy of these associations—these "little platoons,"
in Edmund Burke's exquisite phrase—is of course the family.
For Burke and Alexis de Tocqueville, two major influences on
Anglo-American conservative thought, these associations are
understood to preserve the freedom of citizens from control and
coercion by central authority. Because they have family bonds
and village associations, churches and social clubs and sporting
clubs, people have less need to approach the central government for sustenance and social connection. The less they rely
on government authority and largesse to satisfy their needs, the
less government authority can demand their compliance and
conformity. For liberal and progressive readers this "voluntary
association" business probably has an archaic if not reaction-
ary feel to it, but writers such as Timothy Carney and Yuval
Levin have argued persuasively that intermediate bodies such as
churches and clubs still play a vital role, especially where jobs
and social stability, and hope, have fled.[1]

What happens, though, when citizens direct their suspicion
not at a coercive government but at their peers, with whom they

find or feel themselves, as parents and families, in competition? I join a chorus of scholars and writers in observing that such a competitive mood abides among parents today.[2] Less noticed is how such competition creates new forms of subservience and conformity among families. In this environment, the intermediate bodies of civil society, cornerstone of the conservative theory of republican liberty, sometimes become demanding bosses, taskmasters, and gatekeepers in the enterprise of winning advantage for our children in a system of zero-sum competition.

It's not that parents today think of their immediate neighbors as direct antagonists in some Hunger Games scenario — at least not the parents I (think I) know. Rather, they play their competitive role simply in absorbing the ambient notion that kids need a leg up to be successful these days. They express their formative agency by arming their children with skills and tools and résumé items. They identify (perhaps optimistically) latent talents in these children and, through a program of training and improvement, try to optimize them. They may not do all or even most of these things, and they may do them haphazardly rather than systematically. But they do what they can, and, knowing that some of their fellow parents are going all out, they color in the difference with self-rebuke and extra worry. There's always more they could be doing.

Under these conditions, the anxious and competitive citizen-parent looks to certain "voluntary associations," certain institutions within "civil society," not as bulwarks against coercive government but as ways to gain advantage over other families, exclusive paths to better futures. From boutique preschools to competitive sports clubs to selective colleges and universities, desirable institutions become bidding objects for future-worried and status-conscious families. It is now common among both scholars of inequality and writers on family life to lament how this dynamic increases inequality, how better-off families claim another layer of advantages through this competition. Who's better equipped to play this game than parents who can pay their way into these institutions, or buy competitive advantages such as private tutoring or coaching?

But an underappreciated side of this competition is the leverage it cedes to these institutions. With families bidding for the advantages they can provide, the private clubs and schools of civil society can set greater and subtler conditions of participation. In the most blatant terms, these institutions can and do ask for money — discretionary gifts and other payments beyond the nominal fees. As I'll describe in Chapter 2, this is a well-known practice in certain high-class preschool environments, and money figures in pretty much all the institutional relationships I describe. But advantaged, educated, and ambitious parents have other things besides money to offer these institutions. Perhaps more basically, they have their outsized feelings of agency, their belief in their own power, and their willingness — informed by their anxious awareness of the stakes — to work.

As Annette Lareau documents these differences in her landmark book *Unequal Childhoods*, modern parents, especially better-off and -educated parents, differ from their own parents and grandparents, as well as from less-advantaged parents today, in how they throw themselves into the job of child-rearing. From the first queasy hints of pregnancy to the wrenching parental rite of college graduation, raising a bourgeois kid has become a total thing. There's so much information available, so many parenting tools, so much insight and advice from kid science and brain science, from BabyCenter and Moms.com. Of course, when it's your kid, the *ability* to do things that might be conducive to their future success translates into the felt *obligation* to do these things. In other words, the presence of all this advice, the swelling of our parental agency thanks to all this helpful knowledge, makes us parents guiltier and more anxious. To learn of possible pathways to success for your children is also to imagine new routes—should you be lazy or remiss in applying this knowledge—to failure. The crude parental logic of this is: *do more*. Do as much as you can, because among the many things you're now empowered by knowing is that there are a lot of parents out there who are doing as much as *they* can.

As a measure of how modern parenting seems to require this more-is-more logic, consider two trends that have risen together: the working time of educated women, and the time spent in direct parenting by both mothers and fathers—but especially mothers. College-educated mothers spend more time in salaried work than their own mothers did, on average, and then, when they come home, they also spend more time attending to their children than their mothers did.[3] Where in these busy days does this new parenting time come from? Parents, mainly mothers, can apparently alchemize it into being from other substances, such as sleep.

It's not just the amount of time devoted to parenting that's increased, but the conscious intensity of the parenting as well. For those who live or move amid the community of bourgeois parents in America, and especially for those who were parented differently themselves, the intentional, systematic, unremitting *activity* of parenting is a conspicuous if not comic feature of

life. The underlying impulse manifests in small ways, but ubiq-
uitously. Perhaps informed by an NPR piece about the developmental advantages of exposing kids to an abundance of words,
for example, many bourgeois moms and dads practice a method
of parenting that might be called *never shutting up*. Like some
combination of baby-talk David Attenborough and preschool
Socrates, these parents keep up a ceaseless patter of narration
and questioning as they drive or stroll or handhold their little ones around town, or sit with them at bakeries and burrito
stands. "Your cookie was made from flour and butter. The flour
is made from wheat. The butter is made from milk. Do you
remember where milk comes from?" "You have one taco and I
have *two* tacos. If I gave you *my* tacos, how many tacos would
you have?"

Having your little kid in front of you, and being burdened
with this new knowledge about words, and having a sense of your
formative potential as someone with an adult-sized vocabulary,
and faced with this combination of nervous parental energy and
all these gawping silences you might fill pedagogically—these
things are enough to bring an endless stream of vaguely instruc-
tional chitter-chatter out of your mouth. I've spent years observing this, and, of course, I spent years doing it myself.

Funny as it is to observe, I've come increasingly to see these
gently overwrought ways of parental engagement as *output*, an
expression of this optimizing, more-is-more logic. They are an
early signal of just how much parenting we modern parents are
ready to do. Are these silences that parents are so desperate to
fill also, as the awful phrase has it, "teachable moments"? Dude,
every moment is a teachable moment. The future will be one of
countless teachable moments you're either seizing or wasting.

The lazier parents of earlier generations were leaving so much young potential unaddressed, untended, untaught. It's not that it's not nice or pleasant, this hands-on parenting. I probably enjoyed my time with my young kids more because I was so powerfully *intent* on them, and my sweet memories of that time are surely more vivid thanks to the manic states of hyperawareness in which I spent it. Nor is it useless, as a formative method, though the most reliable ways in which it's helpful might surprise parents eagerly building their kids' mental powers with early challenges and enrichments. In other words, setting simple math problems for your little kids and then waiting for them to solve those problems adds less to their cognitive math powers than to their noncognitive motivation and endurance, their tolerance for sitting with the minor discomfort of tackling mental tasks, their willingness to be messed with by authority figures. In any case, this sort of early engagement shows how readily parents will up their effort, increase their output, especially when the future they're launching their children into looks like a scary time of high competition.

And when this effort is directed toward institutions ostensibly useful in this project of conquering the future, then our dire and beautiful commitment to our children can transform itself into compliance and conformity. Parents' identification with their children can become identification with the institutions that dispense—or rather, are *reputed* to dispense—the best advantages. This fierce commitment, so expressed, gives institutions surprising leverage. Families are bidding against each other, with effort and money and agreeableness, to be allowed in. They're also teaching their children the habits of tactical pliancy that they exhibit in these crucial moments.

You might think that American civil society, the array of voluntary associations that conservatives celebrate, might ease these bidding pressures. A key feature of these bodies, after all, is often their sheer numerousness, the many liberating choices they offer the free citizen. And the number and variety of such bodies are indeed remarkable. In the United States bookish pastors wandered the land founding colleges in places that weren't even United States yet, technically. It has over 2,500 four-year colleges. Two thousand five hundred college choices! With that in mind, parents can just chill out about college admissions, can't they? Their kid will find a place. For my part, as a graduate of no-repute Central Michigan University who learned and grew a ton during those five and a half years, I know that a curious kid can fashion a good education almost anywhere. But these many options do not have equal value to applicants and their parents, and the value they do have is not really based on the amounts of "good education" the schools might provide anyway. It's based on something else. America's bounty of colleges has sorted itself into a pyramid, a status hierarchy.

But the schools aren't just sitting around, content with their place in this pyramid, sure their current ranking is safe. Like families, they're anxious and ambitious. They're neurotically aware of this status game they're tangled in. They're constantly trying to improve their position, burnish their institutional profile. The alternative is losing their position, slipping down the pyramid. My dear old Central Michigan would like to become Michigan State in people's minds, as Bowdoin would like to be Amherst, but not nearly as keenly as Michigan State and Amherst want *not* to be Central Michigan and Bowdoin. This institutional psychology expresses itself in marketing, branding, image-mongering. More prestigious colleges want their distinctness from less prestigious colleges to be vivid and salient in the minds of high school students and their parents. High school students and their parents have strong incentives to take the results of this image competition at face value, and to seek the highest-possible place in the status pyramid it generates. Thanks to college guides and the internet, everybody has the same information now. Everybody knows the rankings, which makes the rankings more exact in their status meaning. And if prestige is the most important criterion, and prestige is in part a function of the number of schools below you in the rankings, then more total choices means more prestige, more desirability, for the top ones. The larger number of options doesn't ease the competitive pressure in this type of status wrangling. It intensifies it.

In other regions of civil society, too, the abundance of options can make things more rather than less stressful for parents. In certain preschool environments, parental worry about simply getting kids into a preschool turns into worry about getting them into the *best* preschool, thanks to the teasing pedagogical claims of the preschools themselves. Parents who've put their kids into club sports face a constant temptation to move over to a different club or up to a better one, for more playing time or better exposure to college coaches. And those who stay lament how mercenary and unstable the club cultures are, parents and players ever comparing their options, restlessly hopping about.

Parents, anxiously involved in this calculating and choosing, are readily put to work by these institutions. Just as they're eager to fill the empty minutes of early child-rearing with pedagogical mumbling and other hypothetical brain stimulation, parents remain on call throughout the nineteen school years.

Institutions, noting this parental readiness to work, and feeling the leverage they have as dispensers of marginally better advantages, and having many functions to fill, turn to these parents and say, "OK. Do this. Take this job. Fill this need in our organization with your effort and your time and your money."

Now, this sort of voluntarist participation might sound kind of healthy, especially to the conservative who champions civil society. And I admit I still respect the theory and affirm some of its practical expressions. But in the context of family competition, and especially competition related to college admissions, it takes on certain obligatory features, something of a compulsory feel. When they serve as stepping-stones to educational advantage, or attractive lines on a college application, our "voluntary associations" become, if not *in*voluntary, then sort of semi-voluntary. Sure we can opt out of them, but only with the nagging feeling of paying a long-term cost in competitive viability, achievement points, future-mastery. Many of the institutions we deal with throughout our children's lives extract our effort to varying degrees, but college admissions is worth considering in particular since it is the consummation of all prior efforts. Moreover, the terms it's able to set for participation are the most intimate and presumptuous, and, with these invasive methods, it raises the sharpest and darkest questions about institutional power.

What children and parents are doing as they curate extracurricular selves and labor over cutesy essays and take on more AP classes than there's time to study for is not educational, either by design or, generally, in effect. It is administrative, and disciplinary. With the effort they put into admissions, families are performing the administrative functions of distant bureaucracies. Applicants are induced to generate information, largely irrelevant to the core matter of their ability to succeed academically at a given college. This information helps college admissions offices do their jobs more effectively—qualified applicants struggling to make themselves more legible than the other qualified applicants by, as admissions personnel sometimes say, "standing out."

These procedures increase the influence of the admissions bureaucracies both within their colleges and upon the home lives and personalities of their applicants. With their college admissions efforts, then, these empowered American parents and their striving children concede the real power to the admissions office.

For years, the admissions departments of desirable schools had more power over applicants than they realized. Even before the "admissions crunch" of the early 1990s, when application numbers began to explode, a vague sense was growing among ambitious college applicants that they might help themselves by striving against each other, but this competition was intuitive and unsystematic. Kids added extracurriculars as a competitive mood set in, a general worry that fine grades and high scores might not be enough to get them into the best schools. Then they added more as this worry fed into itself and the competitive mood intensified, and they began to hedge their bets by applying to more and more schools. Gradually, admissions people came to grasp that the selection power this competition had given them was also a deep and subtle sort of moral power. With their flattering abundance of applications, they could now tell their applicants which extracurriculars were *better*, and which sorts of personal confessions were more pleasing in admissions essays, which sorts of person, as manifest in these essays and extracurriculars, they liked more. They could now induce their applicants to become such people. You might think these admissions people weren't actually *telling* their applicants to change themselves to serve their evolving administrative needs, weren't consciously using their newfound leverage to manipulate teenagers. You might see their heightened influence as merely incidental, which it was, at first. But recent initiatives from the admissions world, promoted as raising the ethical pitch of the process, show that they know now how much power they have, and they like having this power. They want more of it, because, for some reason, they think they earned it.

This parallels the emergence of another powerful force confronting parents and families today: digital technology, networked computers, tablets and smartphones—the linked array of machines and behaviors I call "the internet." Like the machinery of college admissions, the internet gathered its power from the busy output of individual people before anyone quite grasped how great this power was, or how to optimize it through conscious design. Observers, entrepreneurs, engineers, and venture capitalists knew the surge of human output through these digital channels was somehow consequential, indeed epochal, a massive new stage in the history of human behavior and business possibility. It *had* to be a big deal, this explosion of activity on the internet, this hybrid system of people and machines. But what *kind* of big deal would it be? Would it be newspapers making huge profits via some not-yet-divined business model? Would it be selling groceries? Pizza? Dog food? It turned out that the biggest deal by far, business-wise, wasn't the virtual versions of these age-old ways of making money. It was an entirely new way of making money, built from the very thing that was building the internet—us, people, users. It was the activity itself.

Well before they knew how it would make their business viable, the founding geniuses of Google intuited that the deep imperative of a search engine had to be maximizing the users' own production. Searches would be refined by data, and data would be produced via movements of users' fingers. Users would contribute to Google Power by creating data, typing away like little data clerks in reverse, generating rather than retrieving information, initially, and then generating more when they eventually retrieved some for themselves. Unlike its competitor Yahoo, with its busy home page of blue links, Google based its user experience on a goading blankness. A struggling company with no real revenue model, leaned on by investors to start making some damn money finally, Google was dogmatic about this blankness. Its founders *refused* to muck up their page with banner ads and other eye diversions. The point of Google was *search search search*, which is to say: harvesting data about searchers. For the user, the searcher, there was nothing to do when you got to the Google page but start typing. Then after the typing there was the clicking, which was at least as precisely confessional as the typing. When the commodity value of our data was revealed, most famously and lucratively by AdWords, Google's automated program for targeted advertising, the builders of the internet experience were electrified with business purpose.[4] They now had a trillion-dollar incentive to hack the clicking and scrolling instincts inside our brains, which we were already revealing through our early thralldom to the primitive, undesigned internet of the nineties. They would do this by combining the unglamorous trades of computer programming and rat-lab psychology into something known as "behavioral design" at Stanford University, where it's taught.

Like the other zones of family striving, digital technology has a sort of bait-and-switch character: what seems like a way to increase your power leaves you entangled with and bound to an outside system, which somehow gains in its power over you as you express your agency through it. Like the general system of family competition, digital technology presents itself as inescapable. In its unstoppable momentum, the internet poses a choice to families that feels more like an obligation: "Are you going into the future with us or are you gonna stay stuck in the past?" And so, reluctantly or not, we hitch ourselves to this force, hoping to increase our powers and those of our kids by merging them with *its* powers.

As I mentioned above, the main functional benefit of modern hands-on parenting is not that it makes kids smarter but that it makes them better at sitting still and sticking with the irksome tasks that schools, colleges, and employers will assign to them throughout their lives. On one hand, we'll be reassured that, if we're parenting in this way, we're giving our kids a marginally better chance at a successful life. On the other hand, we might be a little chagrined at the idea that the selection needs of college bureaucrats and the behavioral preferences of corporate managers have come to inform our parenting methods, that their priorities have somehow taken up residence in our home lives, as our priorities. For my part, as a fretful and yet skeptical and contentious dad, I'm open to both the reassurance and the chagrin. I'll want my younger daughter to succeed as a good corporate team member, if that's the job she wants and gets, the track she ends up on. But the idea that, unwittingly but systematically, we *raised her to be a good corporate team member* might complicate my fatherly pride just a little.

But modern hands-on parenting is also nice and rewarding—all the together-time, all the tender encouragement instead of the yelling and ignoring of earlier parents, all the forehead kisses and "good jobs" and so on. That we end up doing the work of distant institutions simply in being attentive as parents is a spooky irony, perhaps, but not really a bitter one. The sharper ironies involve the institutions we encounter more directly, in a more consciously competitive or self-empowering spirit—prestigious preschools, embattled public schools, the high-involvement clubs of competitive sports. You enlist them in your family's quest for advantage, and then you find they've reached into your family and made it an extension of their institutional functions. Looming in the background of most of these relationships is the specter of college, getting into college, a good college, the college admissions process. Even the internet is hard not to approach with this end point somewhere in the back of your mind, especially when your kids are little and it seems this ingenious technology might work their plastic brains into Harvard shape.

This, the looming influence of college admissions offices, is where the sharpest ironies abide. If you consider how many parents intend to send their children to college, and if you add up the time, energy, rumination, and competitive calculation these parents devote to the crucible of college admissions, and if you consider how these reflexes and priorities permeate the culture of schools and the home lives of families that aren't even thinking of competitive colleges or selective admissions, you might begin to realize how much social power reposes in the college admissions process. Think of how many movies—from

Risky Business to *Lady Bird*—have as a major or minor line of drama the question of college admissions. It's in TV shows and TV commercials—the high school senior screaming as the unfolded acceptance letter shakes in her hand. This process is truly one of the most influential forces for the steering of human behaviors and the formation of human attitudes in the United States.

But as I will discuss in Chapter 7, the internal lives of families have in fundamental ways been rewired to satisfy not the expectations of college professors, nor the demands of the twenty-first-century workplace—but rather, the selection imperatives of admissions offices. These imperatives, once they move beyond the numerical nuts and bolts of academic performance, are a mix of administrative make-work and shifting, arbitrary standards of moral assessment—which also function as administrative make-work. Among the things that inform these standards is a notable strain of contempt, among influential deans and other admissions personnel, for the parents of their applicants.

This is predictable. Simply having so much direct power over other people, being in a position to receive their desperate entreaties in the grudging attitude of someone who has only so many favors to hand out, would naturally breed a sort of looking-down attitude. My discussion of this process, its offices, its personnel, and their attitudes toward parents like me occupies the latter part of this book. This is where the fighting mood I mentioned earlier, and warned about as counterproductive and fraught with irony when applied to the competition among families, comes rising up again. I don't know if it's finally productive at this point, but I'm pretty sure it's justified.

chapter one

Parenting in Public

A Speculative Theory of Overparenting

LOVED IT WHEN OUR KIDS WERE BABIES, ESPECIALLY THE first six months—holding my infant child, the ecstasies of obligation and unease, being bound to serve a baby's primal needs for adult humming and staring and ignore my own irksome needs for food and constant movement. But things were especially good with our second and third kids, because in the early months of their lives I also slept great. Juliet co-slept with those two, in a separate room, on a mattress on the floor next to the empty crib, so that the baby could nurse on demand and Juliet didn't have to sleepwalk down the hall several times each night, and I could enjoy six months of peaceful nights in a queen-sized bed I had all to myself. But then my sleep vacation and the baby's blissful deal of sleep-nursing would end when Juliet returned to the queen bed and we trained the kid to sleep alone in the crib. We used the "cry it out method" of sleep training at this point, which sounds harsh for the kid and was definitely agonizing for the parents, but we suffered through it only briefly—like five or ten minutes a night, for a week or so with both kids. We had to do something different. We'd botched the sleep thing so badly with their big sister, who raged against sleep through her first year and began escaping her crib as soon as she could—sounding that alarming *thump* as, in her final bid for liberation, she released her grip and her little body hit the floor—and who was still defiant and manipulative at bedtime when her younger sister was going down quietly and sleeping through the night.

These are dear memories—there's even some proud amusement in the ones about our oldest thumping heavily onto her bedroom floor, headfirst for all we knew. So it's kind of sad to imagine having submitted them, as confessions or advice or requests for advice, to the Internet of Parents. I mean the magazines and blogs, the message boards and social media threads where the "sleep training wars" rage, simultaneous with the "breastfeeding wars," which are partly subskirmishes in the "mommy wars," but are also partly their own separate things. (The term "mommy wars" generally denotes online arguments between working and stay-at-home mothers.) We'd have been criticized for the co-sleeping, which, according to the American Academy of Pediatrics, increases the risk of sudden infant death syndrome. Devotees of attachment parenting might denounce us for our sadistic sleep training. Someone sensitive to gender inequities would probably object to our parental sleeping arrangement, the woman bearing the sole burden of nursing labor, the sleep privilege seized by the entitled man, his preening grossness in describing it. When you read the magazine articles and blog posts, or follow the threads on the message boards, this is what you find: parents highly but insecurely invested in their own methods, wishing to support other parents in their parenting labors but ready to read other people's differing choices as personal attacks on their own choices, and, of course, ready to defend themselves against these attacks.

In other words, it's a touchy business, raising kids, being a family in twenty-first-century America. Parents often find themselves looking over their shoulders, feeling exposed to a lineup of ungenerous gazes, hostile judges both real and imagined. This is a little counterintuitive, if you think about it, especially in America. The Anglo-American ideal of family life stresses its social separateness, the veil of privacy that is supposed to surround and define the family unit, delimit the sacred zone of children and mothers, and sometimes fathers, from the fallen world outside, the grubby world of wage work, social trouble, and nosy government. This ideology dates back to the Victorian era and the Industrial Revolution, but its romantic view of domestic life persists, in the dreamy aspirations we entertain for our home lives, the immersive child-rearing and spiritualized consumerism through which we seek not just personal fulfillment but a sort of religious transcendence. That may sound critical as I describe it, or at least ironic, but it's pretty much how Juliet and I are trying to do it. And, I have to say, when it all comes together, it *is* pretty great. It *is* transcendent. I highly recommend it. That we still observe their model of family as a unit of higher meaning suggests those romantic Victorians were onto something.

But all the meaning in our little families ends up overspilling its homey vessel, the domestic sphere. Being so important to us parents, being so rich with emotional pleasure and moral duty and existential risk, the private little world you make with your spouse and kids turns out to be really interesting to other people and other institutions as well. You're in charge of your children, in other words, but you don't *own* them. You're not free to do what you will with them, in the government's and the police's view of family things, even inside the metaphorical fortress or castle or haven that is your private home. And if you go online to read up on what other parents in your situation are doing, you're going to find some strong opinions. You may find people judging the very things *you're* doing in your private haven in sharply public language, language that brings the government and the police into the matter, at least notionally. You may find yourself accused of child abuse (sleep training), or child endangerment (co-sleeping).

And when you bring your child out into the world because kids need vitamin D from the sun and you need caffeine from coffee, the emotional language you share with your little one is still the private idiom you wrought at home, though perhaps with the silly and sloppy and angry extremes shaved off (or perhaps not). You don't adopt a conference-call manner with your child just because you're at Starbucks and strangers can hear you. You coo, you cuddle, you sing, you love, sometimes you chastise. If you're a newish mom you might nurse, in the light of the big sidewalk window of a franchise coffee establishment. As a parent toting or strolling a child, you've shown up using certain gear, in a certain mood, wearing a certain expression and certain clothes, about all of which certain strangers might be forming certain opinions. Your child, being a child, might do things notable to nearby strangers, like suckling from a woman's breast, or giggling, or crying, or crapping. And these things being notable from strangers' perspectives, strangers will note them.

Here is the curious nature of parenthood, as a legal predicament and a lived experience. It is a public thing done in private. Indeed nothing opens private life so fully to public interest and intervention as the vocation of parenthood, the presence of children. And as it is a public thing done in private, it is also a private thing done in public. Your kids are still *your* kids even when you're out on the street or at the mall or at church, even when they're fascinating and charming and irritating strangers. A person has to cross a chasm of etiquette to correct a child in front of her parents, and so it's not often done. But, in the difficult and embarrassing moments to which selfish children subject their vulnerable parents in public, the parent knows, the parent *feels*, that just because strangers are holding their tongues, that doesn't mean they're withholding their judgments.

Child-rearing places parents in a web of interest and attention, which can provoke a robust sort of self-awareness in them, some mix of pride in raising adorable members of the next generation and anxiety that people might think they're doing it wrong. As a parent out in public you absorb the warm regard of pro-child people who smile at you on the sidewalk, and you register the varieties of impatience and disapproval, expressed or implied or imagined, from the other sort of people.

I started thinking of these parenting-in-public dilemmas after having to discipline my kids outside the house, among different sorts of parents. Now, as many social scientists of family life have noted, today's educated, middle- and upper-middle-class parents tend to practice what's known as "authori*tative*" discipline, rather than the "authori*tarian*" discipline more common among working-class parents in America—that is, we never hit or spank, and we *explain* instead of yelling, and we *listen* for the child's perspective rather than demanding that kids just shut up and obey us.[1] Of course Juliet and I mostly use the method proper to our social class: the talky, solicitous means of correcting our children known as authoritative.

But I was raised the other way. When it came to disciplining his six children, and especially his four sons, my suave, kind, self-cultured eightysomething father was the same sort of Old Testament dad all my friends had in the Detroit neighborhood where we lived until I was in middle school. The model of fatherly discipline I absorbed in my own childhood was fully authoritarian. I could get away with talking back to my mom, as long as it wasn't so egregious she told my dad, but there was no debating with my dad, no respectful back-and-forth, no heartfelt giving of fatherly reasons why I should have acted differently just then. He didn't give reasons. He gave orders. He didn't express humanistic disappointment when I screwed up. He unleashed the thundering anger of fathers throughout time. And in response I swallowed all my wise comebacks on pain of, well, pain. Indeed I can neither remember nor imagine having argued with him in the way my kids argue with me all the time. As a father I accept the research that says physical discipline might not be the best way to manage your kids, but I loved and respected my dad then and hold no grudge against him now. The authoritarian reflex is deep inside me, even if I generally ignore its parenting advice.

So when I find myself dealing with my unruly kids in front of parents I take to be working class, and who are using the same style of discipline my parents used on me, I'm frankly torn. In the small Michigan town where my parents now live, where I spend several weeks a year, these parents tend to be white, while in Oakland where I live they're usually African American. In such cases I have a deep, almost visceral sense of needing to look respectable to these parents through my style of discipline, as if I'm performing parenthood for my own parents. I might even change how I act a little, under the (imagined) gaze of the black mom using direct orders in a sharp tone to manage her two little kids in the food court. I might sharpen my own tone, speak with heightened impatience, in the imperative voice, give my dawdling or misbehaving kid the verbal equivalent of a smack upside the head, like the real one I might have gotten had I been so distracted or disobedient. In these moments the image of myself following the parenting protocols of my social class—dropping to one knee and gently, vainly *explaining* to my bothersome kid the *reasons* why *Papa is upset right now*—strikes me as dishonorable, if not weak and pathetic. To the mom in the food court—I can't help it—I don't want to look weak. I want to look as respectably tough as I remember my dad being.

Of course this confession doesn't illustrate the superiority of one sort of parenting over another. But it does suggest how unavoidably *social* the experience of being a parent is—how social attention converges on parents, how parental self-awareness radiates into social space, especially when that space contains other parents. A more typical example was presented to me by another dad recently. I'd dropped off my son at school and was walking home when a five- or six-year-old boy, barely noticing me under his big helmet, wobbled toward me on a scooter he was quite bad at riding. We were set to pass each other at a little bottleneck, a spot where the sidewalk was narrowed to one lane by someone's untrimmed landscaping. So I stepped aside to let this boy through just as his father, a few steps behind him, called forward, "Henry . . . make room!"

Now this parental plea was nominally directed at little Henry, but unless you understand it as meant for me it makes no sense. Not only was little Henry concentrating too hard on his wobbling handlebars to note his father's words, but he was at the very limit of his ability to control the scooter at all. Had he actually diverted the mental resources needed to attend to his dad and then "make room" for me, who'd now stepped off the sidewalk, he'd have driven off the sidewalk himself, if not just toppled over. I was perfectly charmed in standing aside like a bullfighter and waving the little guy past me, but the dad trailing him couldn't assume that, or he didn't want to *appear* to assume that, or to assume anything about my view of his scootering son. His son couldn't and didn't bring me under his consideration, but his dad wanted me to know that *he* had. I've said that kind of thing many, many times in sidewalk traffic, a comically futile bit of parental guidance. At the shallowest conscious level, as I said it, I surely thought of it as parental guidance, but it was really a gesture of consideration to an adult who might be inconvenienced, minimally, possibly, by my kid's unadult way of moving through space. "Careful!" "Remember to look up!" "Someone's coming!" Never has the unseeing, unsteady passage of any of my kids been made safer or more convenient for strangers by my saying these things, but with them I have acknowledged to many strangers: *Hey . . . I see you there . . . I don't know if you're one of those people I need to apologize to about my three-year-old veering in your way because she's a three-*

year-old . . . but if so . . . I don't want you to think we think we own the whole sidewalk. The valence of this signaling changes when you know the other adult is another parent. When it's another parent you might be less worried about the rank disapproval of anti-kid people, the ones who roll their eyes at obnoxious brats and entitled parents increasing global warming and thinking they own the whole sidewalk, but you do want to present yourself as competent and considerate, at least as competent and considerate as that other parent is.

In other words, parenting in public, among other parents, is by nature comparative and thus subtly (or overtly) competitive. I don't mean to say it's egotistical or vicious, or even unfriendly. It's just the natural expression of the fact that humans are socially sensitive, status-conscious beings, especially in public settings that bring them under each other's gaze, within a shared practice, as equals—an academic classroom, a pickup basketball game, a dinner party, raising your kids among other people raising their kids. As parents, we're paying attention to other parents, who, we suspect, are paying attention to us. We want to look good to each other. We want to give a respectable showing, conducting our private labors of raising children in the public world we make and share with other parents.

These social rigors have only grown in the last few decades as parents have become more involved in their kids' daily lives, in ways that, I suspect, have further intensified this involvement. Parents being more involved with their kids has involved them more constantly, more systematically, with each other, as parents. Parents chauffeuring their kids to school and parks, practices and games and playdates, instead of letting kids schlep themselves to these things, has exposed them, much more so than previous generations of parents, to the nervous, comparative gaze of other parents.

IT'S A SOURCE OF QUIET PRIDE BETWEEN JULIET AND ME that we throw minimalist birthday parties for our kids. Over a decade of birthday parties where our kids and their guests always have a great time, we've never rented out a facility or an establishment for one of these parties, nor hired anyone to clown for or paint the faces of the little guests. We always hold our parties at home, and we tend to keep the guest lists small. Of course our local circumstances let us pull this off and, so, help obscure our commitment to doing as little as possible, birthday-wise. Unlike me and many of our parent friends, Juliet is from Oakland, where we live. Her parents and sister live here, and her sister's husband and their two little kids, and her brother lives close enough to make it to most of his nieces' and nephews' birthday parties. So even before classmates and friends have been invited, the guest list of our kids' parties already has four or five extra adults on it, plus two siblings and two cousins. This way we can invite only three or four of the most obvious candidates among the birthday kid's friends and still achieve that party feeling of noise and chaos. And somehow the presence of six or seven adults of various ages lends an aspect of substance, of ceremonial bigness and variety, to a party whose actual ceremonial outlay consists of a delivered pizza, a cake, and a half gallon of vanilla ice cream.

But it doesn't take much self-reflection for me to wonder if, in making these ceremonies so much easier and cheaper for ourselves than they are for our fellow parents, we might be violating some ethical compact. Maybe we're shirking. Maybe in observing one scruple, not overindulging our children, we're violating another, reciprocating within the social system of kids' birthday celebrations. Once they're in the crazy swim of a minimalist party, kids don't care. The novelty of the day and its surroundings, their license to make noise and run around and eat cake, with several more friends than normal, is enough to convince a small gang of eight-year-olds that what they're at is a party, and the party is good, even if there's been no trip to Bouncy Land. And if the kids are happy with a bare-bones party—and everyone's less vulnerable to the manic buildup and tearful disappointments and logistical snafus of an elaborate party—it's hard to see why parents should choose the harder, more fraught, more expensive sort of party. That is, unless we understand the norm of bigger parties as rooted not in squishy parents indulging bratty kids but in socially sensitive adults operating within a web of tacit obligations resembling what Marcel Mauss, the great French anthropologist, called a "gift economy."[2]

I'm not the first person to apply Marcel Mauss's landmark 1925 work *The Gift* to the ceremonial side of family life. Many sociologists and social historians have compared today's lavish weddings to what Mauss calls the "potlatch," the feast in which a tribal leader hosts a visiting rival and attests himself a great man, in front of this rival, by lavishly wasting his own possessions. (Mauss argues that the potlatch is found among "archaic" peoples all over the world, from Polynesia to the Arctic. Accounts from colonial America clearly show that the native peoples had a view of economic exchange much less utilitarian, much more ceremonial and honor related than the Europeans they traded with.)

Mauss describes the potlatch in this form as a "purely sumptuary destruction of wealth that has been accumulated in order to outdo the rival chief." The tribal potlatch features not just the wasteful outlay of food and possessions but, sometimes, their active destruction, the intentional, theatrical smashing of pots and bowls, for example, as a chief's demonstration that he has a wealth of pots and bowls to smash. In the academic's wedding comparison, the modern stand-in for the tribal chief is the bride's father, who looks on with nervous indulgence as his wife and daughter plan a reception that will cost—per his ritual obligations—more than he can afford.

Were sociologists and historians to take up the expensive kid's party as they've taken up the lavish wedding, they'd probably view it as yet another modern-day potlatch. We are, after all, talking about a big party. But in a potlatch the status contest is explicit. The rivalrous pairing of chief and chief frames the whole drama. It's not like that with a birthday party. Rather, the system of kids' birthday parties resembles the network of ritualized giving—the "gift economy"—of tribal people in the *same* group. We parents might be rivals in some very specific or very abstract sense—competing over our kids' playing time in club volleyball, their future job prospects in the global economy—but we're also friends, or members of the same school community, or whatever you call the relationship of near strangers who text back and forth for several days about a playdate. In very few cases will the birthday parties we throw have a bowl-smashing feel. In our world, to carry on like a tribal chief, to make an overt bid for greatness in party throwing, would be considered a little gross.

Still, as Mauss describes them, the everyday relations and gift exchanges are also governed by standards of honor and status. They are "agonistic" and competitive too, only much less overtly so than among rival chiefs. You give because a past generosity obliges you, as a matter of honor, to give. You accept because accepting says you're an honorable and able person, unafraid to take on the obligation that accepting entails, that is, to give at some time in the future. A gift economy is thus a system of *reciprocal* gestures. This reciprocity is both cooperative and competitive, communal and individualist. In a society built upon gift exchange, people preserve social relations, paradoxically, by tending their own status.

An advantage that tribal peoples have over us modern parents is that they generally know what's expected of them. The exchange of gifts among these peoples is often closely scripted. Each gift belongs to what Mauss calls a "total" system. In the tribal settings he describes, every act of giving is understood as part of an unbroken history of such reciprocal gestures. The integrity of the social system mapped and nourished by these exchanges is taken for granted.

We parents aren't so lucky. Our social worlds are much more broken up. Like tribal peoples, we feel expectations of reciprocity, but they are vague and merely implicit, and they probably apply, on the top end, to grandiose gestures rather than minimal or miserly ones (at least I hope so). You'd hesitate before criticizing other parents for being unreciprocally stingy with their kid's party. Maybe they're secretly broke, or going through a rough patch. Indeed criticizing other parents for not being extravagant is a good way to make yourself look cheap. So being *over*extravagant is more likely to strain social relations. A dad proposing to take your kid and twenty of his friends to the Super Bowl would be both an obvious boon and a niggling communal problem.

Perhaps without even realizing it, people would take offense. Unlike in some tribal settings the offending people wouldn't be ostracized, or beaten to death by their relatives, and some parents might find the outsized generosity admirable, or be so happy their kid got to go to the Super Bowl that they overlooked the normative breach. But the offense against reciprocity, making your peers look poor or stingy in front of their kids, would probably register in other ways, eye-rolling between spouses, critical confidences among the other moms and dads about Tom and Doris, the show-offs.

But even where you don't have outliers and megalomaniacs blowing the proportions, such a balance as there is remains an unstable one, with a constant bias for novelty and slight excess. You can see how such a dynamic, being hard to read, might get out of hand, parents signaling to each other, as part of this system of reciprocity, but through ceremonial gestures designed to make a public declaration both heartfelt and a little complicated. They're proclaiming their love for the birthday kid to the kid herself and to other parents, while extending generosities to these other parents' kids proportionate to the generosities these parents have extended to *their* kid. The uncertainties multiply in this setting. The question lingers whether you've done enough for your kid, and whether other people will think you've done enough for theirs, and whether this gesture is truly in keeping with the tribal history of kids' birthday parties, and whether the core patrons of this party, their kids, will think so, and whether the other parents will think their kids think so. Some kids are hard to please, or so you've heard. Some parents are weird about their kids, or so you worry. You just don't know for sure. So the safest thing is to maybe go a little overboard to placate these imagined worst-case versions of your party guests and their parents, your fellow participants in this uncertain, unstable gift economy. It would take only small initial changes in the way parents treated their kids, small increases in the time they spend out in the larger social world with these kids, for these changes to grow and intensify as they pass through the social circuitry made by these parents. From, say, baby boomer parents resolving to be warmer and more present with their children than their own chilly and detached postwar parents were, could grow a whole civilization of overparenting simply because parents, in their function as parents, now made up an anxious and besotted social system with each other. This system, since it's the result of feedback loops still in place, would continue to grow more anxious and besotted all the time.

I think—or, I'd like to hypothesize—that the practice known by the derisive phrase "everyone gets a trophy" is rooted in a similar dynamic. I don't mean the generic practice of lavishing excess praise on kids, which that phrase is used as a sort of synecdoche to represent. I mean the literal practice of giving participation trophies to Little Leaguers and youth soccer players and other young athletes. I'm interested in these discrete moments of social parenting, the webs of expectation we come to occupy simply in sharing public space with each other, as parents, operating in public under each other's judging gaze, in ways earlier parents did not.[3] An important detail here is that—at the youngest age levels, where the competitive pressures are lowest and the participation trophy most common— the coaches I'm talking about are almost always parents.

Giving participation trophies seems to have expanded into a common practice in the early 1990s, and this coincides with the emergence of the belief—incorrect, as it turns out—that kids need high self-esteem to succeed in school and life, and so commenters have naturally fingered the latter belief as a cause of the former practice. Together they make an efficient way to mock narcissistic "Millennials." But these things also coincide with an increase in the practice of parents simply showing up, being present, in public, for everything their kids do.[4] A Little League coach giving his players a send-off at the end of a season is going to have a different, heightened sense of ceremonial obligation if those kids' parents have been hanging around all season, lingering at the margins of every practice, never missing any games.

That is, a coach who arrives at the last game or the end-of-year pizza party with a duffel bag full of trophies for nothing in particular is probably worried less about his players' self-esteem than he is about his own relationship with those kids' parents. He's tackling the ceremonial quandary posed by their constant presence. They've been hanging around all season, unlike when he was a kid and he and his friends rode their bikes to Little League practice, and maybe *one* of their parents went to *most* of their games, and parents weren't even invited to the end-of-season party. Back when he was in Little League his coach didn't look up from hitting fly balls to the outfield to see eight or ten adult faces just beyond the first base line, chatting with each other, perhaps about the coach, and casting eager, loving, hopeful eyes on their little sluggers.

The coach's feeling of obligation would be very different from his own Little League coach's—for the simple reason that it's not kids' expectations he has to consider, as it would have been for his coach, but their parents'. A few of these parents have complained about playing time. A few others have expressed high hopes for their kids' baseball future. One has confessed that her son is struggling academically, another that her boy is being bullied. Both boys cry at night. He knows how *he'd* feel if one of his kids was crying every night about subtraction homework, the sadistic bruiser in the lunchroom.

In all, because it's kids and parents mixing together amid minor injury and thrilling success, unavoidable failure and occasional disappointment, it's been an emotional few months. Some parents seem kind of invested—exactly *how* invested it's hard to know. It's hard to know what gesture best concludes these months of kid baseball and parental looming and confiding. He doesn't think his players care one way or another about a little trophy unattached to any achievement. He knows his own kid doesn't. But their parents are another matter, and he has to consider them, since they've been such a presence all season, and this is America, where the default uncertainty in social relations makes the extra gesture or gift a prudent step, and, also, they've started selling participation trophies at the trophy store.

Philosopher Kwame Anthony Appiah's wonderful book *The Honor Code* describes how a destructive practice that derives from a self-fueling status economy—such as dueling among European gentry, or the foot-binding of Chinese girls from aristocratic families—can be discredited and eliminated through a public reaction that places it in a shameful light. For those caught within them, these honor circuits are hard to step out of without grievous loss of status, *until* respected outsiders turn scorn upon the practice, and the destructive choice one makes to preserve one's status begins to damage it instead. It became much easier for young country gentlemen to opt out of a duel, or choose a less deadly way to answer a slight, after celebrated writers in London started mocking the duel as idiotic. Likewise, disapproval among high-status foreigners eventually made the binding of girls' feet dishonorable within China, which was surely a relief for many Chinese parents who didn't relish torturing their daughters, not to mention the daughters themselves. The participation trophy, belonging to a much more benign status economy, seems to be meeting a similar fate. If my experience as the parent of three kids who've played various low-intensity sports is any indication, you're a lot more likely to hear derisive reference to the "participation trophy," as a signifier for whiny college kids and entitled young employees, than you are to see your kid holding a participation trophy. In other words, the tainted meaning of the participation trophy makes it easier for coaches to go back to the traditional practice of rewarding no achievement with no trophy.

I'm speculating here, obviously, trying to tease up underappreciated aspects of contemporary parenting for a few reasons. First, they're amusing. When I think of my own parenting in public, my reflexive signaling to other people and other parents, I find myself amusing—the mindless element in the most mindful thing I'll ever do. Second, things like the participation trophy and the elaborate birthday party have become cudgels and clichés. They're too easily fit into formulas of generational insult and cultural complaint, which critics tend to use as stand-ins for actual thinking. People are more interesting than such formulas would have it.

Third, grasping this social, comparative circuitry of parenthood is crucial for understanding the more serious predicaments we find ourselves in as parents raising children to live in an uncertain future. Thanks to a confluence of economic, social, and institutional forces in twenty-first-century America, it's easy for parents to assume that the main purpose of family life is the fashioning of polished competitors in a lifelong struggle for opportunity and advantage. The social feedback loops that make our everyday relations the comical communal challenge I've been describing become something different when the signals we send to each other concern achievement and competition, the grinding work some parents and kids are doing so they can triumph, in a scary future of scarce opportunity, over other parents and their kids.

It's probably easier to find your parenting-in-public experiences as amusing as I do if you're a dad like me, and not a mom. The highly educated moms who write parenting articles and books, at least, don't find the social pressures they face from other parents amusing at all. They find them oppressive and exhausting. Even when popular writing on motherhood is about other things, even when it attributes parenting troubles to other sources, it often turns, as if automatically, to the social side of these troubles, the condition of being watched and judged that I call parenting in public.

In its very title, Ayelet Waldman's book *Bad Mother* evokes the mother's feeling of being gazed upon and judged in public. The book begins with the story of Waldman, not yet a mother herself, sitting on a city bus and watching a mother roughly managing her young daughter, and judging this woman a "bad mother." Here Waldman is telling a story of her own smugness, as someone who didn't yet know how reasonable it can be to be a bad mother. She's identifying with this mother, retrospectively, not just as a bad mother, which Waldman is now confessing to be as well, but because, as a mother, in public, she's under surveillance, furtive and casual and constant. This woman and her child attract a sort of moral attention as a matter of course, just as Waldman attracted such attention when she published a now-notorious essay in the *New York Times* where she confessed to loving her husband (the great novelist Michael Chabon) more than her children. With a sort of muted relish, Waldman recalls in her book the storm of outrage she provoked with this essay.[5]

On its first page, the 2004 book *The Mommy Myth* conjures a harried mother in a supermarket trying "to avoid the stares of other shoppers who've already deemed you the worst mother in America."[6] Judith Warner's book *Perfect Madness* is not just a critique of the ideology of total motherhood, the expectation that American mothers should exhaust themselves raising their children and then feel guilty for not doing enough. It's a description of how the social circuitry of American motherhood makes the expectations this ideology generates so hard to ignore and escape. The norms of this ideology are propagated not just authoritatively, from experts and authors, but intimately, in the looks and comments one gets from other moms on the street and schoolyard and playground. Are you doing it right? Are you doing enough?

In 2009 the *Atlantic* ran an article by Hanna Rosin with the eye-poking headline "The Case Against Breastfeeding." Of course Rosin's case was not actually against breastfeeding but against the tendency in American parent culture to idealize breastfeeding and stigmatize bottle-feeding. But the article is also an unhappy study (and perhaps an example) of the culture of parenting in which strong opinions about such things as breastfeeding circulate as cutting personal judgments on parental comportment and conduct:

> In my playground set, the urban moms in their tight jeans and oversize sunglasses size each other up using a whole range of signifiers: organic content of snacks, sleekness of stroller, ratio of tasteful wooden toys to plastic. But breast-feeding is the real ticket into the club.

Time magazine was calling out to this highly reactive readership when, in 2012, it paired a cover article on "attachment parenting" with a cover photo of a woman, slender and pretty and blond, standing with her right hand sassily propped on her right hip and her tank top pulled down so that her son could suckle from her left breast. Overstamping this photo was the goading title-question "ARE YOU MOM ENOUGH?" The key detail here is that the boy, standing on a small chair, is no baby, or even, apparently, a toddler. He looks like he might be grabbing a milky snack before T-ball practice. In the photo both the woman and (oddly) the boy are looking directly into the camera, as if echoing the challenge in the titular question: *Well, are ya?* Are ya mom enough to nurse a monster like this? The manipulative intent of this magazine cover was so blatant as to be a winking metacommentary on both manipulation and blatancy. If people should not let themselves be provoked by obvious attempts to provoke them, no one should have been provoked by this cover, and yet the online reaction was fierce. Indeed, even people noting the obvious manipulation, commenting on *Time*'s sly cynical means of provocation, were provoked into personally insulting the lithe blonde mom being suckled by the big son.[7]

I can't really blame people for overreacting to such provocations, since their touchiness illustrates my sympathetic point about how primed we are, as parents, to judge ourselves according to what other parents are doing, even, or especially, if what other parents are doing seems a little loopy, a little crazier than the parenting methods we—as yet—can commit to.

"NO ACT WAS TOO ASININE," WRITES JUDITH WARNER IN *PERfect Madness*. She's talking about how far—during the 1990s, when by her account the ideology of total motherhood took off—some women were going to meet its demands. A New York mom, for example, bragged about quitting her job to devote more mothering time to her preschool son after "testing showed that his 'pencil grip' wasn't right."[8] But, as much as she may like to, Warner can't dismiss this extreme reaction as a niche worry. After all, "no act [is] too asinine" to reflect the ideal and, thus, to at least get you wondering. In this environment the pencil grip mom can be both a comical example of deranged mothering and a standard of parental commitment you might feel kind of bad about not meeting yourself.

It was this anxious readiness to bring the extreme case into the center of our thoughts that made Amy Chua's *Battle Hymn of the Tiger Mother* such a publishing sensation. Chua's book is a memoir of her struggle to raise her two daughters as she was raised by her Chinese parents—with unbending expectations of not just success but supremacy, which requires constant hounding and yelling from Chua and, for her daughters, a nunnish cloistering from pretty much everything that isn't school, homework, or music practice.

On one hand, it takes barely a page of Chua's book for a more typical American mother to realize she could never raise her kids as Chua does, and she would never want to. Chua herself makes no bones about the extremity of her methods. Indeed, she seems to relish if not exaggerate her angriest, harshest mothering moments for comedy and drama (and sales). So, as a practical matter, the parent reader should be able to take Chua's often funny confessions mainly as entertainment.

And yet the outrage of her readers suggests they took her lurid confessions personally, as judgments about their own commitment as parents. I'm one of these readers. I can't deny it. I neither could nor would want to raise my kids as Chua raised hers, but I felt a little competitive sting in reading her book, a little self-rebuke at my unfitness for the job of putting such a demanding parental philosophy into practice, had I been responsible enough to come up with it in the first place.

Why, though? Why should I care what Amy Chua says? Let her raise her kids her way, and I'll raise mine my way, right? But the comparative reflex that comes with public parenting makes the extreme counterexample something you at least have to consider. Now that you've entered the popular discourse of child neurology, as all mindful parents end up doing, you can't *entirely* dismiss the mom who quits her job to attend full-time to her son's pencil grip, without, at least, some follow-up. You have to ask yourself: What's *that* about? What's a weak pencil grip a symptom of? Now that I'm thinking of it, how's my kid's pencil grip?

And other examples, nearly as quirky, might be harder to dismiss. It might be the nonorganic snacks the patchouli mom was declaiming about in the schoolyard. It might be a stroller less implicated in head flattening than your stroller is. (Is your stroller flattening your baby's head? Sounds absurd, but you'll probably look it up anyway, once the other mom at the playground mentions how her stroller is scientifically designed not to flatten the heads of babies.) And when it's a question of your children's success in life, or failure, and you can't *entirely* deny that extreme methods *might* help them achieve the one and avoid the other, the extreme approach can start to feel downright rational. If the primary fact of my family's life is that I'm arming my kids to fight for something, and if the thing I'm arming my kids to fight for is the same scarce thing that Amy Chua's arming her kids to fight for, I might have to read her book as a direct challenge, and not just a funny memoir by a mom who's clearly top percentile in the "hard driving" department.

This is the predicament many parents feel they're in now, the competitive challenge their child-rearing methods are deployed—systematically or haphazardly—to meet. The idea that your child may have a specific future calling that matches his or her character or virtues or interests has been subtly displaced by the idea of a single competitive struggle, one slippery pyramid of achievement you can't even get a place on unless you graduate from college, and you can't get a good place on unless you graduate from a good college. (There's a whole other lower, damper, lumpier island of life chances your kid will be left to scrabble for survival on if that bachelor's degree proves too hard or too expensive.) For his future, your college-bound child will be assigned a slot within a single hierarchy of opportunity and advantage, and this assignment will be based largely on his inner quantity of a single human alloy, a mix of honed intelligence and field-tested motivation and documented achievement that might be called

Accepted-to-Harvard. How much Accepted-to-Harvard can you fill him with in your precious few years together?

This is surely an exaggeration, grown from our natural parental vigilance and protectiveness, which becomes a shared, self-sustaining fear—a feedback loop—under the conditions of involved, public parenting. This sort of feedback loop will inevitably generate an oversimplified, fear-distorted picture of reality. It replaces the substantive, ethical questions of parenthood and child-rearing—discerning your child's nature and cultivating its better parts at the expense of its worse; raising a good and happy person—with quantitative standards of competitive fitness, abstract calculations of risk and reward. This fear leads us to focus on the risks even more than the rewards, and to work like crazy to minimize those risks. Unfortunately, such fears tend to be not just self-reinforcing but self-fulfilling. The more we translate our future worries into high-investment, competitive child-rearing, the more we goad others into sharing our fear and imitating our extreme methods.

America is a highly competitive society. Many people think this is a good thing, but it's clear that this competitiveness exacts real and growing costs on both individual families and society as a whole. As a father of three, I can attest to these costs. From the outside, for some nonparent who can calculate the stunning cost of three college educations but doesn't know the infinite privilege of raising and being borne up by three new people, the idea of fewer rather than more kids, or no kids rather than one or two, of not getting married and making a family at all, is growing increasingly persuasive. Many people have also pointed out that the new dynamics of family life magnify socioeconomic inequality by favoring the high-investment style of parenting more available to better-off families. And many people have pointed out the costs—in terms of straitened finances and exhausting effort and constant stress—faced by middle-class families struggling to stay in this competition.

I'm preoccupied by these things, too, but I also want to point out a further cost to this competition, which goes to the heart of family life as a political institution. Early in this chapter I mentioned the Victorian ideal of family life as a place apart, a "haven"—as the saying goes—"in a heartless world." You don't have to accept the entire ideology behind this ideal—sometimes known as the "cult of domesticity"—to appreciate it. In the sort of mass industrial society taking form in the Victorian era, with its high mobility and the extreme vulnerability of people to opaque, arbitrary, alienating, and very powerful economic and technological forces, the family sphere stood as an irreplaceable zone of human connection. Here family feeling—spousal commitment built on romantic love, the love and commitment of parents to their children—was a sort of everyday opposition to, a living critique of, the inhuman forces that ruled the outside world. I don't buy into every part of this ideal—its sacralized view of femininity, for example, has worked to both elevate and constrain women—but the oppositional reflex it expresses remains powerful today. The idea that the family sphere is ruled by different, deeper, more human values than govern the outside world is at least as compelling now as it was in the nineteenth century.

But as we indulge the competitive fear that lives and grows in our parenting world, the anxious feedback loop that families unwittingly generate together, the inhuman, instrumental rules that govern the outside world are colonizing the inner lives of families too, changing our very conception of what the inner purposes of family life *are*. American institutions are emerging and growing to administer the competition of families against each other. And it is easy for anxious parents to recast their priorities in the functional terms prescribed by these institutions, to reimagine the vocation of parents as creating mere contestants for this competition.

We absorb this competitive logic constantly, as parents, but we hate it, or at least many of us do. I've seen this on the faces of parents I encounter on my daily and weekly dad rounds, walking my kids to school, picking them up, standing pitch-side at weekend soccer games. Parents would learn I was writing a book that criticizes the spirit of anxious competition in American family life, and their initial response was often a small, quick change in their posture, a slight sagging of the shoulders, a little melting inward of the chest. These were parents of grade-schoolers and middle schoolers, instantly, visibly deflated at the mere mention of the achievement war they'd been drafted into through the wonderful act of having kids. They'd been trying not to think about this predicament and also haunted by it, already, well before I came along and brought it up. It wasn't that they didn't want to try hard for the sake of their kids, or thought their kids shouldn't have to work for what they might get in life. Rather, they were recoiling against the competitive system *in its particular nature*. There's something alien and artificial in its specific demands, they sense. Giving their kids over to the machinery of fretful striving seems at once compelled and unwholesome, like entrusting them to a drunk neighbor in a sudden emergency. What are their other choices?

For my part, as both an anxious and a pugnacious dad, the idea that this great competition into which my wife apparently birthed our children requires us to submit the inner workings of our family to the needs of an alien, amoral, technocratic, utilitarian system of achievement kind of pisses me off. And the idea that I have to suck up to certain guardians and gatekeepers of opportunity within this system, and my parenting should be devoted to urging my kids into this sucking up as well, roils my fatherly pride. It makes me want to recommit to the idea that my family is a place apart, a vantage from which I can look upon these forces and these people and tell them, No.

This defiant retreat has a romantic appeal, I admit, and it might be a healthy move for parents to make in the short term. But as a general outlook it is counterproductive in the longer run. It takes for granted our atomized predicament as families, and thus reinforces it. Admitting this leads to some ironic conclusions that might be hard for America's more conservative defenders of family life to accept: that the autonomy of families is actually undermined by our system of individualized competition; that reorienting the nuclear family away from this anxious striving and toward its traditional rewards and inherent virtues might require heightened solidarity in our social outlook.

chapter two

Getting into Preschool

Early Education in
Agreeableness and Conformity

I T SEEMS LIKE IT SHOULD HAVE BEEN A PONY, IN RETRO-
spect, but it was actually a horse. A nearby preschool was
holding an open house, and, even though pony rides would
have been more in scale with the occasion, this open house had
horseback rides. At the time we were thinking of preschool for
our first kid. She was still two, small even for a pony ride, but
I went ahead and handed her up to horse level anyway, so she
could sit in front of the young woman in the saddle, grab the
big pommel with her little fingers, and take a lazy lap around
the parking lot. I thought she'd be excited, or maybe scared, but
she just looked really focused, a two-year-old concentrating on
the huge fact that she sat on a horse. Though I am a worrier I
wasn't worried, looking up at her. In such cases I always trust
the judgment of people whose business is getting children to do

risky-looking things in front of their parents. The idea of legal jeopardy in these settings is so flagrant as to be reassuring. There must be a reason a lawsuit hasn't killed this tiny business yet.

It was a raw, unpleasant day, as I remember, and the horseback ride was an anticlimax, and the school itself was just a big old house filled with kid furniture and familiar books, and these things cast a quotidian shadow on our visit, which was also reassuring. I figured the desultory stagecraft signaled a relaxed process overall. This was our first go at preschool, and I didn't want anything intense and competitive. I didn't want to be presented with some glimmering option we wouldn't get because everyone else would want it too. I wanted all the sales pitches to be mediocre, which they were. If there was a secret of toddler pedagogy that was going to help certain Bay Area children get into Harvard, our local preschools were unanimously not in on it. This was a relief. It let us choose our preschool because the people there seemed nice, and other parents we knew seemed to like it, and it was close enough to home that we could walk there if we wanted.

But I wasn't just looking for ease. It was more serious than that. Letting competitive worry and fussy academic standards guide my preschool search seemed both natural, an easy thing for a nervous dad to do, and wrong. This attitude felt to me like part of some larger system I should want to keep as far away from my family as possible. It's fitting to call it a "system," I think, because the competitive worry of parents is self-fueling, the sort of feedback loop I referred to in Chapter 1. Worried parents coping with an uncertain future by arming their children for competition prompt other parents to top their efforts, which pushes other parents to exceed *these* efforts, and so on.

For me, as a student of various critical philosophies that treat autonomous systems as threats to freedom, this was a philosophical issue. For Juliet it was more a matter of inclination. Being an optimistic person, unlike me, she simply doesn't go around worrying about the future. Luckily, this tends to land us to the same place, practically speaking. Indeed, her steadier nature makes her a better agent of my philosophical designs than I am.

In this case my philosophical designs consisted mainly of wanting our choice of preschool to *not matter*. My conflict here was a pretty abstract one, I admit. Our submission to an alien system built on parental worry was less direct and literal than it was hypothetical. It was the *idea* of this submission that bugged me (as it was the idea of needless worry that bugged my wife). But in other, more straitened and competitive preschool environments, the submission is more real and personal, and more ironic. It's real and personal in that, in these environments, the market in preschool openings means that certain parents sort of have to, well, beg to get a favorable look from certain schools, behavior that the schools themselves encourage and sometimes require. It's ironic in that the parents most willing to beg in this way tend to be empowered ones, the ones with high incomes and a vital sense of their own agency, parents who know in detail what they want, and expect to get it.

"Why Your Children's Day Care May Determine How Wealthy They Become." Imagine being the parent of a one-year-old and stumbling across this headline, which appeared above a 2017 story in the *Washington Post*. You'd want to dig right in to see which "day care" facilities are putting their students on a straighter path to wealthiness. But if you're a middle- or upper-middle-class parent for whom day care, or preschool, involves the sort of choice implied by the headline, the article attached to it will have the odd effect of undermining all the worries that made you read it in the first place. (I will use the two terms, "preschool" and "day care" interchangeably, both because a distinction between the two is generally not observed in academic studies, and because, as we'll see below, the greatest benefits of preschool arise from what we think of as its "day care" aspects.) The *Post* article is not, in fact, about how preschool choices will determine how "wealthy" kids end up as adults. It's about a body of research showing that, by various important but very basic measures, disadvantaged kids who attend quality preschools do better throughout their lives than those who attend low-quality preschool or no preschool at all. This is an urgent matter of public policy, obviously, but this urgency, on the matter of raising poor children from disadvantage, has a way of moving into the preschool talk aimed at more affluent parents, and thus, ironically, stoking the struggle for advantage among such parents in ways that probably make the gap even wider.

The policy story is worth outlining, both because it's interesting in its own right and because it helps illustrate that the preschool worries and struggles among better-off parents—beyond the basic question of getting into one at all—are overwrought. As we'll see in Chapter 4, American education offers few triumphant or even hopeful public policy stories. Large-scale policy interventions at the primary and secondary level usually end up as costly and onerous disappointments, but research on preschool offers the prospect of education policies whose ambitions

aren't mocked by their outcomes. For decades, the general social scientific understanding of public preschool programs such
as Head Start has swung between promise and disappointment.
Early studies of Head Start showed that children who'd passed
through the program performed better academically than com-
parable children who had not. This was great news, if true. It
was already known that poor children face serious disadvantages
at school, and that these disadvantages are rooted early in life. If
a single government program could limit these disadvantages,
bring poor children closer to the academic level of better-off
children, this would be a huge public policy victory.

But later assessments showed that these academic gains were
transient. By the end of grade school, Head Start graduates had,
on average, reverted to the same academic level as their disadvantaged peers who hadn't attended a good preschool. This
phenomenon came to be known as "fade-out": academic gains
from a good preschool program emerging, measurably, and then
receding in a few years. People dubious about publicly funded
preschool took this to validate their skepticism.

Yet more recent research presents a surprising and hearten-
ing revision to this disappointing story. The fade-out on strictly
academic measures seems real, but other, long-term benefits
from these programs have begun to stand out in the data, and
these benefits are important. One well-regarded study noted
that "most evaluations of early education programs show that
such programs improve children's school readiness, specifically
their pre-academic skills." Some programs also seem to generate
"gains on achievement tests," but, as other studies had shown
already, these gains "typically fade over time." *However*, "some
studies of children who attended preschool 20 or more years

ago find that early childhood education programs also have lasting effects on children's later life chances, improving educational attainment and earnings and, in some cases, reducing criminal activity." The study goes on to note these benefits from "high quality early childhood education programs" might be so great that they offset the cost of running them.[1] Head Start and other such programs, expensive as they are up front, might be a fiscally prudent thing for governments to do in the long run.

Nobel Prize–winning economist James Heckman of the University of Chicago has built something of a crusade for early childhood education upon this argument that the costs of such programs are more than offset, in concrete fiscal terms, by the benefits.[2] (Heckman declares that "fade out is a myth," but then concedes that purely academic fade-out is real and turns his argument to preschool's other benefits, which seem to persist over time.) And the case for these benefits has received compelling indirect support from a study on kindergarten by another star economist, Raj Chetty of Harvard. As with recent studies of preschool, Chetty and his coauthors find that sound early education (in this case a standout kindergarten teacher) boosts the academic achievement of disadvantaged students—though only temporarily. Also echoing these preschool studies is their finding that the benefits of an excellent kindergarten teacher show up later in life. "Students who were randomly assigned to higher quality classrooms in grades K–3 earn more," they write, "are more likely to attend college, save more for retirement, and live in better neighborhoods. Yet the same students do not do much better on standardized tests in later grades."[3]

If this latest turn in the preschool research is as robust as it looks—and questions remain—it justifies the urgency and optimism with which these studies have been treated. What interests me is how this urgency about preschool for disadvantaged kids moves into areas where it doesn't really apply, and so fuels the general competitive outlook of middle- and upper-middle-class parents, whose children's prospects almost surely do not hinge on where they go to preschool. This is partly about the sort of misleading headlines I note above. Another example of these is a story from the Washington, DC, news radio station WTOP, which carries this parent-goading headline: "The Most Important Year in a Child's Life? Research Points to Preschool." The article quotes an "education researcher" who says that in preschool children "learn about math concepts — not just the names of shapes or the names of numbers — but how you use math."[4]

The reference to building math skills in preschool is the sort of thing an ambitious parent wishing to use the preschool years to optimize his child's plastic brain will seize upon. But, as the balance of preschool research shows, the most important thing about preschool is not how much math you learn there but some deeper long-term capacity simply to be and stay in school, which children from disadvantaged homes need help with in ways that the luckier, better-off kids do not. As economist Helen Ladd of Duke University notes, "preschool is likely to generate larger benefits for children from low income (or low SES [socioeconomic status]) families than for those from higher income (or higher SES) families." This is because, "compared to low income families, higher income families have the capacity to invest more in their children's wellbeing and development."[5] The things that anxious, ambitious parents from the middle and upper-middle classes want preschool to do for their kids they're probably already doing themselves.

Though this mixing of two different preschool stories is partly a matter of news outlets hungry for attention, it's also, in some places, about preschools and parents—preschools selling their wares to parents in a competitive environment, and parents appealing to preschools for reassurance and advantage.

A THING THAT SUPPOSEDLY HAPPENS IN COMPETITIVE PRE-school markets, such as New York City and San Francisco, is unborn kids being entered into the preschool admissions process—expecting couples writing the prechosen names of their buns in the oven onto the waiting lists of prestigious day care centers. I'd read and heard about this a number of times before I attended the 2019 San Francisco Preschool Preview Night, a yearly meetup of parents and preschool representatives staged inside the San Francisco County Fair Building—which, despite its name, is not a barnlike structure smelling of hay and manure but a tasteful wedge of mid-century modernism, glass and brick, tucked into the southeast corner of Golden Gate Park. I wasn't looking for the waiting list thing here, kids competing prenatal to get into the best preschools. It was too blatant a cliché to actually expect, and so I'd let myself forget about it. And how would I have conducted my investigations anyway? Would I have skulked around pretending to stare at my notebook while scanning the abdomens of women, to see if any of the hundreds attending this event was showing—as the tabloids say—a baby bump? As a detail to pursue it was neither seemly nor feasible.

But then as I stood at a school's information table this detail found me. I was browsing pamphlets when a school representative, chatting with a couple to my left, a tall man and a tall woman, asked them how old their child was, their preschool prospect. There was an awkward buildup and then all three had a cathartic laugh and the representative said, "Oh yes, I forgot . . . *negative* . . . how many months?" The couple, then, were expecting. Their preschool applicant was negative months old.

At that point I admit I did a quick sideways scan of the tall woman's abdomen and made out a baby bump.

This seemed to confirm the gist of the stories in which this pregnancy detail usually appears, that overcompetitive parents are making a madness of preschool. I'd read and heard convincing testimony that it was happening in New York, and since San Francisco, like New York before it, is becoming a weird money-polished version of itself, I was ready to see at least some of the same madness at this Preschool Preview Night.

Preschool Preview Night was indeed full and busy, with nearly a hundred schools for the hundreds of parents in attendance to consider, but it didn't exactly feel touched with parental madness, at least compared with preschool events in Manhattan I'd encountered in articles, TV news stories, and one feature-length documentary. One reason, perhaps, is that San Francisco doesn't suffer from the supply problem that parents face in New York. Several preschool teachers at this preview event told me that new preschools seem to be opening up all over the place in San Francisco. I visited the tables of many newly opened schools. Some school personnel spoke of rigorous, competitive admissions processes, which I'll discuss more below, but most described their admissions procedures as pretty low-key.

Another sign that things were less intense than I'd feared was the pedagogy proclaimed by the various schools. If there was one phrase that dominated my conversations on that topic it was "play based." "We're play based." "Our classrooms are play based." "We practice play-based pedagogy." I'd figured that, among private preschools in a tech-focused city increasingly viewed as the meritocratic capital of the STEM economy, many would be proudly, aggressively academic in their focus. But nearly all the teachers and administrators I spoke with said, no, the important thing for preschool-age children is "social-emotional" learning, which they sought to effect through play. There was, humorously, some competition among schools on this front. One teacher, aware of the irony, chuckled at herself as she told me her school was *more* play based than a lot of other schools. These schools, she said, mouth the slogans of play-based pedagogy, but they practice a rigid, secretly academic version of it. The schools where all the drawings on the wall are of the same thing, she said, are the ones that aren't *really* play based. For some reason I imagined frogs, from some frog-morphology exercise, green-crayoned onto white paper, hung in a line high on a wall, trying and failing to resemble each other.

Though the talk at most tables was about play-based learning of social-emotional skills, nervous parents could still feed their achievement anxiety with the general message that emanated from the posters and pamphlets, which was that these preschool years are crucial and irreplaceable for your child's development. You already feel that way as the parent of a toddler, in this era of competitive and scientific parenting. Your child has passed from his first babbling year to expressing clear signs of human intelligence, potential you feel an urgent need to realize because it's beginning to show itself on its own.

Despite myself I too had fallen into this urgency when my first child was this age, simply reading and thinking about her brain. I wasn't wondering how to improve her social-emotional skills through play-based pedagogy, so that she could merely tolerate school long enough to earn a bachelor's in something. I was thinking about math. I was wondering if there's some way to maximize her math power that I was in danger of not exploiting, and maybe to make her a reader at three or four, so she could enter kindergarten with the sixth *Harry Potter* tucked under her arm. Juliet, by contrast, said we should not teach her to read precisely so that she'd have something exciting to learn in kindergarten. If the research about preschool is sound, then my wife's calm judgment was right and my anxious paranoia was wrong. Our daughter was getting plenty of brain enrichment at home from her attentive and voluble parents, and the many books she had read to her every day. Her life prospects would probably be uninjured by our sending her to the easygoing preschool up the street, whose central pedagogical instrument was the monkey bars.

Still, there's one area of preschool pedagogy where real academic stakes are undeniably in play, in just the sort of time-sensitive terms that concentrate the minds of ambitious parents. That of course is language acquisition. Everyone knows that young kids' brains are designed for picking up languages. Really young kids learn new languages without even realizing they're doing it. I remember living in Germany as a graduate student and straining to improve my German, not just because it was important for my studies but because, more fundamentally, I viewed fluency in a foreign language as a badge of cultural honor.

And so I also remember the odd envy I felt toward an American friend's four-year-old daughter, whose German, after less than a year abroad, was not just fluent but delicate and beautiful.

And it was at the tables of the language immersion and bilingual schools where I caught the clearest hints of parental competition I'd read about. Indeed the tall couple hoping to sign up their unborn child were talking with the administrator of a French immersion school. I spoke with a different representative of this school, a short woman with a heavy French accent and a dead-serious way of explaining herself, and she described her school's admissions as an "intense process" that is "very competitive." The head of a Mandarin immersion school said her school typically receives about a hundred applicants for entering classes of about thirty students. But since these new classes come already partly filled with siblings of older or prior students, the rejection rate can be closer to 75 or 80 percent. (The head of one language-focused school had little interesting to tell me about its admissions process, but the school is worth mentioning simply for the marvelous fact that it was a *tri*lingual preschool—Mandarin, Cantonese, and English.)

But how are admissions choices in these intense processes made, such that one desirable two-year-old is picked from four or five less desirable ones? They don't have GPAs to compare. They don't have test scores. The obvious answer is that they aren't choosing kids. They're choosing parents. The head of the Mandarin immersion school said that her process looks to get an "overall picture" of the applicant, which is to say, a "picture" of their families. What the school really wants is "hands on" families. Perhaps I'm wrong, but I understood "hands on" to mean "willing to give time and effort and extra money, beyond tuition, to the school." The head of another selective school—not language focused but a sought-after school located in the wealthy Pacific Heights neighborhood—described her school's admissions in a way that sums up the criteria of the lucky preschool desirable enough to *have* criteria: what they're doing in their admissions process, she said, is "assessing the parents."

I don't mean to suggest that there's anything sinister in what these schools are doing. It's perfectly natural for them, in their situation, to use the information they have available to them to help their little childcare institutions thrive. I do want to suggest that preschool admissions, conducted in such an environment, give a case study of how the American way of distributing the most rarefied sorts of advantage places families in a state of pliancy toward the institutions that have this advantage to dispense. These little institutions, humble as they are in absolute terms, have the leverage to set high expectations of "hands on" agreeableness and munificence from, ironically, the best-off, best-positioned families.

Just as the preschooler's personality is conditioned to a long toleration of the hassle of school, the affluent family that has successfully bid against other families for a rarefied preschool slot is also beginning a long process of formation and conditioning. Parents gain early knowledge of what gatekeeping institutions want and then refashion their family's inner workings to present a convincing semblance of this thing. With time, through successive stages of their children's lives, parents come to think of their family as a machine for producing this institutionally desirable thing over and over again.

IN 1999, AS BANKING GIANT CITIGROUP WAS WOOING COMMU-
nications giant AT&T for a future deal, Citigroup chairman
Sanford I. Weill asked one of his stock analysts to "take a fresh
look" at the rating of AT&T's stock. This wasn't just any stock
analyst. This was Jack Grubman, known at the time as "the most
powerful telecom analyst on Wall Street." After Weill's request,
Grubman surprised Wall Street observers by upping his rating
of AT&T from "hold" to "buy." The apparent result of this fresh
look from Citigroup's Grubman was that AT&T took a fresh
look at Citigroup's courtship efforts, awarding the bank "a cov-
eted role selling shares in AT&T's wireless division." In conducting this sale, Citigroup "reaped lucrative fees."[6]

Other details, believed to be linked with this Citibank-AT&T
deal, later came to light. Citibank pledged a donation of one
million dollars to the 92nd Street Y, a storied Manhattan cultural institution with a prestigious and extremely choosy preschool. After this rich pledge, the twin two-year-old daughters
of Jack Grubman, the powerful stock analyst who unexpectedly
went long on AT&T, were admitted to the 92nd Street Y. Weill
later confirmed he "called the school on behalf of Grubman's
children." Grubman likewise described to a friend that Weill
had helped his children get into the exclusive preschool.

These events came to light in the fall of 2002, spurring
several investigations and a busy round of semi-scandalized
commentary. The general focus of this commentary was, understandably, parents. Grubman became a stand-in for all the
rich and selfish New York parents who scheme against each
other for access to the city's most exclusive nursery schools.

The scandal-loving *New York Post* sounded this note after
Grubman's special treatment came to light. "Private schools,"

the paper lamented, "are always under pressure from the rich and famous to accept their kids."[7]

But the view of elite New York preschools as woefully pressured by the rich and famous is incomplete. The *Post* article, for example, reports that, thanks to their dad's preschool conspiracy, Grubman's twins later found themselves blackballed from the city's private *kindergartens*. The article quotes Victoria Goldman, author of a guide to New York preschools and a prominent observer of the city's preschool madness, who, as coda to the Grubman scandal, added this revealing bit of Schadenfreude: "The schools wouldn't touch him. They knew, of course, he could afford to donate a new library or new gym, but they have just as many other top candidates with more money and much better ethics."

The rich people need the schools much more than the schools need any particular rich person. This means that the rich people have to bid against each other in an auction for admissions, where the schools graciously permit the candidates with better ethics to give them new gyms and libraries and such. But what I'm interested in is less the big financial inducements than the personal adaptations this competition generates, the ways in which the inner attitudes of these affluent, competitive families are changed as parents sacrifice meaningful chunks of their personal dignity to win the big prize of admission to a prestigious day care facility. A valuable glimpse of this process of ethical formation comes in the 2007 documentary *Nursery University*, which shows five Manhattan families as they navigate the island borough's notorious preschool admissions process.

Now, I would hesitate to use a film from 2007 as an ethnographic resource, but the dynamic it illustrates within New York

City has by all accounts grown more intense since its release. And, in their intimacy, a few of its portraits are simply too vividly and instructively mortifying to ignore.

New Yorkers like those shown in *Nursery University* are often described as "status obsessed." This is ironic, because when we think of societies where status is (or was) an explicit feature of social life, we tend to think of traditional, "honor-based" societies, where proud men might go to violent extremes to protect their reputation, their *name*. In these societies, the flip side of honor, the thing one guards one's name and status against, is *shame*. But in the competition for preschool slots among affluent New Yorkers, supposedly status obsessed, one thing you find, among the more ambitious parents, is a willingness to submit to a little shame. We've already seen that one stock analyst was willing to sacrifice his greatest asset, his reputation, to win approval from the admissions personnel of a nursery school. In *Nursery University* we see various Manhattanites striving to win the preschool status contest by, ironically, groveling.

The movie begins with a tall, mannerly Upper East Side dad being interviewed by the head of a highly selective preschool, a gray-haired woman in a black leather jacket. She bids him to tell her about his daughter, and he lists several traits—"ball of fire," "very loving," "very verbal"—that, presumably, make his little girl a stronger candidate for this woman's preschool than other parents' little girls. Then he urges his daughter to write her name with the crayon she's holding so that the preschool head will be impressed and accept her into this school, a girl barely two who can write her name, perhaps, after a fashion. The child shows no intention of writing her name for the nice lady in the black leather jacket, and her dad grows uncomfortable and tries to coach her into it when she fails to take his cue and start scratching. She never does write her name, and so he has to go back to arguing her case directly. It's only after several minutes of him telling the preschool head what he thinks she wants to hear that she gives him the bad news: with two hundred applicants and only a single half-day slot open, there's basically no way that ball of fire's getting into this preschool. He doesn't—as I hope I would—stand up angrily at this point and ask why the hell she didn't tell him that in the first place. Why didn't she tell him he was sucking up to her for no reason?

This is the signal feature in the movie's portraits of parental striving. The most advantaged of these families throw themselves into a pointless competition, from which grows a shared belief that some lifelong benefit rides on which fancy day care facility their kid attends, that there are fine grades of preschool quality at stake in this competition. The fancier preschools cultivate this delusion in these grasping, gullible parents. At an admissions event for one elite preschool, the school's head begins what sounds like a skeptical gloss on the whole Manhattan preschool mania. "There are some parents who believe that preschool is the first step in getting your child into the college of your choice." This idea, she says, is "crazy." "*However,*" she goes on, "if your children get a really good preschool education, they have a leg up." For the anxious parents she's addressing, there's no effective difference between the belief she's rejecting as totally nutso and the cold truth she's avowing as a sober-minded preschool administrator. Is a "really good preschool education" like ours a first step? No! That's crazy! It's merely a leg up.

This sort of institutional double-talk is very common in college admissions. Admissions deans curate a process guaranteed to stoke the competitive fears of applicants and parents. Then they position themselves as the final line of defense against madness when their process plays out as it's designed to. They deride overanxious parents, share lurid stories of unbalanced applicants. Predictably, journalists who write on the topic of college admissions generally do so from the perspective of the admissions personnel they interview. In this reporting, the dominant parental figure is the crazy or scheming one.

But, as *Nursery University* shows, the main parental type in these settings is not the crazy one who skirts the rules in search of an unfair advantage. It's the agreeable one who really wants to know what the rules are, so he can show himself to choosy administrators as following those rules with all his heart. Here the distinction between self-interested calculation and tearful conviction collapses. With things like admissions essays for kids who aren't yet two, these parents take on entirely artificial exercises. At one level they must know they're artificial, but they're obliged to treat these false chores as filled with merit. The Upper East Side dad is seen flipping through a thesaurus for lexical help in answering the application question: "What makes a good educational program?" For a two-year-old, that is. Lacking a real answer to this question, as most parents would, he sets out, thesaurus at hand, to write an unreal answer. It's a difficult scene to watch—a man making an exacting effort to craft something totally insincere in its content, totally made up, but totally committed in its eagerness to please.

The most discomfiting example of this parental striving is an ambitious West Side mom whose son gets rejected from one of her "top two" preschools. This rejection sends her into action. "This is a school," she says, "where I distinctly remember them saying, 'Every time you call us you get a little star next to your name.'" "I haven't called," she's alarmed to realize, "and I haven't gotten any stars." To prove her commitment she dashes off an emotional letter about her son and runs it over to the school, to hand deliver it to the school's director, and finally, retroactively, earn herself a star. (It doesn't work.)

The obsequiousness of these affluent parents is matched by the disdain toward them from the preschool heads they're trying to please. When preschool staff get together or speak into the camera, they like to dish about the dumb and gauche and pathetic things parents do. When they advise parents, it's to emphasize how they're the ones, the parents, whose conduct is *really* under the microscope. An admissions seminar features a litany of emphatic and belittling *don'ts* for parents to observe on their preschool visits—any of which, it is implied, will result in one's toddler being rejected from that school. To knowing laughter from the other preschool professionals, the elite preschool head quoted above says, "*Don't* Purell your hands right after you've shook hands with the director."

The ironic thing is that these imperious preschool workers are creatures of the very rich people to whom they dictate these rules of parental behavior. Indeed, there seems to be a direct relationship, in the film, between the socioeconomic status of the parents and their degree of inner pliancy. The best-off families seem to grant, automatically, that the process and its demands are legitimate.

A less affluent couple from Greenwich Village, however, express justified distaste at an admissions exercise where their daughter joins other two-year-olds in a big room, as the preschool's teachers and administrators assess these children from behind a one-way mirror. "I don't know what they're looking for," the dad says. Of course not. What could they possibly be looking for? It's two-year-olds! Why, then, are he and his wife being put through this belittling exercise, having to sit by as preschool workers scribble mysterious judgments upon their toddler, her competitive viability as a preschool applicant? The Upper East Side dad has a much less disorderly attitude. "We were very aware of the process," he says, "and respected the process."

On one hand, the New York preschool environment is uniquely intense, compared to other American preschool markets. In other obvious ways it's all too typical, a microcosm of American family life in general, the anxieties that drive it, the stratagems it inspires, the psychological adjustments that turn these stratagems into family folkways, and the striking leverage it grants to institutions, even little ones the size of preschools, that have better chances at brighter futures to dispense, and fewer openings than they have applicants or aspirants. The Grubman scandal, after all, was recently reprised at the college level, with more explicit forms of fraud and bribery, by Hollywood celebrities. But the darker, truer parallels have nothing do with the scandalous exception. They have to do with the dull procedural rule. Anxious parents are encouraged to believe that, in our struggle against each other, the likely winners are those who, above all, respect a good process.

chapter three

Not Playing Around

Youth Sports in America

T WAS THE FIRST GAME OF THE INDOOR WINTER SOCCER season. My eight-year-old son was playing on the east field of the Bladium, a converted airplane hangar on a shuttered naval base in Alameda, California. This field was only part "field," actually, and also part "rink"—a turfed patch in the dimensions of a hockey rink, enclosed by white hockey boards topped with high, thick panes of plexiglass, as at a hockey rink. My son was gathering with his new teammates, and I was peering through the hockey glass onto the soccer pitch, chatting with a dad whose son was on my son's team. I noticed something nervous and uncertain in our talk. It was as if we were trying to explain to ourselves why we were there at all. He mentioned extra training he'd put his son in, plus the boy's success in baseball. I listened, waiting for a discreet way to mention that my son had scored a ton of goals for his under-eight team in the fall.

As an English professor might say, we were in a "liminal" position, as soccer parents. In more colloquial terms, we were like ghosts, as ghosts are often described. That is, we hovered, indecisively, between the two worlds of youth soccer, the recreational and the competitive. Our sons' team was rec. We'd had the competitive route put before us as an option. We'd gotten the emails the previous summer announcing tryouts, but we'd chosen the other route, for our various reasons. The time commitment of competitive soccer—three practices a week, games every weekend, frequent travel to distant tournaments—was too onerous. The $3,000 price tag was too much. The idea of sports tryouts for seven-year-olds was kind of obnoxious.

Yet we were here, weren't we? The other rec soccer families were somewhere else today, doing things unrelated to soccer. They weren't at the drafty Bladium on a cold rainy Sunday of late January. And wasn't my son—unlike all his rec teammates from the fall—doing Winter Soccer School on Monday nights? And hadn't the other dad put his son in the fall session of the same program?

We'd made our decision, but now, it seemed, we were waiting for it to be overturned by some fait accompli of soccer performance. Our sons had been very good or even dominant in little-kid soccer, the no-goalie, four-on-four games that boys and girls under eight play in our area. We'd watched our fast, focused boys dance through or run past their distracted opponents. So we were waiting for this first game of the winter indoor season to tell us we'd chosen wrong. We *must* reconsider. We *must* go the competitive route after all. The gods of soccer talent, having seen our sons, simply dictate it.

Our first game would be a nice test of these vanities. This off-season league was sort of a mishmash of rec and competitive, and the opposition was a competitive team from one of the area's top clubs, kids who'd had far more practice and skill training than our sons had, but these players were a year younger than our team's, and this was the club's "White" team, the lowest-level squad for its birth year. Maybe our kids would show their irrepressible talent against the year-younger scrubs of the Montclair Soccer Club. Maybe my little guy would do the same nifty jukes around them that he'd done around all those rec players back in the fall, and I'd know.

Now, another fact from the folk science of ghosts is that ghosts are caught in their liminal state because they don't realize the world has moved on without them. Ghosts are human spirits who don't know they're dead. It took about thirty seconds of this first game for me to see that, in the mix of indecision and ambition that explained our hovering presence in this drafty building, the other dad and I were as ghosts. The world of youth soccer had moved on without us. Those year-younger, third-level kids were playing a whole different game from our kids. They were speaking a whole language with their feet, of which my son, whose sly, intuitive dribbling had given me such pleasure to watch in fall rec, knew just a few simple words. Maybe with some frantic overcommitment I could help him catch up—pricey individualized coaching, a battery of private clinics, backyard drills informed by YouTube videos—but that wasn't the tacit deal I'd made (and, frankly, that's not the kid he is). I was waiting for something undeniable, a blaring declaration from the soccer gods, and it didn't come. The soccer gods were silent on what I "must" do with my son, which was a relief, actually. It let me honor the choice Juliet and I had already made, consciously and, in her case, unambivalently: to avoid the byzantine logistics and manifold stresses and epic time and money suck of competitive soccer—or, as she puts it, to "keep it simple."

Still, did our decision have to be so final? Was I really ruling out serious soccer playing for my son, for the rest of his life, if I didn't put him into "competitive" now, as an eight-year-old? Opinions differ on this among my more informed acquaintances. The owner of a soccer store we frequent, a longtime competitive coach and a youth soccer fixture in our area, told me he thinks the age cutoff is nine. My son's winter coach, who's something of a social reformer and egalitarian crusader in this world of pay-to-play opportunity, thought this was too pessimistic.

But it wasn't really on my son's behalf I was troubling myself. We think of a tryout scheme like the one presented to us as a means of selecting players, but it's not the young athletes who are being chosen in this moment. Competitive soccer clubs, with their several tiers of talent and their organizational need for members and fees, will make room for many if not most of those who show up for tryouts. So the real units these clubs are selecting in this tryout moment aren't the little players, but the players' *families*. Implied behind those emailed invitations (and, as we'll see, explicit in the training literature of many competitive soccer clubs) was a question that was also a challenge that, once answered, would become a commitment, a sort of moral contract with the institutions of youth soccer: Is your family ready to turn itself into a different kind of family, a soccer family?

THE OASIS CHARACTER OF BETTYE WILSON SOCCER COMPLEX in far northwest Las Vegas is mostly obscured by the hundreds of sand-colored houses and the several big retail complexes and one big sand-colored high school that now surround it. By contrast, the oasis character of James Regional Sports Complex, in far southwest Las Vegas, is manifest. Bricks and pavement buffer the Bettye Wilson soccer experience from the desert experience. At James Regional, on the other hand, the desert experience is pretty much a part of the soccer experience. You just have to lift your gaze a few degrees to see, beyond the two or three contiguous soccer pitches, depending on what game on which lush green field you're watching, an expanse of yellowish land covered in jagged space rocks and desert dust. It's also the case that James Regional, when I visited it, was still being built. Seven of the planned sixteen soccer pitches existed only as rectangles of yellowish land that differed from the surrounding desert only in that they'd been bulldozed flat and scraped of their space rocks.

These were only two of the seven soccer complexes hosting the 2019 Las Vegas College Players Showcase, comprising only nineteen of the forty-eight total soccer pitches at these parks, on which nearly five hundred teams from around the country— ranging in age from under thirteen (U13) to under nineteen (U19)—were playing over a three-day weekend of early March. This was the Boys weekend. The following weekend would be the Girls College Showcase, which would be even bigger, a lot bigger, with almost seven hundred teams playing on the sixty-six pitches of fifteen different soccer parks.

I was there to observe and talk to the soccer parents who'd driven or, more likely, flown to Las Vegas with their soccer-playing sons. I have to admit up front that there was a sort of gender bias in my sample, in that I shied from parents who were visibly writhing or growling to themselves or cursing inspirations to their son and his teammates, or darkly narrating the game to a remote party through a phone. These tended to be dads. Also, gender-grouped parents met me very differently. Moms gathered in twos and threes generally turned friendly, interested faces to me when I interrupted them with a question. By contrast dads gathered in groups eyed me warily and answered curtly when I summoned the nerve to bug them. Solitary dads were more approachable, especially ones who'd put obvious distance between themselves and the tenser parents bunched near midfield, and I talked to a good number of these dads. This—another organic bias in my ethnography—may account for the unexpectedly high levels of rueful irony I encountered.

For someone who played competitive sports mainly through my small-town middle school and high school and who'd never been to a club soccer tournament before, this busy event had a conspicuous absence: the team bus. Despite the surfeit of teams at play on the many pitches, there were no frozen caravans of yellow buses waiting near the main venues. Instead people arrived family by family, generally in cars rented at Las Vegas's McCarran Airport. At some point boys of the same age dressed in the same "kits" would find each other in the park and hang together as teams, but the general movement into the park and back out to the parking lots was familial, generally a mom and a dad, and a kid in a soccer kit, and sometimes a younger sibling or two tagging along.

Since my sly intent was to find out how the protean system of youth sports entangles families, I began by asking parents about their travel burdens. For years I'd been hearing complaints from fellow Oakland parents about mandatory weekend drives to cities like Sacramento (70 miles) and Fresno (175 miles) for soccer tournaments. Also, my own experience with club sports travel began when, as a sixth grader, my older daughter signed up for Oakland Lacrosse (an urban outreach program of US Lacrosse), and her team's first competition—just a few weeks after they'd picked up lacrosse sticks for the first time—was a doubleheader up in Sonoma County. Their actions were identifiable as "playing lacrosse" only because they were wearing helmets with cage masks and clutching metal rods with nets at the end, and yet a squadron of parents had to wake up at six on a Saturday morning and drive over an hour both ways so this doubleheader could happen. The assumption that this was not just possible but reasonable seemed significant to me.

The travel burdens these Las Vegas soccer parents described to me varied widely, and, if they confirmed my assumptions, they did so undramatically. The higher you rise in the youth soccer hierarchy, the more rarefied the competition and the farther you have to travel to find your weekly rivals. I spoke to a mom from a Michigan team whose travel for an elite midwestern league took her and her son as far as Chicago, Indianapolis, and St. Louis, *every weekend*, and a Minnesota mom whose son's team just orbited the Twin Cities on weekends and who, understandably, seemed glad they hadn't played their way onto the elite level. But then I spoke with a mom from Los Angeles whose son's elite team made fairly short trips each weekend, because Southern California is both full of people and a soccer hotbed. The teams in his elite league were bunched within half-reasonable driving distances. Their largely middle- and working-class team had made expensive soccer trips only a few times in the previous year, this Las Vegas trip, plus tournament trips to Hawaii and Spain.

A strange thing happened during many of these conversations. Answering questions about their travel burdens forced these parents to describe the competitive system in which their sons' teams played, and how this tournament fit into that system—that is, for what competitive reason they'd flown their families to Las Vegas in the first place—and many of them couldn't. They'd start out describing their team and league and, perhaps, what this Las Vegas tournament meant, competitively, but then they'd end up shrugging and trailing off. They didn't really know. The system is so darned complicated. One dad confidently described for me the tiers of competition in which his son's game fit, and I thought: *Finally! Someone who can tell me what the hell is going on here.* But then I found out later that he had the leagues wrong.

I sympathized with them. The system *is* complicated. Leagues and their governing bodies are morphing and splitting all the time. The confident dad had said we were watching an NPL (National Premier League) game, but the NPL is part of US Club Soccer (USCS), while this tournament was hosting US Youth Soccer (USYS) competitions. Both USCS and USYS operate under the umbrella of US Soccer, the organization that runs the US Men's and Women's National Soccer teams, which in turn operates under Concacaf, which oversees soccer in the Americas, which operates under FIFA, the global soccer organization that runs the World Cup. USCS split off from USYS in 2001, and the two now oversee parallel youth soccer hierarchies, more or less competitively. Perhaps as a result of this competition, the two organizations are constantly creating new playoff systems and tiers of leagues, or reforming and renaming their existing leagues—each league claiming to optimize the competitive experience of the clubs, on behalf of the individual players, or the individual players, on behalf of the clubs. I'm honestly not sure which one. It's hard to keep up with. Two different moms told me that their sons' teams played in the Midwest Regional League (MRL) of USYS. But when I went searching for more information about this MRL, I learned that USYS had disbanded it the year before. It was now something else, with different boundaries and different teams.

In certain formal ways, this competitive system is the creation of the organizational bodies themselves. They're the ones organizing and reorganizing the various competitive tiers and the various regional and national leagues. But when it comes to funding and fueling this large and complicated apparatus, and feeding it most of its personnel, the most important figures are parents and families. This is a parent-driven system. And yet parents don't control it. Rather—in the concrete sense of how they spend their free time and dinner hours and weekend days for ten or eleven months of the year, along with a healthy chunk of their money—it controls them.

To frame the strangeness of this predicament, the evolution of sporting play by children into a complex and disorienting system of administration and scientific training, I will take a brief, somewhat philosophical digression into the nature and deep importance, for humans, of play itself.

HOMO LUDENS IS A 1938 BOOK BY THE DUTCH HISTORIAN Johan Huizinga that, it seems, almost everyone who writes about youth sports and childhood play gets around to citing at some point. *Homo Ludens* is indeed a great book, and Huizinga is a titan among historians, but the book's lessons are not just historical. They are philosophical and political, and these lessons pose a stark challenge to the understanding of childhood play that has come to dominate family life in our competitive age. Huizinga's delightful, unnerving, and revelatory portrait of the central role of play in human action deserves detailed (and perhaps slightly difficult) exploration, for this reason, and also because his philosophy of play has bold parallels with the philosophy of family life that informs this book.

Homo Ludens is Latin for "playing man," or, "man, whose nature is to play," and, indeed, Huizinga makes the surprisingly persuasive argument that play is central to human existence, indeed that the "play-spirit" generated human civilization itself. At their deepest roots, religion, philosophy, law, even war express the human tendency to engage with the world through play. Early humans faced the alien mysteries of nature—storms and sunshine and nightfall, the violence and vulnerability of other animals and themselves—and made sense of these things, for each other, through "representation," that is, metaphor, word-play.[1] The shaman or priest was a performer of these representations. He staged plays through which world-ordering meanings were created. And so, at the origin of the unfolding history of culture and religion, sits the play-spirit.

The dialogues of Plato, in which the shambling idealist Socrates engages his young acolytes and takes on the cynical Sophists, grew from the popular tradition of argumentative performance and competition perfected by these Sophists.[2] Thus the Western philosophical tradition—and arguably Western science—emerged from theatrical play contests that entertained the public and were utterly unserious about the pursuit of truth. Until recent centuries, organized warfare was commonly draped in play forms, featuring decorative clothes, ceremonies of fair engagement, shouted challenges. With its powdered wigs and *adversarial* proceedings, the Anglo-American legal tradition bears "obvious" connections to ancient legal suits that, Huizinga shows, took the play forms of performance and struggle, from contests of boasting and insult not unlike a rap battle to elaborately staged, hand-to-hand fights sometimes known as, well, trials.

But *Homo Ludens* is also a lament about the narrowing range of the play-spirit in modern life. Today's science- or business-minded observers—some of whom can be found garlanding their management books with Huizinga quotations![3]—are quick to reduce play to a function or impulse. A playing child, we hear, is discharging a subconscious play *instinct*, or she's engaged in the important *work* of brain growth or social learning. For a management consultant, the proneness of even adults to fall into play, to make a game of things, is something to be harnessed for worker efficiency and office comity. But Huizinga scorns a utilitarian view of play, and he uses the phrase "play-spirit" in pointed contrast to "play instinct"—*instinct* denoting an unconscious, automatic discharge from the animal brain programmed by evolution, *spirit* suggesting an emergent condition of metaphysical freedom, the conscious activity of a human mind. Huizinga, then, uses the nature and persistence play to give a rough practical answer to the enduring philosophical question: Are we free, or are we mere machines, bundles of biological function?

To make his case he shifts the perspective from that of the scientist, who views play as a biological function, to that of the player herself, who surely does not experience her play as a function or an instinct. She experiences it, rather, as a conscious, creative, indeed subversive activity. What ensues from human play—real, persistent, socially shared, historically fertile *meanings*—cannot be folded back into the scheme to which "instinct" belongs, the causal unity imagined by natural science. On large scales and small, play creates *culture*. To a brother and sister playing with their Star Wars Lego kit, this play is not brainwork or instinctual output or social training; it's a last-ditch effort to get the *Millennium Falcon* up and running before the Empire locates its signal. That they can return to this story after bedtime has broken the thread shows that the world of meanings made in their play has a separate reality from mere nature or instinct, and this reality persists in time. Play thus makes a world beyond nature. The specific meanings generated and shared in play can in no way be comprehended by any materialist model of human agency. As Huizinga writes, "in acknowledging play, you acknowledge mind, for whatever else play is, it is not matter." Play is a sort of effective, everyday metaphysics, then, a mode of freedom both abstract, as "mind," and real, as the texts and artifacts, memories and invented scenes it leaves behind to be recalled and replayed.

As conscious play stakes out a "spiritual" reality distinct from material nature; it also stands against the functional needs of what Huizinga calls "normal life." Everyday survival requires us to obey the machinelike needs of the economy. Household management requires a steady labor of cooking and cleaning. Children must surrender to the rigid schedules and procedures of school. In modern life, the binding force of these social processes grows and grows. They dictate what's practical for us, what makes real sense, what must be done, and from their perspective, the exceptional worlds made and treated seriously in play are "nonsense." Normal life can't make sense of play, and wishes to limit or smother the play-spirit.

Play, then, exerts an antagonistic force against normal life, and this force is intensified by its communal pull. Play brings people together and spawns secrecy, and this secrecy, when shared, creates solidarity, conspiracies of playful nonsense hatched against the sensible functions of normal life. For children, Huizinga writes, "the charm of play is enhanced by making a 'secret' of it. This is for *us*, not for 'others.'" Even for adults, "the feeling of being 'apart together' in an exceptional situation, of sharing something important, of mutually withdrawing from the rest of the world and rejecting the usual norms, retains its magic beyond the individual game."[4] It's only now that I'm an adult, and a parent, that I can really understand how important and meaningful it was for my parents to escape from their six kids occasionally, and join their friends in games of bridge and late-night poker.

This would seem to point toward the intense bond that forms among sports teammates, but about this Huizinga is strangely ambivalent. He speaks of the modern sporting *crowd* as evincing the play-spirit, in its swooning seriousness before the game drama down on the court or pitch, but the professional sports *teams* they're watching make him suspicious. It's the permanence of such teams that bothers him, the whiff of administration that rises from this permanence, the idea that, with play being taken over by organized sport, and sport being regularized by the modern corporation and nation-state, the play-spirit is being killed by "systematization and regimentation."

I'm not sure he's right about sports teams, even professional ones.[5] He might underestimate this play-spirit he describes. On the pitch or the field, the court or the rink, the play-spirit of pro teams seems strong enough to transcend the financial and administrative systems that assemble and pay them, reignite itself from the mere existence of a ball, a drawn field, a set of rules that guide play and frame its drama. Still, if Huizinga were to see how much more "systematization and regimentation" there is in professional sports now than when he wrote, he would at least feel vindicated on the matter of modern organizations. And if he were to see how thoroughly a spirit of "systematization and regimentation" has come to form the worlds of children engaged, ostensibly, in the *playing* of organized competitive sports, he would be alarmed and depressed.

IN THEIR PAMPHLETS AND WEBSITES, YOUTH SPORTS CLUBS express the modern ways of thought that Huizinga saw killing the play-spirit. Generally they declare that their mission is not to enable the contained nonsense of play but to enact a machinelike process of improvement and refinement upon individual children and the teams with which they are grouped. This intent is often expressed through some form of the word "develop." In my area, for example, the Montclair Soccer Club describes its "vision" thus: "To *develop* skilled and highly motivated players."[6] Marin FC soccer club was "founded in 2004 as an alliance of five local Marin youth soccer organizations [and] created specifically to support the *development* of elite competitive soccer teams and players in Marin County."[7] As it is with youth soccer clubs in the Bay Area, so it is with our youth volleyball clubs. "Marin Juniors has been *developing* outstanding volleyball players for over 30 years."[8] Golden Bear Volleyball Club of Berkeley is "first and foremost . . . an educational organization. We believe the underlying values we teach are fundamental to players' *development* as athletes, students, and people."[9]

Mere play is stuck in its nonsensical present, but competitive sports clubs know that what really matters is the future, which has the potential to be much better developed. There are several reasons for this intense future orientation of youth sports clubs, their default view of themselves as agents of systematic and regimented development, rather than as mere enablers of the playing of serious sporting games for children. For one thing, children seem so malleable. It's very easy to imagine that submitting them to prodigiously early training and then making it prodigiously intensive over many years will yield something like an investment account brimming with developed talent. And there are sports that conspire in this by nature. Soccer, for example, carries a certain crude, indeed quantitative developmental logic, which prescribes that gaining hand dexterity in your feet is achieved by maximizing the raw number of "touches" a young player gets, and indeed private soccer clinics often advertise themselves on this numerical basis. A clinic near me promises "a thousand touches per session." Just reading the phrase "a thousand touches" must provoke a sort of thousand-touches lust in the hearts of players and their ambitious parents. It does in my heart, and my kids play rec. That the secret of excellence in such sublime skills can be expressed in such blunt formulas is oddly rousing. It brings a piquant sense of agency and optimism from the sports parent.

By stressing development, in other words, a youth sports club tells parents: "Look, we're not playing games, so to speak. You're thinking about the future. *We're* thinking about the future, too." Whether or not a mother is thinking about how volleyball pertains to the future of her second-grade daughter when she first signs her up for Marin Juniors, it probably takes very little messaging to get her to link the one with the other, because she *is* thinking about the future. Some of her most urgent thoughts about her eight-year-old daughter attach to moments a decade or more into the future. It's tough out there in the future.

This project of reaching a more highly developed future is necessarily a technological one, an application of material means to the stepwise achievement of practical ends. It's almost comic to recall Huizinga's concerns about the regimentation and systematization of professional sports teams as you read the following passage, which is directed to parents who are thinking of letting their second and third graders play club volleyball:

> At Marin Juniors, we understand that expert training in volleyball techniques is the foundation of great teams and great players. However, we also know that in order to develop truly amazing teams and for young players to get the most out of their volleyball experience, development must go beyond simply serving, passing, setting and hitting. In order to develop the complete athlete, Marin Juniors is determined to provide support around some key areas and have [sic] partnered with experts in the areas of sports nutrition, team dynamics, mental toughness and fitness.[10]

For today's grade school athlete, "expert training" in the various "techniques" of the sport is not reductive enough, not when pediatric sports science allows us to break the promising young mechanism down into its eating, breathing, sociability, tissue repair, and psychic-resilience functions.

But what kind of future *is* this, such that these laboratory methods seem necessary for realizing it? How long and hard is the haul, such that a fourth grader—or even a seventh or ninth grader—might be helped by an expert in mental toughness? On the first page of the Marin Juniors website, the first two sentences under the heading "Indoor Volleyball" give a suggestion: "The most experienced coaching staff in the area will teach, train and inspire teams to reach new heights. Our age-appropriate, consistent training methods will prepare players for the next level."[11]

The next level. This phrase is ubiquitous in the testimony of youth sports clubs, as sociologist Rick Eckstein points out in his informative book *How College Athletics Are Hurting Girls' Sports.* When they involve themselves with one of these clubs, parents are immediately thrown into the imagined future in which their scientifically developed child athlete has ascended to a different, next level, which, obviously, is college. The club's website will probably have a page listing its prestigious alumnae and the colleges they've gone on to play for, and the schools their oldest current players will be playing for next year, and the schools whose coaches are supposedly recruiting their somewhat younger players right now. Some clubs have pretty impressive lists. Seeing three or four players from *just last year* playing varsity soccer or lacrosse or volleyball at Division I schools, and seven or eight current players receiving the attentions of, or with active commitments to, serious colleges, must be pretty arresting for parents pondering a sport and a club, while also pondering the cost of college, for their little kid. And to give all this distant, dreamy college stuff a rough patina of realness, the website might note that the club has its own counseling program for players navigating the complicated process of college recruiting. At some point, some of these clubs will come out and put the prospect of college before younger players and their parents, as a reason for them to stay in this high-intensity, high-involvement relationship. Eckstein quotes a speaker at a meeting of the National Soccer Coaches Association of America exhorting his listeners on this theme: "You have got to start telling the parents early and often that your team and club will be a ticket to the next level. Don't wait. Start right at U9 or even earlier so they start thinking about travel as an investment in college."[12]

In this world things go from just getting your athletic kid into a sport to a big project for tackling the future pretty fast. This is why—in addition to the word *develop*—the literature of club sports teams often contains the word "commitment" or its equivalents. You and the club are in it for the sake of the future, and it takes commitment to make your mark on the future. To be clear, the commitment sports clubs typically invoke does not bind the *player* to the club, or not just the player. It binds the player's *family*. When I get a glossy postcard or pamphlet from a California soccer camp, this mailer is addressed not to my soccer-playing kids but to the Feeney family. When clubs lay out their "Expectations of Commitment," these expectations are addressed to the family, or the parents, as much as the young player. If your child signs up with Spurs FC of El Cerrito, for example, "you and your player are committing to all the other . . .

players and their families that your player is going to show up, day in and day out—on time and with a good attitude."[13] If your son starts playing with Montclair Soccer Club, you are warned that "competitive soccer requires a high level of commitment from the players and families who participate."[14] If your daughter plays for Walnut Creek Surf, the club requires "from families and players . . . a personal commitment to be the very best soccer player and person."[15] The practical upshot of commitment in these terms is the procession of households I saw moving into and out of the tournament grounds at those Las Vegas soccer parks. Their kid playing soccer entailed a commitment to do several of these family schleps every year.

This leads us to some curious institutional facts. When you look at the latest bracket for the NCAA men's basketball tournament, or the playoff brackets of the NBA or NHL, or the regular season schedules of these sporting organizations, and you think of the games being played, the players arriving and departing, eating and sleeping, you don't stop to ask yourself: Wait, who's making all this *happen*? You just assume the teams are, of course, and the leagues or other organizational bodies, big-money businesses or organizations making more big money through these competitions. But if you look at the even more elaborate competitive hierarchies and brackets and schedules by which competitive youth soccer clubs play out their travel-league schedules and take their tournament trips, and you think to ask yourself these questions, your answer won't be cash-rich teams and leagues making money for all the money they're laying out. Your answer will be: parents. Parents on the internet, making plans. Parents in cars. Parents on planes. I'm not saying it's wrong or bad, necessarily. I'm just saying it's curious, if you think about it this way, and kind of remarkable, that the massive, byzantine, nationwide system of soccer play and soccer travel is bankrolled and actuated through the private funds and Expedia accounts of individual families, moms and dads like you and me. It is *at the prompting* of the clubs and leagues that this system is created, and according to blueprints drawn (and then adaptively redrawn) in club or organizational offices, but most of the effort and nearly all the money come from families. Maybe the Commitments page of soccer clubs' websites should say, "When you sign up your child for competitive soccer, you are making a commitment to fuel and thereby constitute, with your family's money and time and energy, a sublimely elaborate organizational and competitive machinery to which you will also be beholden in ways you don't foresee and won't fully understand. Just so you know."

In her excellent book *All Joy and No Fun*, Jennifer Senior cites the Suzuki method of violin training to make a trenchant point about intensive parenting that applies here. "At the heart of the method lay a very generous theory, which is that all children are capable of musical accomplishment." Now, behind this theory lay the stern assumption that the child will show "a high level of commitment." However, Senior notes, the "truly unusual" thing about the Suzuki method is the "high level of commitment [it requires] from parents too." Parents become teaching assistants, or support staff, "attend[ing] music lessons and pay[ing] attention to what's being taught."

Senior notes that the Suzuki method is now used "to teach all kinds of musical instruments, not just the violin." This is also "a pretty good metaphor," she continues, for how, "everything [parents do] . . . has to be full-saturation involvement," parent and child working together. It's "not just the violin," but "making the pinewood derby car for Cub Scouts," "playing the role of sports agent" during soccer season, "curating summers at six different kinds of camp."[16]

Senior stresses the parent side of this phenomenon, and with good reason: the change in the conduct of middle-class American parents over the last thirty years—the generalization of Suzuki-style commitments of time and effort—is indeed remarkable. But it makes the picture even fuller and more instructive, if also a good deal weirder, when we bring the organizations or institutions back into the frame. The expectations behind the Suzuki method, after all, come from music teachers, not parents. These teachers simply expect that parents—being the devoted sorts of parents who submit their children to the notoriously difficult process of mastering the violin—will make the logistical and devotional efforts they request. The broad, optimistic, vaguely democratic conceits behind the method carry their own motivational power, no doubt—that this mysterious skill of violin playing is not in fact mysterious, not a measure of rare innate talent, but rather a technical output of maximized inputs, conditioned more by will and grit and time-at-task than by musical gifts. How inspiring for the parent with a flexible schedule. It's not unlike the promise of making your child into a soccer star by multiplying the thousands of touches she gets in the extra clinic sessions you drive her to on the two days a week she doesn't have a game or a practice.

When parents choose the Suzuki method for their children, they take on an entangling commitment, much as the parents who sign up their kids for a serious club sport are exhorted to make a commitment, or informed that by enrolling their child they *have* made a commitment, on behalf of their family unit, to the club. The sports organization has selected the child, nominally, in its sign-up or tryout procedures, but the more important unit of selection, from its organizational perspective, is the child's family.

What I'm saying is that the era of intensive parenting is defined by the rise of a sort of hybrid entity, an institutional cyborg that is part organization and part family. The boundary between family and organization has broken down, or been redrawn as porous and permeable. Parents and organizations become components of each other, agents of each other's functions. The competitive sports club staffs itself with parent officers and parent volunteers and parent board members, and relies on the massive logistical and financial input of players' families. Families, observing the fullness of their commitment to the organization, become defined by the functions the organization has deputized or obliged them to carry out. They drive, they feed, they fly, they keep time and buy snacks and staff boards of directors. They pay for chiropractors and personal trainers and orthopedic surgeons. When the organization takes on a child as a player or member, it is simply understood that it is also enlisting his or her family, and the family's time and effort and money, as resources for the larger enterprise of the organization. In having your child join a competitive youth sports club, as I said above, you make your family, perforce, into a youth sports family. "We're a soccer family!" is not just a cute thing you say that means your kids have a sport they like to play and you try to watch them when you can. It means that you've fused yourself with the hybrid entity. You're part of the institution. And the institution's part of you.

SCHOLARS AND WRITERS WHO FOCUS ON THE EXCESSES OF youth sports usually eventually take explanatory recourse in that familiar megavariable of academic sociology: capitalism. Here is Rick Eckstein, the sociologist, noting how his investigations into youth sports confirm this explanatory reflex of his discipline: "The notions of corporatization, commercialization, and commodification are deeply embedded in sociology's historical roots, and it was both intellectually exciting and morally depressing to watch them at work in the milieu of girls' youth sports."[17]

As to how these forces work, and on whom, he writes: "Parents and other adults who place too much importance on youth sports were making conscious decisions, but they were making them under social and historical conditions not of their own choosing." In his reference to choices constrained by unchosen "social and historical conditions" he's speaking of *ideology* and *false consciousness*, more or less in the Marxist sense. "Social and historical conditions," according to Marx's theory of ideology, radically limit and shape the perspectives and choices of those who live and think, moralize and legislate, within those conditions. In a capitalist society, those conditions are capitalism, or, as Eckstein puts it, "corporatization, commercialization, and commodification."[18]

I find this unpersuasive. Eckstein's right that money is a malign influence in youth sports, but viewing the competitive machinery of clubs and leagues through the critique-of-capitalism lens mischaracterizes the predicament of the families caught within that machinery, precisely in this core act of "choosing" and its conditions. An illustrative contrast is the very different kind of machinery that dominates high-level youth sports in Europe, especially soccer (football). This is the club academy system. In this system, quite unlike in the United States, the training of promising young footballers is undertaken and paid for by professional football clubs (FCs)—smaller clubs like Girona FC and Middlesbrough FC, big and famous clubs like Manchester United FC and FC Barcelona. Almost all the clubs whose top teams play in the top leagues have youth academies. European football is dominated by huge and glamorous business entities that operate under much harsher conditions of capitalist competition than do American pro sports leagues—which function as cozy socialist cartels in which wealthy owners share revenue and cap salaries, and where teams don't get dropped into the minor leagues for being terrible. And, while American professional sports leagues observe the genteel practice of "trading" players, in Europe pro footballers are *bought* and *sold*. Youth academies are a key part of this capitalist machinery. As the father of one Dutch academy player put it, the kids in this system are "capital."[19]

The key difference between European and American systems of youth soccer isn't the presence of money or capitalist influence, then. It's the presence of *parents*. In Europe, young players are brought into the academy system by scouts working for clubs, not via the bespoke development and competitive strategizing of ambitious moms and dads. These scouts visit schoolyards and junior games looking for little football standouts, prodigies of raw talent or soccer intuition, to whose parents they might later pay a Sunday visit and pose the fateful question: Does your lad want to join our academy?

Compared to sports parents in Europe, American parents have far wider latitude for seeing and choosing how they might involve their children in youth sports, far greater decision power, far greater control over the details of their kids' sports careers. They participate far more directly in the organizations that oversee those careers. The entire structure of youth sports in America is a monument to the enlarged agency of bourgeois American parents. Many clubs and leagues are founded and run by parents. Many of the peculiarities and excesses of these leagues come from the indirect influence or direct intervention of empowered parents.

Even the overtraining injuries often mentioned in discussions of American youth sports bear the causal stamp not of "capitalism" but of "American parenting"—or, this hybrid entity of parents and the sporting institutions, which carries a certain structural bias for doing things to excess. Recall the Dutch father I cite above, who refers to his son as "capital," private property of the Dutch company AFC Ajax NV (*Naamloze Vennootschap*, Dutch for "Nameless Partnership"—nomenclature that, in English, sounds like something from a satire of capitalism). He uses that term, "capital," not to evoke indifference or abuse at Ajax's hands but to note the care and caution with which the club treats the bodily health of its young players. "They do not want to do anything to injure them or wear them out," he says. "They're capital. And what is the first thing a businessman does? He protects his capital."[20]

How might it be that nameless partnerships in the people-selling business are better than American sports parents at protecting the health of the young athletes in their care? It is obviously not because nameless partnerships love their players more than American sports parents love their children. And it is obviously not because American parents are more capitalist than profit-driven nameless partnerships. It is, rather, that the nameless partnership is better positioned to make cool-headed, cautious decisions about how much training a child should be asked to handle than are American parents. This is not to say that European sports academies are good or healthy for the children who live and practice within them. For many reasons—young children's separation from their families, the shoddy education they often receive, the predictable hazing and other *Lord of the Flies* aspects of dormitory life—a sports academy does not sound like an experience I would want for my own children. Indeed, this is another indication that American sports parents are more empowered than their European counterparts, and less constrained in their decisions by economic conditions. In America, competitive club sports are largely a middle- and upper-middle-class pursuit. In Europe, the stereotypical academy boy comes from the working class.

The problem of overspecialization further illustrates this point. Many critics, from coaches to psychologists to orthopedic surgeons, point out that America's young athletes are specializing in a single sport, and playing that sport year-round, when they should be sampling many different sports. Specializing too early is bad for many reasons. Kids can burn out emotionally and psychologically when they play one sport all the time, especially under the intensive conditions of training and coaching and traveling typical in competitive club sports. They get injured at higher rates, in ways specific to this early specialization. That is, they suffer direct "overuse" injuries to the muscles and bones and joints their sport tends to stress, and they suffer what might be called disequilibrium injuries that come from having overdeveloped muscles and ingrained movement habits useful to one sport but harmful to overall physical resilience and structural balance.

For all the reformist complaints about these injuries, the institutions of America's high-involvement youth sports seem to view them as a lamentable but inherent part of the club sports bargain. The website of a St. Louis youth soccer club contains this paragraph under the heading "Length of Season":

Missouri Youth Soccer Association rules set the seasonal year from August through July of the following year. In practice, fall league play wraps up in less-intensive winter activities like futsal [indoor soccer played with a smaller ball, on a basketball court] or indoor [indoor soccer played on a smaller pitch of artificial turf] with very limited or no practice sessions. Spring League games typically start in early March and run through mid-May. Older teams participate in State Cup in June. The younger teams, U11 or younger, recess for June and July.[21]

To recap, "older" players play organized soccer eleven months of the year. "Younger" players, given a longer "recess," play only ten. As a darkly comic sidenote, when I came upon this paragraph there was an ad right next to it, in the margin, for a suburban St. Louis chiropractic office. This, in its entirety, was the ad's copy: "Specializing in soccer related injuries and performance enhancement."[22] Apart from burnout and injury there's the basic matter of getting good at your sport, which early specializing actually hinders, according to many coaches.

So it seems it's in everyone's interest to restructure competitive club sports to make them more relaxed, to allow more space for players to play several sports. Well, maybe not *all* the interests, of *everyone*. The interests of the clubs and coaches are mixed. On one hand, a more relaxed approach, with kids sampling several sports, might make their players better in the long run. On the other hand, clubs like the fees that come from year-round programs, and coaching is what coaches know. They want year-round coaching jobs. But they're not exactly dictating terms to families. Parents run many clubs, and they have considerable influence at most. Why aren't these influential parents steering coaches to these more holistic methods, which are not just safer and healthier but more effective?

Unlike in Europe, with its top-down organizations—based in professional clubs, national federations, or some collaboration between the two—there's no person or body in the United States that can take these helpful insights about healthier training and make them mandatory, or even propagate them with a semblance of authority. If a prominent coach or parent-officer in an American youth sports club, infused with a crusading spirit after reading all the bad stuff about overuse injuries and overspecialization, were to declare to her coaching peers or fellow parents that everyone needs to tone it down, make things more fun, shorten their seasons, and let their kids play several sports, the response of her audience would have to be: *you first*.

For both parents, whose kids are competing with other parents' kids, and clubs, which are competing with other clubs for the best players, moving to a partial-year schedule that encourages multisport participation looks a lot like unilateral disarmament. Sure, that strategy might offer long-term benefits. But it's hard for parents to look at the long term, given the short-term need to simply keep your kid in the club *now*, moving up through the colored ranks *now*, getting playing time *now*—because the alternative is having his participation in the sport *end*. What choice do you have? You have to assume that other families are driven by the same short-term thinking you are, because they assume you're driven by the same short-term thinking they are. The same goes for clubs, which need to stay attractive to these *now*-based parents *this year* and can't risk letting their guard down against the other clubs. Because no one's in a position to force everyone to adopt the judicious long-term position, doing so unilaterally can put any parent or club at a decisive short-term disadvantage. And even if parents somehow reached an armistice that stopped this all-year competition, the incentive to break the agreement—"defect," in the language of game theory—would persist. It's parents after all. They want the best for *their* kid. Indeed, you can see the entire structure of club sports as a sort of social-contract scenario in reverse, the result some primordial act of defection, in which a nice arrangement—scholastic sports, in which kids conveniently played their sports in the same place where they spent their days, starting, reasonably, in seventh grade—was unraveled by some original defector dad in the misty theoretical past who, wanting a leg up for his kid, founded an out-of-school club for sixth graders, after which the arms race took over.

To be clear, I'm not *blaming* this problem on individual parents. I'm pointing to the competitive logic in which their family commitment to club sports entangles them. The maniac parent is a stock figure in commentary on youth sports, and I'm sure there are a lot of them scattered around. It's a big country, and they tend to stand out, and it feels good to blame the bad things on the bad people—the crazy stage moms, sideline dads berating their kids or threatening coaches or punching referees. But it illuminates very little. You glimpse the deeper tendencies not through the villainous exception, but through the much more sympathetic rule.

I spoke with several parents in Las Vegas who were fully concerned about the toll that year-round soccer was taking on their sons, teenage boys who had either suffered injuries or shown early signs of burnout, or both—and they, parents and sons, had discussed these things together. The Los Angeles mom I mentioned above related some difficult conversations she'd recently had with her son. "I don't know if I can keep doing this," he admitted to her at one point. He was just coming back from an Achilles injury. He was tired. He was a serious student with excellent academic prospects who got inadequate sleep and had very little free time. And she was fully willing to let him quit, if that's what he wanted. But they'd made this commitment years ago, and he had some college coaches interested in him, and, deep down, he still loved playing, and so he decided to keep going. His little sister was dribbling a ball in front of their mom and me as we talked. She'd just joined a competitive club. Somewhat wearily, her mom said she was ready to do it all again.

CAPITALISM IS NOT *ABSENT* FROM SUCH A DYNAMIC. ENTER-prisers can indeed make money by setting up shop at the margins of an arms race and selling competitive gear to the adversaries. But that is very different from saying that they are responsible for the arms race. And besides, the main elements of the "youth sports industrial complex"[23] are a pretty unimpressive lot—

medium-sized towns building big soccer and baseball parks so they can feed tournament traffic to their struggling businesses, small groups of former college players who start tiny companies to run for-profit skill clinics, the thousands of small, local, non-profit clubs. The idea that the empowered American parents running their kids through the all-year rigors of youth sports are doing so because their consciousness has been taken over by the "industrial complex" of small-city mayors and former Division II midfielders does not pass the laughability test.

Pointing out a confusion that dogs this focus on capitalist persuasion helps us see the real predicament of sports parents, and the real economic inequities the system generates. According to articles and books criticizing the youth sports industrial complex, parents are duped by capitalist marketing into spending gratuitously on their kids' youth sports careers. But often the same article or book will bewail the class bias in the pay-to-play system: it's mainly well-off parents who afford the hefty club fees and elite skill clinics that give kids a leg up in winning the big prizes, college scholarships, or at least preferred college admissions as recruited athletes. In the former case the parents can't see their own interests thanks to capitalism. In the latter they're crafty elites, hoarding advantages for their own already advantaged kids.

The latter complaint is sounder than the former. Eckstein documents how well-off parents discovered and exploited the new sports niches that opened up in the early 1990s, when the US Department of Education began enforcing Title IX more stringently—that is, interpreting a law broadly dictating gender equality in education to mean that, for men and women, intercollegiate sports opportunities and scholarships should be numerically equal, or as close to equal as possible, at individual colleges and universities. Opportunities for female athletes to play at an intercollegiate level rose dramatically, and so the number of valuable scholarships and desirable preferred-admissions slots exploded too. At this point, Eckstein shows, empowered, savvy, forward-looking parents of school-aged girls moved into or created or built up clubs and leagues, especially in posh sports like lacrosse and crew, where the competition was initially weak and through which their daughters might win spots on the new women's teams that colleges were forming.

This expansion of women's college sports was a sort of parenting arbitrage opportunity for those who saw it first. Of course, better-off parents saw it first. Eckstein cites a study of ten Division I college programs in women's field hockey and soccer that found that scholarship athletes in those sports "had family incomes roughly twenty-one percent higher than those of students as a whole."[24] To be clear, the family incomes of these field hockey and soccer scholarship recipients were not higher than *athletes* in other sports, such as football and basketball, but higher than the general population of students. So the explosion of girls' club sports under Title IX is, at least partly, another story of empowered parents using their existing advantages to seize even more advantages. Indeed, peering through a critique-of-capitalism lens, one might view the ubiquitous "girl power" marketing motif, in its commercial origins, as ideological cover for moneyed people gaming the college admissions process.

AND YET ECKSTEIN'S BOOK IS ALSO A CATALOG OF THE TROU-bles these families suffer thanks to their involvement in these competitive systems. The parents are run ragged and stretched financially. Their daughters drive themselves to burnout and injury through ceaseless training and travel and competition—all to gain those elusive scholarships, or at least preferred admission as recruited athletes.

And, except in major sports like football and basketball, most of these scholarships are merely partial, and at the smaller schools, in the NCAA's lowest competitive tier (Division III), there are no scholarships at all, merely the promise of preferred admission for those designated as "recruited athletes." Indeed, whatever the value of their scholarships, athletes in every NCAA division enjoy this admissions bonus, which grows in its perceived value depending on how selective the school is. That is, a college coach or athletic director identifies an applicant as a "recruited athlete," and the admissions department typically waves the kid into the school, as long as he or she meets some basic academic standards.

In most sports, then, only the very best players will win full-ride scholarships. The likeliest prospects for even elite players, coming from popular club sports like soccer and lacrosse, feature merely partial scholarships, while for other players who excelled at the club and scholastic levels, the biggest prize to look forward to is preferred admission to the schools that recruit them.

SUBMITTING YOUR KID AND YOUR FAMILY TO TEN YEARS OF expensive and exhausting club sports involvement for a chance at some partial scholarship looks irrational, then, and reformers and critics cite statistics that seem to prove it *is* irrational. In a *Time* magazine article on the big money moving into youth sports, one reads, "Only 2% of high school athletes go on to play at the top level of college sports, the NCAA's Division I." This seems dispositive. Giving up your life to a pricey club sport for a one-in-fifty shot at a partial scholarship is obviously nuts. But if you probe this statistical vessel even a little, it starts to leak, and the calculations of committed sports parents start to look a little sounder. If you change high school athletes to *varsity* high school athletes, for example, the percentage would increase, and if you refined that category to "varsity athletes who also played clubs sports competitively through high school" the percentage would increase further, and if you found some way to adjust for the intensity of involvement in the club sport, including the hours of specialized clinics and outside training these athletes received, your percentage would probably go up more still. And if you replaced "play at the top level of college sports, the NCAA's Division I," with "gain any kind of college scholarship or admissions preference," the percentage would multiply several times.

In other words, the percentage of athletes whose families made and sustained a commitment to competitive club sports from their grade school years through their high school years, and augmented that commitment with private coaching and other custom enhancements, who then received *some* college-related bonus for their efforts would have to be, at the very least, nontrivial. The number is surely well into the double digits, perhaps as much as a quarter or a third, and even higher for some of the more obscure and rarefied sports that colleges underwrite for their various terrible reasons. This is a case where what economists call the "sunk cost fallacy" may not be a fallacy, where the yearslong commitment is its own justification: the longer your kid stays in, the better her chances get, not least because of simple attrition among your competitors.

This tendency to downplay the likelihood that these parents will achieve *some* payoff mischaracterizes their deeper—what you might call philosophical—dilemma on the matter of sticking with it. To me, their philosophical dilemma is worse than the critics think because their calculations are better than these critics claim. In other words, the problem with intensive youth sports involvement is not that it's a delusional quest for illusory prizes but that it's a trap of marginal rationality. That is, sports parents look into the future and—adjusting for the variables that the critics omit but remain within their control as parent managers of their kids' sports careers—decide it might just make sense. It might actually be rational, *marginally* rational. There's a half-decent chance that spending all this money to recast the inner and outer life of your family as part of a demanding ad hoc bureaucracy of some youth sport, while increasingly testing the physical health and psychological well-being of your athlete child, over ten or so years, will end up being worth it, sort of, depending on how you define "worth it."

It's not crazy to think it could pay off, at the margins. You can imagine the ad hoc accounting of a sports parent taking this form: "Maybe Chad's partial scholarship over four years of college won't exceed our gross expenditures over his ten years of club lacrosse, but maybe it will. After all, the value of those quarter scholarships is going up at the same dizzying rate as the price of college, and, to be fair, we should really only start adding up the cost, for the sake of comparison, from the point where we started thinking about this lacrosse thing in college terms, which was . . . roughly . . . U14? Okay, U12. Also, if he's good enough to be recruited by a few programs, and you cultivate coaches at the right places, his 'recruited athlete' status should get him into a better school than he'd have gotten into otherwise, with *his* grades, and isn't that what really matters?

"And we're here, aren't we? We made it this far, so we might as well keep going another year. If we start counting expenses from this point, the college thing makes even more sense."

EARLY IN THIS CHAPTER I MENTIONED HOW, WANDERING BEtween the pitches of the big Las Vegas soccer tournament, I was often drawn to solitary parents watching from farther down the sidelines, the ones who'd put an obvious gap between themselves and the parents of their sons' teammates. I didn't expect this physical detachment to betoken other, more abstract sorts of detachment. I just figured they'd be easier to talk to. Perhaps my being a writer doing research on youth sports—I tried to admit this right away—made these moms and dads self-conscious, and they were just saying what would make them look smart and knowing in the book I was writing, but, even so, I was often struck by how jaded they sounded. I came expecting to pick up tasty nuggets of parental crazy talk, and instead, in these cases, I got something closer to social criticism.

One man from the Midwest, father of a sixteen-year-old playing on the pitch in front of us, wanted me to know that *some* of his fellow parents were staking a lot on the possibility of scholarships, but he wasn't one of them. He nodded down the sidelines to our left as we spoke, to the parents gathered more tensely together near midfield. "They're all waiting for a college coach to knock on their door," he said. "They're living the dream." He didn't mean this phrase in its usual sense of "living their ideal life," obviously. He meant "living *in* a dream," "asleep without realizing it." He was a high school wrestling coach who'd wrestled in college, and so he knew the scholarship deal for minor sports. This hadn't prevented him from getting sucked into a decade of high-priced soccer involvement governed, among his fellow parents, by these marginal calculations about college. His athletic son had merely wanted to play serious soccer, and these were the terms of participation—onerous, yes, but no other terms were available. What freedom remained to him to define his family's involvement in club soccer, it seemed, was this critical attitude, his ability to claim that, at the very least, he was free of the stock ambitions.

A California dad I met down the sidelines of a U17 game on the last day of the tournament had the same attitude. He smiled puckishly as he told me—while chewing pistachios and interrupting himself to spit the broken shells between his feet—that he knew his son wouldn't be playing in college. It didn't matter anyway, he said, because the scholarships were too paltry to build any plans around. He took a certain pleasure in informing me that, for this "college showcase" tournament, the college coaches were *paid* to be there. That is, they were paid out of tournament funds, not from their own schools' recruiting budgets, to entice all those distant clubs and families to make the trip. "Wined and dined," he smirked. This would be one of the crowning events in his son's long soccer career, and yet the thing that seemed most important to him, personally, was to preserve some critical space for himself to make fun of it.

Another dad raised the pitch of irony even higher. I'd spoken with his wife on the first day of the tournament, and she'd told him about me, a writer lurking about the tournament grounds, and so when she saw me the next day she was eager to introduce us. He was ready for me, wound up, full of thoughts. From a distance, when she first pointed him out, I might have taken him as a textbook Bad Sports Dad—an intense-looking guy in a tight black T-shirt, with short, graying blond hair, a thick neck, and big chest. I learned he had a high-powered job as an automotive engineer and executive in suburban Detroit, and, indeed, he came on like a David Mamet character, hard-voiced and fast-talking, brash and yet, again, knowing, sharply ironic about his own participation in this event. His wife, whom I'd found watching their son's game down the sidelines by herself, of course, had spoken with gentle optimism about the boy's college prospects, and also about the crushing schedule of his club. Yes, he got home at ten thirty after his weeknight practices, and then he had to eat dinner and maybe do a little homework, and so, with the seven o'clock start of his school day, his sleep was pretty compromised, but he was getting some looks from small colleges around the Midwest, and a couple of these colleges were Lutheran, and their family was Lutheran, so that would be nice, soccer at a Lutheran college. College soccer was a modest but living prospect for her, but not for her husband, who thought the whole college showcase thing was a big joke. "Look at this place," he said, capping a long, withering riff on the sporting apparatus that had taken over his family's life. We were leaving the park at this point, returning to the entrance patio, where tents were set up for the vending of player photos and T-shirts, and he stopped and gestured around, smiling at the timely appearance of these props for his spontaneous lecture. "It's a racket."

The attitudes of this husband and wife were at odds, in some obvious sense, but they seemed in decent balance to me. The kindly mom was making the most of their situation, emphasizing the positive, which seemed entirely sane and reasonable. It's what my sane and reasonable wife would do, in the impossible event she would let our family fuse itself with the institutions of youth sports. The cocky dad was more defiant. It may not have been entirely healthy or adaptive to dwell on the dark side of this sports commitment, the decade of having a series of soccer clubs tell him how his family's time and money were going to be spent, but some mix of honesty and pride inspired a more hostile retrospect on this decade. This, though perhaps not as entirely sane as his wife's smoother accommodations with reality, struck me as equally reasonable.

THE DEFIANT ATTITUDE OF THESE PARENTS MAKES EVEN more sense when you see it as directed at something beyond merely the time and money burdens of their sports commitment. All of them conveyed a sort of moral recoil against the inner, spiritual pressures of this complicated enterprise, the assumption that they should *think a certain way* about youth sports. When we throw our sentimental devotion as parents into mastering a bureaucratic process for the sake of some supposed advantage, this process has a way of moving into us, mastering us. We've addressed it with such loving seriousness, after all. It's only natural that these sodden feelings would transfer onto the objects of our desperate striving, and we'd come to view the organizational personnel who boss us around as mentors and moral guides, and their bureaucratic procedures as liturgy or spiritual teaching. This is what the defiant parents I spoke to in Las Vegas were trying to resist. They didn't want their outer conformity with the scheduled busyness of their kids' athletic careers to become an inner condition of their beliefs as parents, a spiritual trait of their families.

But this attitude is hard to maintain, especially since, as sociologist Annette Lareau has lamented, the inner lessons it's trying to resist might well give the families that learn them a leg up. In her groundbreaking book *Unequal Childhoods*, Lareau describes how the intensive, hands-on methods of well-off and well-educated parents confer subtle skills that will serve their children in the key, competitive moments in their future lives, skills that poorer, less-intensively parented children tend to lack, children raised in the hands-off ways once common among all social classes. As Lareau argues, their heavily scheduled, officially programmed childhoods instill in these better-off kids a sort of general institutional competence. They are conditioned to dwell agreeably in the school building and the workplace, trained in those all-important "time-management skills."[25] A signal part of these busy childhoods, in Lareau's portrait of them, is organized youth sports. And you can see how the most useful thing young people take away from their years of competitive sports, as they move into college and jobs, might be this mix of institutional coping and time-management skills. There's a lot of institutional coping that goes into a youth sports career, and a lot of time managing.

But I would like to bring the great Johan Huizinga back into the discussion, just to note how much of a bummer it would be for him to see what we've done with the primal and subversive play-spirit that courses though all our lives but that defines the lives of our children, how we've rechanneled and repurposed it to optimize their value as future employees by enhancing their time-management skills. In youth sports, not only have the schemes and details of play been "systematized and regimented," in Huizinga's unhappy phrase, but the larger settings of children's play, and our larger understanding of play's role in their lives, have been utterly suffused with, reduced to, the safe, sensible logic of normal life.

To be sure, parents, schools, and national governments have long imagined that the sporting play of children might serve more wholesome ends. But as a former high school athlete who remembers "team spirit" as a kind of conspiracy, an ethos of misbehavior, I'm skeptical that sports teach the useful and sociable and patriotic virtues better than the other things kids do with their time—wage work, hobbies, homework, talking to their friends. But apparently, if Lareau is correct, at a certain level of logistical intensity and organizational saturation, childhood play as it's been remade in competitive club sports really does make kids into better schedulers. Sometimes you even hear these sports praised for this reason, by parents and coaches, and also by college admissions personnel, who, for their own reasons, place a high value on the pliant attitudes and harried busyness of other people's children. The practical upside of hyperorganized play may ease our parental fears, but as the untimely thoughts of Johan Huizinga help us see, the idea that the soundest, most reliable thing youth sports teach is organizational coping is really a sign of what's wrong with them.

Huizinga's portrait of play resonates for a broader reason. When he describes the "magic circle," the secret, conspiratorial space of play, I think, beyond play itself, of family life. Like play as Huizinga describes it, the home lives of families are also, in a certain obvious way, circled off from the outside world, and within that circle, these lives are rich with private meanings, and, indeed, many of these private meanings arise from what is, undeniably, play. Think of how much of what goes or went on among you and your family members is or was actually play, or at least inflected with play. In my own home, with both my children and my wife, when I'm not addressing some practical matter or urgent task—though often when I'm addressing them too—my speech has a play character I would not share with the outside world. I speak in some American accent not my own, often the North Carolina accent I heard during my many years of grad school, or varieties of British accent, which I'm pretty good at (though perhaps not as good as domestic privacy lets me think I am). Juliet has her own range of play accents she uses with our kids, almost as a matter of course. When she and I address each other in calmer, more tender, more romantic moments, it is often in the sort of accent one associates with mountain folk and country music. It was only recently, since my oldest child learned the phrase "dad joke" from her fellow cynics in middle school, that I counted up and realized between 5 and 10 percent of what I say to my kids counts as dad jokes. (The sudden, intense onset of public selfhood in the middle school years is a challenge to the private play-spirit of home, especially but not only in its dad-joke form. The middle schooler at home, entirely shielded from the public gaze, sighs miserably at the dad joke as if both her friends and her enemies are in the kitchen with us, invisibly watching and listening and video recording.)

Our kids themselves, of course, play constantly, interact constantly through play modes, occupy themselves alone through play modes, and these play modes are different from the ones they enact outside the home, with their friends. They're more performative, less guarded, more musical, closer to pure nonsense. This is how it was within my own big family growing up: staged battles, intentionally bad singing, foreign accents, constant interruptions and unserious comebacks, invented sports, Dada silliness—depths of commitment in all these nonsensical things that we could never reach with even our best friends. These shared rituals of play deepened our clannish bonds with each other, etched the circle of our separateness from the larger world, and also from the other big families, who were drawing their own magic circles, their own worlds of private meaning, around themselves.

chapter four

Parents, Kids, and the Internet

Family Life and the Question of Technology

FIRST OFF I THOUGHT IT WAS BEAUTIFUL, THE iPAD MY parents gave me for my birthday in 2010, its different surfaces—clear screen, white border, silver back—barely contrasting with each other, so that, imagining it, I might cast it one time as virgin white in its entirety, and then as a plane of silver so pale it was nearly invisible, and then as a fine wedge of heavy glass. That it was flat, rectangular, lovely and yet visually neutral, made it seem more medium or portal than object. Through it came supernatural powers, whose conjurer and user would be me.

For me, the iPad would mainly be an e-reader. It would give me the power to read better, via the iBooks app, with its bold black letters standing out from their clean white background.

I'd always wanted to read well, but I was and am, in the simple mechanics of the act, a terrible reader, slow and distractible, prone to fidgets. The iPad, though, would make my reading voracious. I would lap up those dark tasty words from that milky surface. But the iPad's true payoff would be parental and pedagogical. We had two daughters by then, and a son on the way, and the thought of all the educational "content" my kids could "access" on that ingenious "tablet" made my heart sing. Snobbishly, vainly, perhaps jealously since I still had a flip phone at the time, I thought there was something decadent in the image of a little kid jabbing at a parent's iPhone. But my iPad was a *tablet*. Somehow, simply in its larger scale, it replaced the suggestion of parental laziness with a feeling of wholesomeness and fitness.

The tablet would give my kids educational advantages I never had. As a kid I didn't learn about the night sky, for example. And knowing about the night sky, placing yourself amid the uncountable bits of immeasurable creation, is like the deepest, most basic educational thing there is, in my philosophy. The tablet could teach my kids their tiny, off-center place in the great universe. So, the first app I downloaded was Solar Walk, which is nothing less than an interactive, three-dimensional, photo-real simulacrum of our solar system, on which you can zoom around from planet to planet, taking the trippy perspective of each one, repeatedly reknowing our Earth as the blueish ball next to the reddish one. Solar Walk was the most educational damn thing I'd ever seen. So I bought its sister app, Star Walk, which blew my mind: an interactive picture encyclopedia of the visible universe that maps onto the real stars, interactively, when you turn your iPad to the sky.

But soon, as I was failing to become a better reader via iBooks, thanks to the iPad's many other tasty attractions, I was also starting to see the tablet's educational promise for my kids as hollow if not false. My daughters learned some quick lessons about the solar system from Solar Walk, and they developed a sort of aesthetic fascination with nebulae thanks to Star Walk, but the major appeal of these space apps, after a while, was clearly just their touch-screen value. They were panels of sweepable stimulation. I'd sit with my little girls and bring up a space app so they could, like, learn astrophysics, but they'd ignore my tutorial efforts in favor of tapping and spinning, unpinching to enlarge and pinching to minimize, more or less randomly, just for the eye-fun of it.

This wasn't what I had in mind. It seemed like my daughters and my iPad were working against me, together, concealing a crude economy of optical sensation within my own dumb hopes for easy learning of difficult things through beautiful machinery. And I couldn't help noting a conflict between the educational philosophy I noted—which stresses that the vastness of nature and the teeming strangeness of human experience are most profoundly understood when we concede our own subjective smallness—and the image of my daughter using her finger and thumb to make the solar system spin around.

It was the defining bait and switch of personal technology, in which the giddy foresense of extended power, when you're considering a new device or have just acquired one, is replaced with a daily experience of dull dependence, fitful compulsion, and trivial diversion. For parents and teachers, wanting this augmented power so badly for their kids and pupils, burdened to realize the brimming potential of these little humans, the urge to see educational magic in this slim gadgetry is hard to resist. I gave in to it even though my training in political theory and continental philosophy taught me a deep suspicion of the abstract power of technology and capitalism, especially when these things are colonizing the human worlds of everyday life, and the larger realms of education and culture. But this gleaming glass rectangle came with education inside it, supposedly, manufactured in vast Chinese factories for the most valuable corporation in the world, and I let myself be persuaded right away. My kids' future was at stake.

It is this, our willingness to be convinced of digital technology's promise, and then resigned before its influence and omnipresence, the simple scale of its claim over our lives, that I want to keep challenging and questioning in my own mental life. It's hard to keep our critical distance from something at once so beguiling and so ubiquitous. You can't escape the digital totality, and besides it comes with all these eye treats and ego puzzles and Wikipedia—so why bother? Still, in the philosophical tradition I was trained in, the fact that something has grown up around us as a totality, even if it's a totality of ease and fun, is reason enough to push it back out from its familiar closeness, to arm's length, where you can better see what it's up to. This is a difficult task, and in fact most people have little motivation to take it up, to ask fundamental questions about a power they can't escape. It's easier to look at the bright side, and go along for the ride. It's not like we have a choice. We're going where it's taking us. And for my part, I can adopt a monkish philosophical attitude toward technology, but I'm still going to twitch inside next time my phone makes the popcorn sound that says I have a text.

But there's a deep difference between my standpoint as a regular guy with an all-too-regular relationship with his iPhone, and my standpoint as a parent. I have no control over the degree to which digital technology rules the world outside my home, but inside my home, all the questions that society has answered, or allowed technology to answer on its behalf, remain open. Digital technology has remade the broader human world according to its powers, but its power to remake your family remains largely within your powers. You still have the power, once an iPad has found its way inside the home you share with your young children, to get rid of it, get the cursed thing out of the house, pass it along to your mother-in-law. It remains within your power to look at the total dominion of digital technology outside your home and determine what its influence will be on the inside. Who else has this power? Who else can create a world in which the extent of technology's rule has been consciously decided by people with powerful reason to treat it with suspicion? Even for parents it's difficult, of course. Even parents feel potent incentives to answer the question of technology in technology's terms, rather than their own.

"IT'S THE DREAM WE HAVE AS PARENTS"—GOOD MORNING *America* correspondent Becky Worley says into the camera, introducing a 2018 segment—"that kids can use their tablet for an hour or so but then they'll spend the rest of the day *climbing trees and playing with friends.*" The italics are in the original. For that last bit about trees and friends Worley sends her voice into a sardonic register, as if to indicate that we parents are dupes of some obsolete Romanticism for even *hoping* to see our kids climbing trees or playing with friends when there's consumer tech in the house. She continues, now in the sharper tone of a cynical TV pundit delivering the dark truth: "But then when reality hits it's only lunchtime, they've been on the device for five hours, and you're yelling at them *again* to put it *down*."[1]

Is that really the reality? Apparently it is, because the segment soon cuts to video of a seven-year-old boy jabbing at a blue-covered tablet, his four-year-old sister sweeping and then staring at a pink-covered tablet, and their ten-year-old brother thumbing his way through a combat game on a smartphone as the harsh video voiceover declares: "*Summertime means screen time.*" The segment then cuts to the kids' parents, who, we learn, harbor the same abstemious vision of tech use that Becky Worley expressed in the opening—kids sweeping and jabbing and staring at touch screens a mere one or two hours per morning. But these parents are helpless to realize this Romantic ideal, "exhausted" from even trying. We cut to video of the little girl sitting at a dining table with a full plate of food in front of her. She's ignoring the food, though, and staring at her tablet. Leaning over her shoulder her mom gently asks, "Are you just gonna keep watching that or are you going to eat your breakfast?" The girl says nothing, but the rigid, elbows-locked posture in which she's propping her tablet on the tabletop, and the animal fierceness of her focus on her screen, tell you that her answer to her mom's question is obviously: "I'm just gonna keep watching."

What's odd about this segment is that its theme, the problem it identifies, the practical question it poses to the *Good Morning America* audience is: What can we parents *do* about kids who spend so much time on their devices? But as I finished watching it, I thought a better theme would be: Why are these parents afraid of their small children?

In giving your four-year-old an iPad or a Kindle Fire, this segment would have you think, you're imbuing her with some mysterious immunity from parental control. Once the techno-cognitive nexus of tablet and child has been established as a domestic entity, mom and dad must humbly defer to its system imperatives. A mom might simply *order* her daughter to brush her teeth or let go of her brother's hair, but if a plate of lovingly scrambled eggs is getting cold because the tablet-child nexus has entered an agitated *Peppa Pig* state, mom has to speak softly and show some respect. The nexus doesn't like to be told what to do.

This is a recurring theme when daytime TV takes up the issue of kids and technology: parents disarmed before the influence of tablets, smartphones, computer games. What strikes you over and over again, in watching such segments, is the *humility* that digital technology seems to induce in parents, their tentativeness about their own parental judgment and authority. Computer devices enter the home and forge a special bond with children's precon-scious impulses, and parents start to feel themselves undermined, their prerogatives somehow under question, like a county sheriff experiencing a recall election.

This is also a theme of the documentary *Screenagers*, whose producers have foregone general release in theaters or on stream-ing platforms in favor of exclusive showings in schools and other special venues. *Screenagers* tells several stories, including one about the filmmaker herself and her husband, who are commit-ted to bringing their sixth-grade daughter into the smartphone stage of her life as mindfully and moderately as possible. They all agree ahead of time that there will be limits—no access at bedtime, for example. The girl's brittle excitement about getting the phone is palpable, and also ominous, given everyone's hopes for a calm transition to a phone regime ruled by sensible limits, mutually accepted. And things do go badly, right away, when the parents try to enforce the limits. For me the most memorable scene in the film was the daughter, now a socially plugged-in owner of a smartphone, slamming her bedroom door in her mother's face—her physician mother, researcher on and filmmaker about children and technology, reduced to a sad, helpless, solitary silence in the hallway. Even grimmer scenes in *Screenagers* feature a stout eleven-year-old boy being raised by his grandmother, who's too frightened of what he becomes when he plays video games to make him stop.[2]

I saw *Screenagers* in a large, very warm classroom in my daughters' middle school. Interest in this film was intense. The screening was sold out and then some. The sweltering room was *packed*, parents sitting and standing, kneeling and crouching. I had an odd feeling about this high turnout, this intense interest, because I knew that nearly all the middle school–aged children of these parents had smartphones. I knew this because my older daughter, then in seventh grade, sometimes complained that she was one of only two people in her whole grade who didn't have a phone.

This complaint has been updated, now that (as I write) she's in eighth grade and, reportedly, the *only* one in her grade without a phone. Strangely, though, it's voiced far less often this year, with much more acceptance. Also, lacking a phone has not prevented her from having an extremely active social life. So far, the most notable result of her and her sixth-grade sister not having their own smartphones—besides my being able to enjoy their undistracted presence at home, and having them remain the voracious book readers they were as grade-schoolers—is that we haven't had to endure the sorts of reverse domestic tyranny featured in *Screenagers*. We don't have any Bruce Banner characters in our family we have to worry about sending into Hulk mode by too assertively being parents, severing the explosive nexus they constitute with their stimulation portal.

Anyway, watching *Screenagers*, I was surrounded by people who, by sitting through this film in these uncomfortable conditions, were expressing how uneasy they were about the influence of digital technology upon their family and their children. But very few of them had addressed this unease by the straightforward expedient of not getting their middle school kid a smartphone. Somehow, at some point, the choice to get our kids tiny two-way media machines for watching pornography and publicly displaying duck-lipped pictures of themselves for other people to judge was taken from us parents and given to the technology.

I exaggerate, of course, using these lurid (and yet extremely common!) examples of smartphone use by kids to make a point about us parents: these things loom large in our parental minds. They give us the creeps. In other areas, with other things that hold a threat of creepiness over our kids, we try to keep our children as far away from these things as possible. We are the most worried, threat-aware parents ever. And yet with smartphones, despite these widely shared worries, the further threat of Bruce Banner transformations reducing our home lives to emotional rubble, we submit. We go ahead and get the phone for the kid. If it were our choice, if it were within our power, we might do it differently, but who are we kidding?

THIS EXECUTIVE DIFFIDENCE, THE PARENTAL HUMBLING that marks this historical moment, evokes a human phenomenon that, with spooky prescience, the exiled German-Jewish philosopher Günther Anders described in 1942. In what has become his most famous work, Anders builds upon an uncanny moment recorded in his journal, when he and a friend are attending a "technology exhibition" in Los Angeles, their home in exile. "As one of the highly complicated pieces started to work," Anders notes, his friend "lowered his eyes and fell silent. Even more strikingly, he concealed his hands behind his back, as if he were ashamed to have brought these heavy, graceless and obsolete instruments into the company of machines working with such accuracy and refinement."[3]

The key word here is "ashamed." The human's humble impulse to recoil from the superior technology he has fashioned Anders calls "Promethean shame," after the Titan from Greek mythology who fashioned humans from clay and then stole fire from Zeus to give to them. Prometheus, known for his cleverness, wanted to pass on the possibility of cleverness to his creation. We humans are now in the position of Prometheus, Anders suggests, cleverly molding our own beings. But these beings threaten both to replace our functions and to destroy us through the growing power they attain with our assistance.

Giving life to these technological forces, and seeing in them a perfection that we can't achieve as mere humans, we begin to see and judge ourselves "from the perspective of machines."[4] Our moral relation with them is thus inverted, so that, instead of asking what they can do for us, we begin to ask ourselves what is "due," from us, to them.[5] So much promise resides in these machines, so much unrealized progress, and it is a travesty for us faulty and limited humans to impede that progress, which, rather, we feel obliged to serve and curate. In a darkly comic passage, Anders compares the future-thrill we get from promising technologies and the hopes we have for our children. As we think of our children we now also think of our machines, as beings filled with "potential and talents." Grimly, Anders calls the hydrogen bomb "the wunderkind amongst machines."[6]

Now, though, the identity of child and machine is much less metaphorical. The helpless parents shown in the various documentary dramas I mention above confront these two elements as a single entity, to which the parents have, so to speak, given birth. They're the ones who got those tablets and phones for their little kids. Through this they created the tensed, volatile being that sends them back on their parental heels. I don't think this is typically done in a spirit of laziness—decadent parents wanting the most stupefying gizmos to keep their kids out of their hair. It's done in a vague but hopeful spirit of child development. It represents a linking of their sense of their children's future potential with the undeniable future-power of those iPads and iPhones and, I suppose, Kindle Fires. When I looked at that iPad my parents bought me, my sense of its power was visceral. As the father of small children, I couldn't help associating that power with my hopes for them, my anxieties about their growth, the development of their brains. Its possibilities and theirs became a fused thing in my mind. They would advance upon the progressive path of that machine. They'd grow with the ever-evolving and -progressing network of other machines to which it connected. Surely their peers were on that rising path, plugged into that network. I didn't want my kids being left down and back. I didn't want them missing out. But then, finally, the toxic uselessness of the iPad became manifest. (An undernoted pleasure of raising kids is when you discover a tool or method purported to help their competitive honing is actually useless or harmful and you can ignore or reject it, which becomes a small act of ignoring and rejecting the competitive honing itself. I like to imagine the pleasure many parents must have taken, after reading the debunking research, in tossing their ridiculous Baby Mozart videos in the trash.)

As they get older and the question becomes when, not whether, to get them smartphones, the existential momentum to which you're obliged to release them is social, on the surface, rather than educational or developmental. But here the issue of missing out is less a vague parental sense and more an urgent and explicit family problem, because your kids will throw it in your face if you hesitate to get them that goddamned phone. Do you have reservations? Of course you do, *dozens* of them. Is it expensive? It's *really* expensive. Are they likely to lose this expensive little rectangle? Their *not* losing it seems the impossible thing. But their social lives have been vacuumed up into those phones. While you dither and question, raising your "philosophical" objections to the "replacement of ontological horizons that are discernibly human with those that are inscrutably technological," their peers are adding followers on Instagram. Do you want that on your conscience? At some point, if you delay in submitting to this pressure, your child becomes an aggrieved lobbyist for society itself, whose realest dimension is now the virtual one.

So far Juliet and I have held up against the lobbying, which, as I note, has abated remarkably in the two years since our older daughter started middle school and found herself an outlier in not having a smartphone. Somewhat like a parent, she has grown tired of the argumentative runaround. Knowing where it ends, she rarely bothers to start it anymore. This will surely change, but in the meantime we've bought ourselves a few years in which certain things Juliet and I quite hate we don't have to have in our home. And I'm not sure our daughter doesn't take at least a little pride (to which she would never admit) in her singular status as an eighth-grade smartphone holdout. I think she respects us for our stoutness in this commitment. She might be unhappy to find herself losing a little of this respect when, finally, we give her this thing she knows we still don't really want her to have.

IN ITS SUBLIME POWER AND BEGUILING SLEEKNESS, TODAY'S digital gadgetry can blind us to how powerful and beguiling yesterday's gadgetry was. *Ha*, we might laugh. Look at those blocky monitors in those photos from the nineties, the suitcase-sized CPUs wheezing under desks cluttered, for some reason, with paper. But the basic features of the internet *experience*, which dominates so much of our lives today, were already present, and already an enthralling force, for people interacting with those slow and clunky old machines. Remembering or realizing this helps us see that our hypermodern system of digital technology rests on the same crude forces it's always rested on, and that the deep nature of this technology was never human progress or liberation, as its visionary defenders sometimes claim. It was always the extraction and use of subhuman impulse and psychological need.

The affirmative rush that kids now experience from seeing new Likes on their Instagram posts, for example, I first experienced sitting in an academic computer lab, on Usenet groups devoted to philosophy and political theory and punk music, in 1994, when a discussion thread on Hegel or Habermas or Hüsker Dü that I'd started or to which I'd contributed showed a new entry. A *reply*. This was a far more intense and rarefied sort of being-addressed than I might feel in a seminar or drunken tavern discussion on the same topics, because online I stood apart, alone, distilled of all ambiguity and confusion, all environmental noise. My personal isolation and the intensity of my psychosocial response were inextricable from each other. For the moment my entire being was some smart-ass thing my rarefied self had typed, two or three or seven hours earlier, because my self had now been addressed by some other self, likewise rarefied and isolated, its whole being likewise compressed to one event of digital typing. For a few minutes, depending on the tone of the exchange, it would feel like a clash of knights, scoring each other's armor with sarcasm, or the swooning "star friendship" Nietzsche wrote about, or I'd get a giddy jolt from another purified self saying mine was funny or clever. I might have joined those newsgroups from some general curiosity about the topics, or a desire to socialize with people who shared my interest in them, but I kept coming back, often several times a day, to see the numbers between the parentheses, which said how many new replies my post had gotten since the last time

I'd checked, then to see the reflection of my self that danced in those replies.

On top of the physical, spatial isolation I describe, there was a further, perhaps deeper isolation in time. This, *time*, is key to grasping virtual engagement as a self-fueling system, and thus a mode of unfreedom. Consider the difference between a living-room conversation, three or four people talking within a shared physical space, and the sequential, intermittent threading of virtual communication and socializing. It's rare in a physical conversation for a thing you say to go entirely unacknowledged, as if no one even heard it, or as if everyone's ignoring you with such perfect choreography it seems like, to them, *you no longer exist.*

This experience would be very troubling, because receiving this acknowledgment is a big reason you spoke in the first place, feeling your self and its reality register with others. But this absence of social feedback is the default experience in virtual communication, and was from the beginning. You write or post or email or text something and then . . . you . . . wait. Every communication you send onto the internet leaves you abysmally hanging. In virtual interaction you are *alone in time,* in a way that you aren't in physical conversation. This is wildly at odds with your programming as a social person, which assumes the simultaneous presence of those you've spoken to, real-time feedback from them that tells you, without any long cliff-hanger pauses, that you are not socially dead.

My point is not that this is bad or harmful, as an experience. We've all had it. We've generally survived and even enjoyed it. My point is that it's very compelling, emotionally and psychologically. Pretty much everything social or communicative you do on the internet throws you into an unresolved future, where human feedback lingers in teasing deferral. For language-having animals like us, whose deep emotional tuning presupposes social nearness, this aspect of online communication means it's perpetually filled with inner drama, and this inner drama translates into preoccupation, need, a compulsive interest in coming back.

A similar time scheme governs the other pillar of virtual engagement—our weakness for cognitive novelty. We often hear about how smartphones are a technology of *distraction*, but the important part of this feature, the thing that fueled the consumer internet from the beginning, was our interest in the *next* distraction, the future distraction teasingly promised by your success in attaining the present distraction. This is the phenomenon described in Larry D. Rosen and Adam Gazzaley's excellent book *The Distracted Mind*—how the possibility of sequenced diversion exploits our brain's natural tendency to "forage" for information. It was adaptive for our evolutionary ancestors to be hungry for knowledge about their surroundings, to hunt around for useful data about food and predators.[7] But instead of rewarding an obsessive search over one patch of ground, the basic economics of foraging prescribed a readiness to get bored and move on when you found yourself searching too long in one spot for too little payoff.[8] This balance, the power to focus on a single task versus a hunger for new stimulation, was coded by evolution into our brains. Entirely by accident, early web technology teased up the restless half of this balance, our evolved readiness to get bored and move on. Crucially, as Rosen and Gazzaley show, continued exposure to this dynamic shortens the foraging cycle. When the restless search for novelty is constantly rewarded with new things, our ability to focus on the old thing grows weaker, and the time we can spend in sustained focus grows shorter. What might be coming next grows more compelling all the time, relative to what's in front of us.[9]

Even with the ancient Netscape web browser, even with data dribbling into your CPU from a telephone line, pumped in from the Bell telephone aqueduct by your dial-up modem, even with the pages taking a minute to unscroll themselves for viewing, often stopping halfway down the screen, the chemical payoff was already enough to flip your animal brain into a foraging jag. You'd focus briefly on the new thing you'd just clicked on, and then ipso facto it was no longer new. What was left was the dying remnant of the secret brain-excitement from the discovery, and the hunger for another hit of this waning thrill, which is to say, the desire to do it again. This sequence of novelty and then boredom and then hunting for more novelty—now neuroscientifically engineered in the platforms and apps that occupy our thumbs—was a basic fuel of mass engagement from the very beginning of the web browser era. The ease of access combined with the sheer number of things there were to click on, the in-effect infinite number of these experiences you could have, meant the tiniest discoveries could keep you clicking after these empty rewards. The evanescence and triviality were key to our deep involvement. Each click, being both a fulfillment and a disappointment, was its own reason to click again.

Pretty much until 2016, when Facebook supposedly helped get Donald Trump elected president of the United States, avid technologists and progressive political observers alike saw the internet as an overwhelmingly liberating force, a miraculous tool of self-expression, a sort of higher destiny for humanity. But, understood as a human system, a mechanism of moral training, the internet was more like a lucky hack. It grew across the world by tapping into and conditioning a random pair of unremarkable but vastly productive human vulnerabilities—our evolved cognitive use for getting bored and seeking distraction, and our powerful social need for recognition by other people. Through its means of engaging these benign tendencies, undesigned and accidental at first, the internet cultivates in us a banal but robust orientation toward the future. Under its influence, we chase through an unspooling series of near futures for relief of minor but persistent social and cognitive needs, which are perpetually regenerated by the very things that satisfy them. Described in this way, the internet seems less like a higher destiny and more like a dumb predicament.

Our mediated experience of the world has thus become almost entirely pathological. By "pathological" I don't mean "diseased" or "insane." I mean it roughly as Kant means it in his moral writings: as physiological or emotional rather than intellectual, as affective, subrational, appetitive, machinelike in its answering to natural force rather than considered reflection. I mean it as instinctual rather than deliberate. Mass engagement with the internet was always pathological, in the Kantian sense. The consumer market in McDonald's Happy Meals, I would argue, is much, much more fully intermediated by the wakeful deliberation of conscious humans than our aggregate participation in the internet has ever been. In its dumb, accidental attractiveness to a couple random functions of our brains, internet technology was suggestive enough to create a worldwide linkage of subhuman impulses before the people who built and programmed it were even suggesting anything.

IN HIS 2016 BOOK *THE ATTENTION MERCHANTS*, WHICH TREATS the history of advertising as prelude to the capture of humanity's attention by internet companies, legal scholar Tim Wu takes a useful detour into the history of reality television. Wu's inspired insight is to see reality TV as a precursor to social media in both human and business terms. Reality TV as it has come to be understood today began with the MTV show *The Real World*, which debuted in 1992.

The important thing about MTV's *The Real World*, for our purposes, is that it solved a programming problem by solving a budgeting problem. The network's whole business model pre-supposed free content—namely, music videos, which were los-ing their youth cachet by 1990. What could replace singers and bands and rappers and record labels willing to trade creative work for the privilege of having this work shown on TV? Who else might be willing to make a similar trade, wherein MTV's financial outlay for its content was as close as possible to zero?

The answer to that question turned out to be pretty simple: people. People, given the odd privilege of conducting their la-bors on TV, would be willing to work for a payment of being on TV. The business model behind this has translated nicely to the internet. It's pretty much what we're all doing on Facebook and Instagram and Twitter, except these social media sites have made the performance side more democratic: Everyone passes the audition! Everyone's in the cast!

Here is the sly genius of social media as a means of produc-tion: its power to incite and harvest our free labor, in the form of compulsive thumbing and tapping, and in the form of the content we generate with our posting. Social media sites "drive engagement" by twining our deep social need for recognition and our deep cognitive weakness for distraction in the same sensory event: the notification. *Ping!* It's a literally ringing endorsement of your social person, which also dopamine-jolts you out of this book you've been reading for two minutes straight, brings you back to your important work of thumbing and tapping, perhaps another risky and hopeful stab at posting.

In other words, the skeptical truism about the internet — "If it's free, you're not the customer. You're the product" — is a little off. You're neither the customer nor the product, really. You're the worker. It's your activity, more than your merely receptive eyeballs, that's being monetized. For Google and Facebook, people sitting slack-jawed and motionless before a TV screen seven feet away is a low-value proposition. The productive capacity of their thumbs, their latent mobility as people with feet and bicycles and drivers' licenses, is totally untapped in that scenario. The internet needs us much more animated than the traditional television ad target, the iconic couch potato whose impassive face glows in the dancing light of the Doritos commercial. Google and Facebook need us on the move, producing content and generating data, thumbing and tapping and typing and scrolling, and mapping our own movements. They need us acting like the unpaid interns of data making they've turned us into.

I NOTICED A CURIOUS THING WHEN I WAS FIRST USING TWITter a lot. It's something totally familiar to any chronic user of social media, I suspect, but I'll describe it anyway, since some people might be unfamiliar with it. What I noticed was that I'd started thinking in tweet form. Something would happen to me in the world, or a kernel of thought would appear in my head, and I would immediately translate that experience, or grow that thought kernel, into something that might sound good as a tweet. I'm not saying I edited my thoughts down to 140-letter epigrams. I'm saying tweeting had become a sort of preconceptual template that shaped the thoughts themselves. Not all my thoughts took this form, but many of them did. Indeed, I suspect that the thought kernels I drew up from the mental silage, the scraps of experience I deemed worthy of conscious notice were often chosen for their Twitter value. If a thought might be written as an ironic aperçu that made me seem smarter than I am, I was likelier, by some meaningful degree, to think it in the first place.

In other words, my private inner life was taking a weirdly public form, and the publicity of its form was infusing its content not just occasionally but systematically. I know I'm not unique in this, and I know that the tweet-shaped thought is only one of the many ways in which this occurs, wherein their imagined success as public theater on social media alters our private and personal moments. I've seen the quirky Twitter personalities sarcastically tweeting all day long, who must be thinking and seeing and living in tweet form all the time, quirkily and sarcastically.

This outward pull on inner life poses several obvious challenges for parents. The psychic and ethical balance between private and public is an enduring subject of modern child-rearing. We want our children to grow up socially competent, of course, but we don't want them to become obsessed with their social image, with their clothes and their appearance, with mere popularity. We don't want them to sacrifice their

morals for some extra bit of social status. But the balance of
forces between private and public selfhood, between the appeal of honest virtue or honed excellence and that of empty
celebrity, has decisively changed with the rise of social media
and YouTube. Young people gaining hundreds of thousands
or even millions of followers for giving ordinary makeup tips
into an iPhone camera, being cute while reviewing toys, being
normal and relatable while relating their normal day. It's hard
not to find a sort of absurdism in this YouTube fame, kids raptly
watching an untalented nobody exactly their age, dreamily
thinking, Wow . . . fame—and feeling so teasingly close to this
highest of all human qualities, by virtue of the famous young
person they're watching's total lack of distinction or excellence.

When the pull of image has become so great, when recognition and renown seem so attainable, at such small cost and
effort, and when their open pursuit has become so familiar and
democratic, the case against these things becomes that much
harder for parents to make. Who doesn't want to be famous for
nothing in particular? How do you convince a kid who sees
empty fame all around him, effortlessly attained, that the real
value is not in being famous but—taking another spin from
Kant—in one's worthiness of being famous?

And it's not just the moral side of this fame awareness that
poses a challenge for parents. I don't know what exactly my
role in the process should be, if it should be anything, but one
thing I hope for my children is that they will develop a robust inner life, a zone of private reflection, of nonconforming
thoughts all their own, a stubborn reserve of character capable of distancing itself from outer opinion, comfortable with

the risks of individuality. The battle between private selfhood and conformist pressures of mass society—which preoccupied modern philosophers from Rousseau to Nietzsche to Hannah Arendt—is something everyone fights. In this way we are all engaged in philosophical struggle.

But young people plugged into the social internet conduct this struggle at a notable disadvantage. I experienced that odd stretch after joining Twitter where my inner life got turned inside out, even though I was far beyond my socially avid teenage years—and even without a constant music of social cues pinging at me from a device I carried with me all the time.

There's a quick, common reply to these worries about social media: we late moderns, with our pop-Freudian idea of self-expression as a basic value, have a strong tendency to look at young people posting on social media and assume they are *empowering* themselves. But the more basic and persistent outcome from expressing yourself on social media is not power but weakness and neediness—the anxious waiting for feedback once you've put yourself out there, the hunger for more feedback after the buzz of affirmation and drama fades out. Yet we hold to this model of empowerment with hysterical fondness. It informs everything from our schooling practices to our clothing commercials.

But equating self-expression with empowerment is naive. Power is dynamic and complicated. It flows back and forth. Self-expression often confers power to the listener and weakness to the speaker.[10] Your child's moment of empowering self-expression through technology is also someone else's empowering instance of listening in—not just their inscrutable "friends" and "followers" on social media, of course, but the social media businesses themselves, and online advertisers and app designers.

IN HIS BESTSELLING BOOK *HOOKED*, TECH ENTREPRENEUR Nir Eyal writes, "The products and services we use [on our devices] habitually alter our everyday behavior. Our actions have been engineered." He continues with a question, "How do companies, producing little more than bits of code displayed on a screen, seemingly control users' minds?"[11]

He seems to be describing a dystopian turn in our society and economy here. Companies engineering human actions by controlling people's *minds*? An author, an insider trained in these diabolical methods of psychological engineering and controlling, who then outlines them in a bestselling book, surely intends to arm everyday citizens against them. That's why he'd write a book like this, no?

In fact, no. *Hooked* is written for future entrepreneurs who, like the profitable companies it profiles, want to learn how they also might make money by controlling people's minds. It describes how they might do this using Eyal's "Hook Model." "What distinguishes the Hook Model from a plain vanilla feedback loop," Eyal writes, "is the Hook's ability to create a craving. Feedback loops are all around us, but predictable ones don't create desire."[12] This sort of feedback loop prompts engagement through a predictable stimulus-reward cycle. But this is plain vanilla mind control. Inspired by the behaviorist psychologist B. F. Skinner, Eyal points out that *desire*, rather than pleasure, is the real fuel for the vigorous feedback loop. When a craving has been established through repeated exposure to some pleasurable sensation, "what draws us to act is not the sensation we receive from the reward itself, but the need to alleviate the craving for that reward."[13]

And the key to creating that craving is *variability*. "Research shows that levels of the neurotransmitter dopamine surge when the brain is expecting a reward," Eyal writes. "Introducing variability multiplies that effect, creating a focused state, which suppresses the areas of the brain associated with judgment and reason while activating the parts associated with wanting and desire."[14] Eyal describes this concept further on a page of his website ("Variable Rewards: Want to Hook Users? Drive Them Crazy") in which he celebrates Skinner for discovering the "powerful cognitive quirk . . . called a variable schedule of rewards." In Skinner's studies "lab mice responded most voraciously to *random* rewards." Sometimes the "mice would press a lever and . . . get a small treat," and sometimes . . . no treat. Unlike the relatively judicious and reflective mice who "received the same treat every time, the mice that received the variable rewards" would "press the lever compulsively."

"Like the mice in Skinner's box," Eyal goes on, humans "crave predictability and struggle to find patterns, even when none exist." The point of cleverly designed apps and interfaces— which was really the deep, accidental tendency of the internet from the beginning—is to make us humans "like the mice in Skinner's box," by exposing us to unnatural doses of "the brain's cognitive nemesis," variability. We fall into a compulsive search for orderly patterns because our deep expectation to find such patterns in our experience is being frustrated repeatedly, by design. This engineered frustration makes this compulsive search, within this busy field of engineered experience, "a priority over other functions like self-control and moderation."[15]

I want to just linger over these design considerations, as they might leap back into my head in the future, when I'm watching my oldest child sweep and tap at the smartphone I'll end up getting her. If all goes to the app designer's plan, she will have become "like the mice in Skinner's box," which were conditioned to "press [a] lever compulsively." What I'll be watching is the Skinnerian triumph of an entrepreneurial app designer over my daughter's "functions" of "self-control and moderation," through the incitement of stronger "functions" originating at an even greater neurological depth and distance from her "judgment and reason." I'll be watching her act upon an internal craving for a patterned regularity she feels but isn't aware of. They will have created this craving at its profitable intensity precisely by their engineered frustration of it.

In other words, what I'll be watching is my child being jerked around by calculating, neurologically savvy app designers, perhaps readers and followers of Nir Eyal, perhaps trained in Persuasive Technology by Stanford's famous B. J. Fogg himself. These designers know that her thralldom in sweeping the apps and user platforms they create will be heightened if they intermittently, systematically mess with her, make her subconsciously beg for neurochemical satisfaction of a craving they've implanted in her. They know, more fundamentally, that it's not the satisfaction but the craving that matters. They are subjecting my child to serial moments of unease and discontent, a state of psychophysiological disequilibrium to which they also manufacture a continuous—but unpredictable and utterly transient—semblance of relief.

When this happens, when my memory of these considerations occurs to me in that moment, I hope I also remember to ask myself why, as her father, I'm letting them do this to my child. I hope I remember to be a little disgusted that my daughter is so intimately engaged in an experience persuasively designed by people with such evident contempt for her, such a low opinion of her worthiness to live a life in which her "functions" of "self-control and moderation" control and moderate the things she does. Maybe I'll remember to be glad, at the margins, that in our fanatical withholding of this phone, we delayed this recurring insult for as long as we did.

In any case, I don't think "contempt" is too strong a word. One app design company, Boundless Mind, which promises clients the power to "Predictably Change [their] Users Behavior," recently renamed itself. Its original name was the majestically cynical "Dopamine Labs," after the brain chemical that drives compulsive and addictive behavior cycles.

This profitable cynicism seems to have generated a secondary response of guilt, perhaps profitable as well. Both Nir Eyal and the Dopamine Labs/Boundless Mind now offer productivity and mindfulness tools engineered to help users escape the feckless and mindless states they engineer with their other products. Still, cynicism would seem to be a deep and necessary mental habit among those who hope to get rich by circumventing the human parts of people's brains, for as many hours a day as neurologically possible, so that the rodent parts are calling the shots.

WHEN IT'S ADDRESSED TO PARENTS, CAUTIONARY DISCUSSION of digital technology tends to have the same focus as most other parenting commentary: risk—the harms and dangers that smart-phones, the internet, video games, and social media may pose to children's brains and bodies. These are serious concerns, but the scientific literature on the concrete harms that "screen time" and digital engagement inflict on children is mixed. My objections to the encroachment of digital technology on my own family's life, though, were never about mental health. The dark intuition that came up when I watched my young children sweeping their way into an iPad trance was not that this device would make them unhappy or unsafe. It was that it would make them unfree. Indeed, what remains the most compelling finding, to me, about the psychological effects of computer use is the one in which this question of human freedom is directly implicated—the possibility that, over time, engagement with digital technologies shortens our attention span, alters the balance of power between our short-term urge to forage for new stimulation and our ability to tame this urge for the sake of sustained concentration. Digital technology erodes the trait that, arguably, makes us human, our power to posit ends for ourselves, consciously, and to pursue those ends with a measure of focus and planning, and to take pleasure in these sustained efforts. Setting and pursuing our ends is how we use our human endowments to form our selves, how we integrate our disparate impulses and appetites into a single life story. Curating these capacities and habits in our children, seeing them grow under the influence of their human as opposed to their rodent tendencies, would seem to be one of our most basic jobs as parents.

Why do those parents on *Good Morning America* get such a bad feeling about their kids using those devices? For parents with kids to occupy all day, all summer, the devices serve their selfish interests quite obviously. And, guided by those interests, inclined to look at the research through their own selfish need to keep their kids out of their hair, they could easily go online and find pundits defending technology use, researchers contending that those tablets don't turn their kids into vegetables or sociopaths after all. Why not let their kids thumb and tap and sweep for five or six hours per summer day, when it makes their own lives so much easier?

Because, perhaps, the specter of it is kind of gross. After some stretch of time, at the beginning of which parents might be gratified their child has happened into an activity so stimulating, they find themselves uneasy with their postures of tireless and fixated (and yet autonomic and pacified) "engagement." This, they sense, is not how a person, a child, should *be*. They sense this because they know the feeling themselves, from when they grab their phone to check their email and find themselves an inexplicable hour later staring at its screen, scrolling through the sequenced nothingness of their Instagram feed. It feels way worse, seeing the subconscious drives and vulnerabilities of their kids taken up like this into the system of digital technology. They have the outside perspective in this moment, a disturbing image of it as a force that visibly shapes whole bodies and conditions whole selves—and it's *their* kids being shaped and conditioned.

What their intuitions are moving toward in these uneasy moments is a realization that the relentless, indifferent force of digital technology and the life of their family are in conflict. This intuition is reinforced by the realization of how isolating that technology is, how it seizes a single gaze and holds it, how the now-ubiquitous earphones and earbuds deepen this isolation, seal the teenage user inside the linkage that digital technology has made with his brain. Parents might attest to the phone's ability to keep them keep watchfully "connected" when their kid's outside the home, but inside, when they're sharing the same room, trying to break into a carefully engineered dopamine trance to start a parent-child conversation, they have to admit that the normal effect is not being "connected" at all, at least not with them. They are, in other words, in a constant power struggle with smartphones and tablets and laptops. This struggle is difficult and nearly unwinnable, but it is not an absurd one to take up. It is not hopeless or meaningless.

The outside world is entirely networked, but how networked your family is is your decision. You can get rid of the iPad, as I did, or decline to buy it because it's mainly a sensation machine and its educational promise is almost totally bogus. You can hold off getting that iPhone . . . another year, maybe two. You can let your kids be bored. You can let them search around for something else to do besides gaming or compulsive thumb scrolling or abstracted ego striving. Often that thing will be reading a book or building something, or maybe even climbing a tree or playing with friends. Sure, there are costs, real ones. You have to deal with their pestering. You have to hear them sigh and complain—costs parents had to pay before iPhones came along. But, on the other hand, you don't have to watch them in that autonomic state of engineered machine engagement. You don't have to brush away the queasy intuition that they're so agreeably distracted because their subconscious channels have been hacked for profit.

And, for Juliet and me, there's an undeniable pleasure in making and enacting this decision. It's oddly rewarding, feeling the relentless disciplinary efforts of the regime of digital technology, and then defying them. And, since the claims this regime makes on you and your family are constant and self-renewing, the pleasure you get from this defiance, should you stick to it, is self-renewing too. Other, more normal and temperate parents might consider taking up the vaguely fanatical aversion to kid technology that Juliet and I reinforce in each other. If they did, they might get to experience the feeling of marital and family solidarity that comes from hearing the persistent demands of this emergent power, and the presumption within these demands that you'll submit because *it*'s calling the shots now, and, persistently, saying "no." Sometimes when we say this we smile to each other conspiratorially.

chapter five

Schools and Families

The Odd Promise of "Parental Involvement"

IKE MANY ELEMENTARY SCHOOLS, OURS CONDUCTS ITS
fifth-grade graduation ceremony as an emotional event.
The poignancy is presupposed and played up, passed down
as an expectation from year to year. "Get ready to cry," you're
told by a parent friend who went through the last one. The ceremony ends[1] with a slideshow of the previous six years of school,
the faces of the graduating fifth graders fading out and returning to the screen in the more babyish forms they had back in
third grade, and first grade, and—*sigh*—kindergarten. Sitting
cross-legged on the floor, the graduating kids watch themselves
move through these younger versions as their parents, standing
farther back, make the telltale noises of nostalgia. Each new
photo gives a little nudge that says, "Remember when . . . ?,"
while the deeper theme of the event as a whole is: The Passage
Of Time.

Now, it's understandable, since we're older as parents than our own parents were, and also less religious, that raising kids would turn us into everyday existentialists. I mean Martin Heidegger–style existentialism, with its focus on the transience and "finitude" of our lives, mortal humans swooning at the supersonic passage of time, groping to shape something solid from its contrails. But I'd like to point out the historical novelty of having our children join us on these Heideggerian head trips. At the very least it makes me chuckle about how we're teaching them to ache like we ache at time's passage, cueing fifth graders to get nostalgic about themselves as third graders.

Of course part of this, beyond the altered existential contours of modern parenting, is just our abundance of pictures. Our kids grow up surrounded by so many personal and family photographs that the sweet self-idolatry doesn't even need to be intentional to be pervasive. When I open my daughters' bedroom closet I'm greeted by a five-by-seven-inch photo print of my younger daughter, my middle child, as a preschooler, which is taped to the opposite wall. On one hand, this picture is jarringly cute. I get a little shock of love every time I see it. On the other hand, *she taped it there herself*, as a fourth grader, just as her older sister, as a sixth grader, curated a collection of evocative pictures of her own childhood—from a much larger exposition of prints already curated a first time from our infinite collection of digital photos—for her personal album. This temporal self-awareness, kids' power to know their place on the graph of time by seeing themselves at all those earlier points, in pictures, is very different from my own youth, as a temporal experience—the hallucinatory fragments of present moments through which I barely noticed myself passing. I didn't learn nostalgia until I had kids, and then, I admit, I took it up with a vengeance.

So this nostalgic grade school graduation rite has a certain obvious basis in both parental culture and recent technology. But it's worth noting the setting for these candid expressions of private feeling—a public elementary school, in whose common spaces, on this big day, we misty parents are milling about with a familiarity that borders on ownership. And at schools like ours, middle-class schools with active and engaged populations of parents, school is indeed an extension of home. Sure your kids spend their days there, which used to mean they spent their days away from their parents, whose absence from the gray institutional space of school once defined that space. But now, on the grounds and in the classrooms of many elementary schools, especially in younger grades, parents are a conspicuous presence, as library helpers and reading aides and math buddies. Increasingly, according to disgruntled school personnel in affluent suburbs, they're coming at lunchtime to eat with their kids, crowding the kid-sized lunch tables with their adult bodies.[2]

But the interest flows in the other direction as well. Empowered and anxious parents seek hands-on influence over the details of their children's education, and beleaguered schools try to enlist family time and parental effort as resources in their own enterprise, the thankless and nearly impossible job of educating America's children to the satisfaction of the schools' various overlords and constituents. For the last forty years a body of research and advocacy has emerged that treats "parental involvement" as fundamentally important for children's education. And politicians and policy makers have taken notice. Exhortations and directives and instructions, explicitly aimed at parents, are now written into major educational legislation at the national level. Schools are under constant pressure to get better, and politicians are under constant pressure to make them so, and some research says that the involvement of parents is key to student success. The political lesson is obvious: let's unload some of this awful burden onto parents. Anxious parents, eager to hear and apply this message, are readily brought into the schooling mix, without quite realizing the role they're playing.

MY THREE CHILDREN HAVE, OR HAD, VERY DIFFERENT AP-proaches to elementary school and its assorted tasks—one fairly dutiful, one aversive and rebellious, one easygoing to the point, occasionally, of laziness (and lazy, sometimes, to the point of passive resistance). Despite these marked differences, they have one acute experience of grade school in common, many times over: they have all cried about homework assignments. They have cried about first-grade homework and third-grade homework. They have cried because they couldn't make sense of the instructions. They have cried because they didn't understand a question or problem. They have cried because they couldn't find a sharp pencil, or because the one sharp pencil had no eraser, only a gouging metal rim around a rubber crater. They have cried because they couldn't think of anything to write. They have cried because there *wasn't* anything to write but they still had to write something. They have cried because I insisted they do their homework when they hoped that I, merciful father, might grant them homework forgiveness, clemency on their penal sentence of homework. They have cried in worry at not finishing their homework. They have cried in panic at forgetting to start their homework. They have cried at being unable to find their unstarted homework and at having lost their finished homework. They have cried, in almost every case, because they'd spent a whole day at school and they were tired. They have cried while bidding the heavens: *Why does there have to be homework?!*

Like many parents, I suspect, and especially when I've had a kid crying onto an unfinished homework sheet, I've posed the same question to the heavens myself. Why *does* there have to be homework? (To be clear, I'm talking about *grade school* homework here. The question I often pose to the heavens about my middle school kids' homework is: Why does there have to be so little middle school homework?) In any case, it's important to describe this moment of cosmic questioning in its details because you can't understand the net benefits of grade school homework without tallying its costs. And prominent if not paramount among those costs, and yet underappreciated by those who defend giving homework to first graders, is that, for kids and parents both, homework is awful.

This may sound like selfishness on my part. It may sound like I don't want the hassle, like I don't want to bear my share of the burden of the valuable practice of doing schoolwork at home. It's true. It *is* selfishness. I *don't* want the hassle. But that doesn't undermine my case. It supports it. I do, precisely in my parental selfishness, want my children to learn in school and succeed in life, and so I'm willing to endure things that push toward those outcomes. But this selfishness is also a reasonable proxy for my family's legitimate interest in autonomy. I'm selfishly protective of my home time with my kids, in other words. If I'm going to sacrifice portions of this time, and this sacrifice in time is going to include some regular suffering, for parents as well as kids, there better be a real academic reason for it. The rationale behind this homework better be good.

And if you're familiar with the research on homework for younger grades you know that, though its costs in hassle and crying are all too clear, its academic benefits are ambiguous, if not null, if not negative. And if that's the case, then you might be justified in viewing your family's relationship to grade school homework in the political terms I suggest, as a matter of autonomy. It's one thing to stand over an eight-year-old child crying desperately at the idea of doing her writing assignment, urging her to venture a task that, in her distinctive after school condition of fatigue and restlessness, is physically repulsive to her. It's another thing to do this with a fairly strong, indeed empirically grounded suspicion that this task is academically pointless.

The recognized expert on the effectiveness of homework is Harris Cooper, a developmental psychologist at Duke University who has conducted a pair of influential meta-analyses of homework research, one in 1989 and another in 2006.[3] These reviews indicate that homework's positive impact on academic achievement is most evident among high school students and diminishes grade by grade until it's imperceptible or nonexistent below fourth or third grade. There remain some large questions about the validity of *these* findings, and about what kinds of homework are effective, and how much of it, and so on. But I leave these aside. I'm interested mainly in grade school homework, and I'm less interested in the substantive controversy about homework's effectiveness, finally, than what the experts' way of discussing it reveals about schools and their relationship to families.

Pursuant to the understanding of homework as gaining in value with age and grade level, many grade schools try to observe the "ten-minute rule," which says that students should do ten minutes of homework per night, per grade. That is, first graders should do ten minutes of homework and second graders twenty, and so on up to fifty minutes per night for fifth graders (or sometimes it's ten minutes for kindergartners, twenty for first graders, and so on). The very modesty of the demands, on these younger students, hints at the ambivalence behind the homework policy, the mix of presumption and uncertainty. The idea that ten minutes of homework per night for a first grader might yield meaningful cognitive benefits or add nonnegligible bits of knowledge is hard to imagine. The kid just spent seven hours in school, and now ten minutes scratching out a sentence of "writing" or executing three math problems is going to augment that? This seems unlikely, but somehow it's important for there to be something rather than nothing.

In the absence of strong evidence that homework for younger kids helps them learn things, proponents of homework often turn to its psychological, or, you might say, *moral*, benefits. Writing in *Education Next*, Janine Bempechat of Wheelock College in Boston, one of the most vigorous defenders of grade school homework, is emphatic on these benefits. She acknowledges that "the relationship between homework and academic achievement in the elementary-school years is not yet established," but she argues that doing away with it "would do children and their families a huge disservice." Even if homework doesn't boost academic performance, there are other factors to consider. "We know," Bempechat writes, "that children's learning beliefs have a powerful impact on their academic outcomes, and that through homework, parents and teachers can have a profound influence on the development of positive beliefs."[4]

One problem with this psychological justification is that the real, rather than hypothetical, relationship between grade school homework and "children's learning beliefs" is not yet established either. I imagine that "through [high-quality, appropriate] homework" parents and teachers *can* aid "the development of positive beliefs" about learning in children, but that's a big "can." What we're hoping for here—what *can* happen if everything comes together just right—is an exemplary homework experience from which a child takes positive beliefs about himself and school and learning into his future. But in the real world of late-afternoon homework tasks, complicating details crowd the scene, and few of them work toward the formation of fond homework memories.

Somehow, these difficulties become their own justification for giving homework. Bempechat notes that, despite its meager academic payoff in younger grades, homework is something teachers use to "foster skills such as responsibility, perseverance, and the ability to manage distractions." This is close to saying that the point of painful homework in younger grades is to prepare children for the pain of doing homework in older grades. A better path to these traits might be to wait until kids have reached the developmental stage where they have them. In any case, what such a triumph of perseverance looks like in practice, from the parent's perspective, is often this: A tired kid melts down about having to do homework, or in the face of his first moment of homework frustration. The unfortunate parent overseeing this episode says, "Look, I know you're tired [sotto voce] *and this meltdown you're having has my teeth on edge and I'd do almost anything to make it stop,* but . . . you still have to do your homework." And then, in many cases, depending on the kid, depending on the day, the meltdown intensifies and then ebbs and then stops and the homework somehow starts and ends up done, though over a time span that probably violates the ten-minute rule, technically. Is that perseverance? Is that the successful managing of distractions?

Perhaps, but it's also several other things—a painful chore for an addled kid, an exasperation for the parent, a stressful and possibly angry encounter between the two, and a portent of more anguished moments in the homework future. The kid's takeaway from such an experience might be a deep memory of power through perseverance, but it might also be an abiding memory of hating that writing assignment, or writing in general, or a hazy association of learning with bitter feelings, or a nagging inner echo of that angry thing that slipped out of dad's mouth.

If, as you're reading this, you're thinking, "Come on, Feeney, quit complaining and let your wimpy kids put in a little *effort*," remember that the experts say, for kids that age, *homework doesn't even help!* What, in other words, is the effort *for?* Actually, policy makers and education scholars have an answer for that question. Homework for children is not just a kind of endurance training for young psyches, frustration practice for their cubicle life in the future, but also a tether between home and school, an inducement for parents to pay attention, be aware of and engaged with their kids' education. You might say that the late-afternoon homework challenge that vectors through your child as frustration and lodges itself in your skull as an adult headache is a conscious policy goal of grade school homework, from the experts' perspective. Here is how one US Department of Education document puts it: "Homework is an opportunity for children to learn and for families to be involved in their children's education."[5]

Homework is part of a fitful effort by educators and policy makers, researchers and advocates, congresspeople and state senators and American presidents, to enlist parents as an institutional resource. Nobody really knows how to meet our standing desire to improve schools, and yet the desire stands. Everyone's impatient, educators and politicians are under the gun, and families are just sitting there, in their homes, an untapped source of motivation and purpose, with strong incentives and a prodigious willingness to work. Homework helps bring parents and their resources into school by bringing school home to parents.

WHEN I DECIDED TO MAJOR IN ENGLISH AS AN UNDERGRADuate, I linked that major to a teaching certificate because it seemed practical. What else could an English major from a regional, no-reputation state university do except be an English teacher? No recruiters from the big consultancies and publishing houses were showing up to CMU for career day. But my teacher-ed classes were so terrible that they spoiled the whole idea of being a teacher for me. In these classes, John Dewey's philosophy of education was treated not as one among several competing theories of teaching and learning, but as an unquestioned starting point, the foundation of everything else. Dewey was the American thinker who translated the hazy and difficult social philosophy of the German idealist G. W. F. Hegel into something perfectly suited to Dewey's own time and place—the growing, bustling, changing America of the Second Industrial Revolution. Dewey's version of Hegelian philosophy was "pragmatism." Applied to education, it meant demoting traditional subject learning from its dominant place in favor of "the subject matter of life experience." Inspired by Dewey, schools would take it as their mission to solve social problems, integrate the disparate parts of America's unstable society into a better whole.

There are unavoidable suggestions of "relativism" in Dewey's pragmatism. To put it crudely, pragmatism replaces such airy questions as "What is true?" and "What is right?" with a more nuts-and-bolts consideration: "What works?" My education professors took these relativist suggestions and pushed them beyond what even Dewey would have argued. The effect of this was not some bracing encounter with philosophical radicalism, but rather an intellectually downcast experience with professors who found the idea of objective truth merely inconvenient for their enterprise, or perhaps too difficult.

For an eager student of the liberal arts, this was simply deflating. And for an academic late bloomer trying on conservative ideas as an intellectual style, it confirmed all too many of my new biases. So even after a successful and enjoyable semester as a student teacher, I never considered staying around and making a career for myself teaching English. And for years after, the memory of those intellectually dim teacher-ed courses nourished my broader conservative political outlook.

This political detail is important. It's hard to overemphasize the boost it gives to conservative commentators, how much it fuels their intellectual confidence and their political will to power, to have the "education establishment" of teachers' unions and schools of education to kick around. The unions and the ed schools not only share a progressive philosophy that conserva-tives hate, but they work together as an anti-market "cartel" that props up teacher pay by limiting the supply of teaching candi-dates. One thing that makes this critical project so attractive and satisfying for conservatives is that, while teachers' unions and ed schools are linked by partisan logic with the Democratic Party, a lot of liberals don't love them either. You have to move pretty far to the left to find people who don't agree with at least *some* of the conservative critique of these things. That is, even many liberals view teacher-education curricula as intellectually weak, and view teacher certification requirements as unhealthy labor protections that reward mediocrity and discourage many smart college graduates from entering the teaching profession. Even many liberals view teachers' unions as protecting bad teachers. And, while reform-minded liberals don't generally share conser-vatives' enthusiasm for market-based voucher programs, they of-ten want to invigorate school systems by introducing new models and options, perhaps a little competition. *Waiting for Superman,* the rabble-rousing, union-slamming 2010 documentary about urban charter schools rescuing black children from bad public schools was, for example, made by liberals. The larger school-reform movement, of which charter schools are a key part, has featured liberals and Democrats at least as prominently as conservatives and Republicans. Teach for America, which lets high-performing college graduates teach in troubled schools without fulfilling those hated certification requirements, has a mixed conservative and liberal pedigree. The existence and mystique of Teach for America are a rebuke, if not an insult, to the professional design of American education.

I don't mean to add new layers to this infamy. I mean only to describe the legitimation problem it belongs to and aggravates. Schools and teachers are in a tough position. A whole cultural tradition conveys the pleasure we take in looking down on the adults who share their workdays with roomfuls of children—the wisdom supposedly contained in such sayings as "Those who can, do; those who can't, teach"; hostile movie portraits such as *Ferris Bueller's Day Off*, where Ben Stein's droning economics teacher is outdone by Jeffrey Jones's unhinged dean of students, whose bloody humiliation is lovable Ferris's moral triumph. And, of course, there's *The Simpsons* and its cast of sad education professionals, kept around for three decades of recurring abuse by that show's merciless writers: dead-inside teachers Edna Krabappel and Elizabeth Hoover, frightened bachelor and boneless functionary W. Seymour Skinner, the school principal. The absurdist extremes of these cartoon portraits testify to how far we're willing to travel with their guiding assumptions. You can say pretty much anything about teachers and principals, flog any stereotype as violently as you want, and people will laugh at the piercing truth of it. One of the psychic privileges of American adulthood, it seems, is taking retrospective revenge on those who, having given their lives to the low-pay, low-respect job of teaching kids essential things, had the temerity to tell our younger selves to sit down and shut up every once in a while.

But it's hard to translate this high-handed critical attitude toward teachers and schools into policies that make things any better. The history of the major education reforms leaves the impression that America's schools are roughly 98 percent as good as we'll ever be able to make them, which is either depressing or reassuring, depending on your perspective. And, as past reforms such as 2002's No Child Left Behind (NCLB) have achieved much disruption but not much reforming, things we might do in the future will help, if they help at all, mainly on the margins. Some reforms, such as charter schools (and possibly vouchers), might invigorate certain school systems, but not others. The boost that charters can give to urban school systems, for example, does not seem to apply to suburban schools. And it's likely that, beyond a certain small number, the benefits of adding new charter schools to a system disappear or turn negative.

That is, after the righteous anger of its viewers has fizzed away, the real prospects of the sort of charter schools advocated in *Waiting for Superman* are . . . *sort of* promising. They might help in some places, for some kids. But it's hard to generalize from the inspiring examples in movies like that. They are, almost by definition, exceptional. The dazzling maestros who start these schools are not minted out in master's programs. You can't rest general education reforms on the lucky appearance of educational geniuses.

Other reforms that sound good at first are likewise fraught with problems of scale and application. Recent research has pointed to the startling variance in quality from teacher to teacher. Kids learn much more, according to this research, under some teachers than under others, and the benefits that come from a single good teacher can not only persist for years but change the very life trajectory of a child, especially a less-advantaged child. From this research would seem to follow a policy focus on hiring better teachers, which in turn would mean testing and other accountability measures that would identify bad teachers, so that we can fire them to make way for good teachers. This in turn would counsel that we turn some political fire on teachers' unions, to force them to stop protecting bad teachers. But these harrying measures would probably lower the social standing of teachers in a way that would dissuade at least some talented college graduates from choosing teaching careers. Of course, no one yet knows how, in their training and formation, good and bad teachers differ from each other. Good teachers can only be identified *post hoc*, through testing what their students have learned. How *would* you create and enforce standards for weeding out bad teachers that didn't make the profession less attractive for potential good teachers? I'm not sure anyone knows that.

Education policy is unbelievably complex at every level. Trade-offs and uncertainty dog questions of how to measure, of what to measure, of sifting causality from mere correlation, of translating the meager few agreed-upon causes into practical policies, and of implementing these policies among the diverse populations of the actual schools of the fifty states of a huge country. And within the knotty mass of education politics there sits, in latent form, a sort of invidious optimism, a hunger within citizens and politicians both to hear and tell an *if-only* story that turns a blanching light on the status quo: this is what we could be doing for our kids . . . *if only*.

If only all our schools could work like this one inner-city charter school started by a visionary genius of learning and recruitment and discipline works. *If only* our education system could work like the free market works. *If only* we could fund schools with the Pentagon's budget and let the Pentagon fund itself with bake sales. *If only* our principals could menace unruly students with baseball bats. *Then* this terrible hunger inside me to see these inequities erased and these policy quandaries solved and my ideological assumptions flattered and confirmed, all at the same time, would finally be sated.

This is the political environment in which your teachers and schools are operating. They are the thing excited people fervently believe *can* and *must* be changed. They are the thing people don't know or can't agree on how to change. In fact, you get the sense that reformist enthusiasm about schools is starting to run out of ways to express itself. George H. W. Bush famously announced, during his 1988 presidential campaign, that he would be "the education president." It'll probably be a while before a presidential contender hangs a phrase like that around his neck again.

You can see why, under this constant pressure to generate big improvements in institutions that have been repeatedly shown to resist even small ones, the main actors might decide that an enticing frontier in reforming America's schools is improving America's *parents*. At the very least, highlighting the central importance of parents helps them—politicians and educators both—off-load some of their unbearable political burden onto families: we're all in this together!

The text of NCLB makes this political burden sharing explicit. It speaks of schools and parents "develop[ing] . . . a school-parent compact that outlines how parents, the entire school staff, and students will share the responsibility for improved student academic achievement."[6] The far-seeing authors of NCLB, it seems, wanted to forge a contractual agreement with the nation's parents to share the blame for its inevitable failure. The text of the 2015 Every Student Succeeds Act (ESSA) does not refer explicitly to a contractual sharing of responsibility between parents and schools, but the aggregate stress of the law on parental engagement (ESSA changes the terminology from *involvement* to *engagement*) makes this sharing of responsibility clear. The California Department of Education, in its literature on ESSA, understands the law's parental engagement provisions in these terms. The law, this literature says, enjoins "schools [to] provide parents and families of . . . students with the information they need to make well-informed choices for their children including more effectively sharing responsibility for their child's success."[7]

I'm not saying parents shouldn't take responsibility for their children's education. Most parents already do this, and all parents should. My point, rather, is to highlight the political logic of government figures publicly, statutorily devolving responsibilities they once eagerly assumed for themselves back onto parents. This reflects the argument I've made in other chapters, about how institutions feed from the energy and resources of families. Here we see politicians and policy makers, facing their own pressures to improve America's schools but running out of policy tools that haven't already been tried, engaged in some combination of throwing up their hands and pointing their fingers: look, parents have to start doing *their* part. The convenient thing about this message, as a political calculation, is that parents are pretty eager to hear it. The fortunate thing about it, for anyone concerned with the success of America's schools, is that this mix of influences might be a healthy one.

IF YOU ARE A PARENT OF A SCHOOL-AGED CHILD, OR HAVE been in the last twenty years, you've probably read or been told how important involved parents are for the academic success of their children. You've probably heard some formulation of this idea, and perhaps passed it on to other parents: the most important factor for children's academic achievement is how involved their parents are in their education. I've heard it put more pointedly, even, than this. For a while a factoid was floating around that said the greatest predictor of children's academic success is, simply, whether their parents go to parent-teacher conferences. When I heard that my first thought was *Yes! That's it!* That was the kind of factoid I liked, combining optimism about kids' prospects—we just need to fix *one thing*—and a handy set of adults to blame for existing troubles: lazy parents with bad values, parents who *don't even show up.*

Among my parent friends and acquaintances, public messaging about the massive educational importance of parental involvement has achieved nearly universal reach. We invoke this importance to each other in a tone that is at once emphatic and offhanded, as if everyone already knows what the biggest thing is. As engaged modern parents we have an ear tuned to "the studies," which come to us secondhand through news stories. I've heard variations on the deep consensus of "the studies" many times, and perhaps uttered a few myself: "All the studies say . . . ," or "The studies all say . . . ," or "Every study says. . . ." You don't have to actually say the second part, what all the studies say. Everyone knows: "parental involvement is the biggest thing."

But what do we mean by "parental involvement"? In my experience, knowing reference to the robust consensus on parental involvement always occurs in conversations about doing things *at school*—volunteering in class or as a library aide, going to PTA meetings, arranging special meetings with teachers, at the very least attending parent-teacher conferences. If you want to put a wise gloss—at once self-interested and scientific—on the reasons behind your time spent picking up granola bar wrappers in the cafeteria, you say, "Of course, all the studies say. . . ."

In case it's not obvious, I'm gesturing at a certain dissonance between the popular understanding of parental involvement and what all the studies on parental involvement actually say. If you're venturing into the literature for the first time, perhaps recently returned from a midday stint as a lunchroom monitor or library aide, or still shaking off the yelling match from last night's PTA meeting, you might find it jarring to encounter these sentences in a 2010 study published in the journal *Child Development*.

> Past research on parent involvement and children's academic skills is mixed (Fan & Chen, 2001). Some studies have found no significant association between parent involvement and academic achievement (Keith, Reimers, Fehrmann, Pottebaum, & Aubey, 1986; Okpala, Okpala, & Smith, 2001; Reynolds, 1992; White, Taylor, & Moss, 1992) and a few have even detected negative associations (Milne, Myers, Rosenthal, & Ginsburg, 1986; Sui-Chu & Willms, 1996). Yet, positive associations between parent involvement and academic achievement have been demonstrated repeatedly in the literature. A recent meta-analysis by Fan and Chen (2001) finds moderate associations between parent involvement and an array of

learning-related or academic skills, such as achievement motivation, task-persistence, and receptive vocabulary, during
preschool and kindergarten.[8]

"Mixed"?! "No significant association"?! "*Negative* associations"!?
After that barrage of deflating modifiers, learning that Fan and
Chen found some moderate positive associations back in 2001
will hardly be enough to reinflate your sense of parental agency.

And, for its part, the Fan and Chen study is something less
than a mustering of all unencumbered parents to lunch duty.
Its abstract begins on an almost dismissive note, describing the
promise of parental involvement as "so intuitively appealing that
both education scholars and society in general have come to
view it as a sort of panacea." Unfortunately, "the vast proportion
of the literature in this area . . . is qualitative and nonempirical,"
and the more quantitative studies show "considerable inconsistencies."[9] The possibility that further study might clear them up
doesn't dull the sting of learning that the quantitative research
on parental involvement is dogged by inconsistencies, indeed
considerable ones. Nobody on the playground said anything
about considerable inconsistencies in the empirical studies.

The Fan and Chen study, which focused on preschool and
early grade school years, did find some positive links, but, like
much of the parental involvement literature, it found that the
type of parental involvement most powerfully associated with
achievement is not volunteering and other sorts of in-school
busyness, the kind of things parents feel compelled to *do* because the future is scary and they have to do something. Rather
it is the educational expectations and aspirations they have for
their kids. The most consequential type of parental involvement,

then, might involve not being super involved in the library and the classroom but rather just, like, expecting things. Other research shows that parental involvement helps with *behavior* but not necessarily academic achievement.[10] Maybe some involved parents, inspired by what "all the studies say" to volunteer at school, are worried about their kids behaving badly in class, but that's not the impression I've gotten over the years. The impression I've gotten is more about, you know, Harvard.

People familiar with the literature on parental involvement will note that I'm cherry-picking here, emphasizing the gloomier aspects of the less positive studies. Those aren't the whole story, obviously. Belief in a smooth consensus on parental involvement didn't come from nowhere, even if what it did come from wasn't a smooth consensus. There are more positive studies, but they tend to impose a certain headache-inducing complexity on our desire to bring school things within our controlling embrace as involved parents. A 2015 meta-analysis from *Educational Psychology Review* offers an encouraging set of findings, but these are conditional on age and grade level.[11] The associations are weaker for younger kids, stronger for older kids.

Makes sense, I guess. You should expect more educational payoff from the Socratic discussions you stage at the dinner table when your kids are old enough to bear up against your puckish questioning. But the link between this variable of "age or grade level" and educational (rather than behavioral) outcomes hints at how complicated this gets when looked at in its many parts. What are you hoping for improvement *in*, test scores or hitting and biting? And how much improvement should you hope for? Seems to depend on what grade your kid's in, at least on the academic side. But the academic side can be further broken down (most conventionally) to reading or language arts versus math. Some studies show improvements in math from parental involvement efforts, but not in language arts or reading.

But this whole discussion started with a distinction between different types of parental involvement—active meeting and volunteering versus the more passive "parental expectations and aspirations," which seems a more robust factor in much of the literature. But even this variable can get tricky when interacting with other variables, such as race and ethnicity. A 2003 meta-analysis summarizes some of this research: "Mau's (1997) findings indicated that although parental expectations were important, parental supervision of homework was very important." However, Mau also found "racial differences in . . . types of parental involvement. . . . White parents were more likely to attend school functions than Asian and Asian American parents," but Asian parents "had higher expectations, and their children did more homework." Mau's work says parental expectations are the main thing, but "other research suggests," without the right parenting style, "high expectations may place an unmanageable degree of pressure on the child."[12]

Got that? High expectations are the biggest thing for boosting achievement, unless you mix them with the wrong parenting style, in which case, hoo boy. Watch out.

Again, nobody said anything about mixing. Nobody mentioned idiosyncratic effects of distinctive combinations of factors related to parental involvement. In parent culture the effects are taken to be basic and straightforward, what social scientists call linear. "The more intensively involved the parents are," as one educational website puts it, "the greater the positive impact on academic achievement."[13] More involvement means more achievement. But the more familiar you are with the research on parental involvement, the harder it becomes to know what kind of involved parent to be, because more might not be more, and some mix of different elements might be bad, depending on the age of your kids, and, perhaps, your ethnic background. Indeed, as worrying, risk-averse parents, we might start worrying about the risks of doing too much of the wrong mix of the different kinds of being involved in our kids' education.

BUT IT'S HARD TO LOOK AT ALL THE PARENTS MILLING ABOUT the grounds of my public school, being helpful in their various ways, and not take this to be a good thing, even if this activity is partly inspired by a theory of parental involvement that's empirically shakier than everyone thinks. Even if all the studies, read together, turn out to tell a confusing story about parental involvement, it feels like there's something real and useful at work here, in our school "community."

I use this word advisedly, and warily. I'm allergic to corporations and bureaucracies using certain nice-sounding words to make their system functions sound human and ethical, and chief among these words is *community*. (You can't get fired so easily from your church community or village community, but your boss can probably use his keyboard to delete you from your corporate "work community.") And indeed this word often appears in the official communication from our school and school district in a way that, surrounded as it is by the therapeutic and administrative jargon obligatory in such communication, makes me cringe, slightly, in critical rebellion. And yet, the collection of teachers, office staff, administrators, custodians, and parents—all these people convened and moved to various sorts of action and collaboration through the shared purpose of educating the six hundred children who attend this school—is by far the sturdiest and realest community I've ever been a member of.

In her bestselling book *How to Raise an Adult*, Julie Lythcott-Haims summons the image of parents hanging around schoolyards in the morning to support her book's larger point about overparenting—all those fretful moms and dads, monitoring their kids until they're ushered into the bricked fortress of the school building. When I first read that I was a little torn. On one hand, I'm neither a practitioner nor a defender of overparenting, I don't think. On the other hand, I was, on a daily basis, a parent in my kids' schoolyard in the morning. I've walked my kids to school for years, not because I was worried about their safe passage but because I loved walking with them to school. For the 2016–17 school year I had all three of them with me on the sidewalk in the morning—and I count that as the single best year of my life. After our little foot commute I hung around for a while as the schoolyard filled up, not to hover over my kids like a helicopter, but to chat for a few minutes with the friends I'd made among the other parents, and with my kids' teachers past and present, as little bodies whirled around us like windblown scraps of energy and happiness. To put it simply, I was in that schoolyard at that time because the schoolyard was a really nice place to be. What a privilege, I've thought to myself many times, to get to spend five or ten morning minutes before work in the midst of so many *children*. And this setting really did, and does, seem deserving of the overused term "community": people sharing friendship and moral purpose, where friendship is anchored in the moral purpose, and the moral purpose is deepened and made more urgent by the friendship.

And maybe the greatest value of "parental involvement in schools" is the creation of this community. Maybe the benefits of our school-based activities consist not in educational advantages we win for our own kids, but the advantages we help secure for *each other*'s kids. This is the contention of a 2017 paper by Sira Park, Susan I. Stone, and Susan D. Holloway of the University of California at Berkeley.[14] Park, Stone, and Holloway take up the disappointing research findings on school-based parental involvement, but they argue that parents' involvement at their kids' schools has real benefits, only not the ones typically measured in parental involvement studies. Evidence is "thin" that parents' busyness in the library and lunchroom is giving their particular little ones a leg up, but the evidence is pretty robust that such involvement makes the overall performance of the schools better.[15]

This goes for schools in both poorer and better-off neighborhoods, but with different underlying features in each case. Schools with higher socioeconomic status (SES) families tend to show stronger benefits from what researchers call "public good" parental involvement—participation that helps the whole school, such as volunteering and PTA membership. Lower-SES schools tend to show strongest benefits from active participation in "private good" activities—participation prompted by or focused on concerns about the parents' own children, such as contacting teachers and attending parent-teacher conferences. Again, even in the latter case these are school-wide, not student-level benefits. The weak or even negative associations sometimes found for public-good involvement in low-SES schools may largely reflect that such involvement is likely to increase when acute problems arise. The problems probably cause the involvement, in other words, not the other way around.[16]

These paths to improvement seem different in their details, but the social achievements in each case may be more similar than they appear—and this similarity may well be captured in this overused word, "community." Park and her coauthors cite the notion of "intergenerational closure," from the great sociologist of education James S. Coleman, to theorize why parental involvement—even its private-good variety—might yield public, school-wide benefits. Powerful features of modern life—not least compulsory schooling—tend to hive off people by age group, especially children in their different age tiers. Instead of apprenticing with an older blacksmith or weaver or working alongside their parents, and perhaps with siblings and cousins of various ages, in fields or homes, modern children are unnaturally gathered in huge, age-identical bunches of other children, where distinctive age-group cultures form. Age-separated children are able to create their own normative atmospheres, whose immanent pressures repel other influences, from other age groups, especially the age group that includes parents.

This is fun and liberating for a lot of kids (and a tyranny and torture for many others). But it also allows kids to separate the normative world of class and grade from that of home and family. For these kids, the administrative sanctions written out at school can be painless and meaningless, compared to the more closely felt penalties handed down by Mom and Dad. At school they work under the official, divided attention of teachers and principals, as opposed to the more intimate, penetrating interest of their parents. The challenges this poses to the learning cultures of schools seem obvious. An absence of parents lets kids treat the separate world of school as an ethically unserious place, or a place whose most serious ethical rules are written by other kids in their own age cohort, and not the adults who nominally run the place.

So, the "intergenerational closure" effected by parents visibly involving themselves at their children's schools helps solve a problem partly created by schooling itself. A communal order—in the ideal, slightly archaic sense of that concept—has all the generations. It has people up and down the age scale, appearing before each other, dealing with each other in a meaningful way, answerable to each other in specific registers. And in a busy elementary schoolyard in the morning, you do see grandparents sitting on benches and toddler siblings wanting in on the monkey bar action, along with schoolkids themselves, and parents lucky enough to have five minutes to hang around at drop-off, talking to teachers who may not even realize the benefits to their classrooms of being seen in this way. It's nice to think of this school community, simply in existing as such, serving educational goals. It's nice to think of the wholesome activity of parental involvement having real benefits, even if they're a little different from the ones we think we're securing for ourselves and our kids when we get involved.

Schools are the focus of intense parental interest, anxiety, and effort, but, in their inner workings, they are not very useful or responsive as objects of competitive striving. One exception, in which a truly private benefit is sought and won through parental angling in public schools, is bossy parents getting their kids switched to the best teachers. I don't doubt this happens, but I do doubt that schools encourage it. Accepted as a general

rule, a set transactional scheme that guides parents' calculations, it would be a huge political headache for schools. Parents
who do this are their own creations, not the schools'.

This lack of responsiveness is actually good for families, at
least those that don't have children with special needs. Because
they can't hold out the promise of a special leg up to individual
students, schools, especially public schools, can't set the sort of
individualized conditions, the transactional demands for compliance and conformity, that one finds in other bodies of civil
society, more finely attuned to the competitive urges of parents. Eager, anxious school parents can throw themselves into
a mode of striving by being "involved," and they may conceive
of this striving in terms of the exclusive leg up it's giving their
little one, but even the most selfish of these parents can't keep
their busy effort from benefitting everyone's kids as well as, and
perhaps more than, their own.

Just as the relative unresponsiveness of public schools, at
the personal level, is a hidden benefit for most families, so is
the lack of choice that the public, neighborhood school model
represents. To have a good-enough school imposed on you as
a nonchoice is something of a liberation. You don't have to
comparison shop. You don't have to weigh opportunity costs or
worry about choosing wrong. And giving primacy to the neighborhood school fits the ideal of the school that's educationally
healthy because a healthy school community has grown up
around it. Lovely and healthy school communities can have
other forms, but the readiest version of it, it seems to me, is the
one that grows from a shared place.

I know that there are downsides to the neighborhood school
model, and that for many families the imposition is an oppres-

sive, not a liberating one. I'm speaking, however, of the neighborhood school *model*. The judicious introduction of well-run charter schools to struggling school systems does seem to help individual students who attend them, and may add accountability and vigor to the systems themselves. But this policy innovation has limits. It's better to view it, and use it, as augmenting the public, neighborhood school model than as supporting the competing model of school *choice*.

That is, embracing the virtues of the unresponsive, good-enough neighborhood school helps us see what we want school reform to achieve, and what we want it to avoid. My argument in this book suggests that even a beautifully run system based on total school choice—all charters, or full vouchers—would impose serious costs on families, adding a new layer of competitive stress for parents. A long, sparkling menu of school choices would become a new arena of competition, in which functionally similar schools would seek a telling edge over their peers on the surface measures of prestige and status, and parents— their status awareness and their future-anxiety twined together, feeding each other—would end up in a parallel competition with *their* peers. We already know that the college admissions process is a disaster, and we know who tends to triumph in this competition. A policy vision that threatens to visit that process upon families during the grade school years doesn't seem like one we should be entertaining, as we trudge on with the endless, hopeless, necessary task of improving American education.

chapter six

Striving Together

Colleges and Families in Competition

F OR ONLINE READERS CONDITIONED TO SAVOR SUCH humiliations, the details of the Lori Loughlin–Felicity Huffman college admissions scandal were delicious. Actress Loughlin and her businessman husband Mossimo Giannulli, wanting very badly for their two daughters to win admission to the University of Southern California, allegedly gave half a million dollars to an associate athletic director at the school, Donna Heinel. In exchange for this bribe Heinel told USC admissions that the Giannulli girls were being recruited by USC's crew team, when, in truth, the girls were largely occupied with posting fashion videos on Instagram and had no association with competitive rowboat racing. For her part Huffman, with no indictable help from her actor husband William H. Macy, allegedly paid her way into a crooked testing scheme whose mastermind said he "could arrange for their daughter's SAT proctor to secretly correct her wrong answers and boost her score."[1]

And then, exquisitely, these cheating, bribing celebrities got caught, by the FBI.

The arrest of Loughlin and Huffman seemed to blow the lid off the half-hidden irregularities in college admissions, to expose the open secrets of unfair privilege and unequal access. Finally, readers and writers were exulting, rich people rigging the admissions process were getting the fist of justice right in the face. But the scandal was actually a distraction that revealed very little of the larger system. Pictures of guilty—and dim-witted and inept—celebrities cringing in courtrooms gave people a simple feeling of moral triumph while leaving the subtler, more systemic tyrannies of college admissions entirely unexposed. By casting the regular admissions process as a virtuous sort of reference standard, the scandal obscured the pathologies that define that process. Indeed, in the adaptations they will likely spawn within admissions offices, the scandals probably made these pathologies even worse.

There are several basic issues that commentary on this sort of behavior, and the college admissions process more generally, fails to address. What role, for example, do admissions departments themselves play in this process? In the Loughlin-Huffman scandal, the USC admissions office was generally depicted as an innocent bystander, if not a victim of these entitled and devious parents. But in fact the competitive excesses of applicants and their families, and the broader condition of stress, competitive striving, and grinding effort that has come to define the admissions process, are inextricable from the colleges' own practices. And an interesting feature of these practices is that they bear strange similarities to what these anxious and exhausted families are doing. The colleges are engaged in a ceaseless battle with each other over tiny margins of status and prestige, and high schoolers are fodder in this image war, which is at once dire in its stakes and absurd in its content.

That such a competition among schools would *harm* their prospective students seems counterintuitive. Choice among many alternatives should, in theory, give more leverage to prospective buyers (college applicants) and make prospective sellers (colleges) more pliable, less able to make demands of their own. But that's not quite how it works in the "market" that matches studious high schoolers with slots in desirable college—which, in America, has been institutionalized as "the college admissions process."

WHEN PEOPLE TALK ABOUT THE PROBLEMS OF COLLEGE ADmissions, they often start with a sort of founding culprit: *America's Best Colleges*, inaugurated in 1983 as a special issue of *U.S. News and World Report*. Most people in the higher education business claim to hate *America's Best Colleges*. They say its criteria are arbitrary, subjective, and unfair, and yet those lofty institutions pay close attention to these empty rankings.

But for families tangled up in the college admissions process, and, really, for colleges as well, the main problem with *America's Best Colleges* is not that it's unfair or inaccurate. It's that it exists at all, an omnibus of college status, a mirror in which, looking into it, both anxious college administrators and anxious college applicants can see themselves and all their competitors staring back at them. *America's Best Colleges* is thus more symptom than cause. Its arrival merely notarized a system that had been evolving for most of the twentieth century.

At the beginning of the century, information on distant colleges was scarce and hard to find, and it had little value anyway, since few high school graduates went to college and almost all of those who did attended colleges close to home. And since America already had an astonishing number of colleges and universities, even those students committed to staying in their city or county or state for college could choose among several schools and settle on a religiously or academically agreeable one. But as travel and communication improved, and popular culture and televised news made distant colleges more visible, easier to dream of attending, this local and regional mottle of college attendance was gradually replaced by, or overlain with, a national system of undergraduate matriculation.[2]

For kids and families participating in this national system of college enrollment, it was natural that the single criterion of academic prestige would predominate. Why else would you shun your low-tuition state universities, the nearby private colleges run by your fellow Baptists or Catholics, fly over or drive past hundreds of others on your way to a pricey school two thousand miles away? It was only natural that the pull of prestige, the fear of losing something real in not chasing it as others were, would spread among successful high schoolers and their parents. And as it spread, it was natural that it would grow in its persuasive power, which in turn would increase and accelerate its spread.

A similar dynamic was building among the colleges themselves, especially in the decades after World War II. As travel improved and college information became easier to find, and as the number of aspiring college students grew thanks to pro-college policies such as the GI Bill, America's colleges found themselves competing for the most desirable members of this expanding student population. The result, for colleges, was a stark sorting, in which the top 20 percent of colleges saw their admissions standards rise, while those in the bottom 80 percent struggled to keep them steady or watched them fall.[3]

So, for those running America's colleges in 1983, the arrival of *America's Best Colleges* must have been a bracing event. There was now a famous publication in which the tortured schema of their inner lives were printed out for everyone to see, the institutional vanities and fears they were already being paid to curate and manage, the status rankings in which they were already placing themselves. And for prestige-minded high schoolers this book put a stamp of precision—artificial and arbitrary but real enough because self-fulfilling—on something their kind had been groping at for decades, using scraps of intelligence from guidance counselors and other half-informed authorities. Indeed, you can see people taking academic meaning from the phrase "Ivy League"—a regional sports conference—as an early solution to this information problem: "If Harvard or Yale or Princeton won't take our young Bradford, then where else *is* there?" Like the precisely numbered rankings in *America's Best Colleges*, the prestige value that "Ivy League" arbitrarily assigned to schools like Brown and Cornell became more real simply in being assigned.

As the 1980s approached, American college administrators were bracing for a disaster. The bounty of applications they'd enjoyed as America's college-aged population boomed, so to speak, was predicted to end. The population of high school graduates would soon be shrinking, and colleges would be looking at fewer applicants, and declining admissions standards, and, perhaps, faltering financial health. Their very survival as institutions was at risk. But the 1980s baby bust did not result in an application bust. Instead, as the economy of the late seventies and early eighties swung from stagflation to deep recession, a growing portion of high schoolers began to find college a wise move. From 1980 to 1985, the percentage of high school graduates continuing on to college rose from 50 to 58 percent. Application numbers held steady, or even increased for some schools, and colleges escaped the fate they'd been fearing. An interesting footnote to this story of demographic crisis, as historians Elizabeth Duffy and Idana Goldberg note in their 1997 book *Crafting a Class*, is that worried administrators decided to make branding and marketing a crucial part of their institutional missions. They would survive the crisis by using advertising to steal applicants from each other.[4] The crisis didn't happen, but, in the meantime, they'd built up all this marketing and branding capacity, which would enable them to conduct their image competition with each other at a higher intensity, and, not coincidentally, claim a larger place within the anxious imaginations of American parents and children.

After this averted disaster, and with a growing population of "echo boom" high schoolers nearing graduation, college application numbers began to increase again. Indeed the rise in application to selective colleges has far outpaced the background increases in population and college attendance. Aided by the growing number of informative websites, especially those built by the colleges themselves, and the fact that the Common Application, first introduced in 1975, moved onto the internet in 1998, more students were able to learn about and apply to more schools than ever before.

This points to a gloomy irony in American college education—everything that seems to empower ambitious students in their quest for a place in a good university increases the competitive stresses to which the system subjects them. This, in turn, empowers the admissions departments of these universities, at the expense of these students and their families. That is, the American system of undergraduate matriculation is another instance in which people rise above prior constraints, thanks to new information and other tools, only to discover they now inhabit a rarefied, denuded landscape filled with an inconveniently large number of people like themselves, fit and motivated, well armed for competitive struggle. And they now confront a body of well-positioned institutions eager to put these striving selves to productive use.

In October 2005, the New Yorker published an essay on college admissions by Malcolm Gladwell. The essay centers on Jerome Karabel's monumental 2005 book *The Chosen: The Hidden History of Admission and Exclusion at Harvard, Yale, and Princeton*. In its function as a review, the essay is typical Gladwell, quick and clear in its writing, judicious in its argument, light in its tone but heavy with fresh insights. But what really stayed with me about the piece was its opening paragraph on Gladwell's experience as a college applicant, because Gladwell is from Canada, and Canada's college admissions are nothing like America's. For years, thanks to this lede, I forgot it was a review-essay on an important book, and I remembered it instead as a whole article on Canadian college admissions:

> I applied to college one evening, after dinner, in the fall of my senior year in high school. College applicants in Ontario, in those days, were given a single sheet of paper which listed all the universities in the province. It was my job to rank them in order of preference. Then I had to mail the sheet of paper to a central college-admissions office. The whole process probably took ten minutes. My school sent in my grades separately. I vaguely remember filling out a supplementary two-page form listing my interests and activities. There were no S.A.T. scores to worry about, because in Canada we didn't have to take the S.A.T.s. I don't know whether anyone wrote me a recommendation. I certainly never asked anyone to. Why would I? It wasn't as if I were applying to a private club.

I recalled this essay more recently, and I wondered if there might be some academic research on the same topic, if any scholarly work backed up Malcolm Gladwell's old *New Yorker* piece about college admissions in Canada.

It turns out there is. Indeed a closely related scholarly article by sociologists Scott Davies and Floyd M. Hammack appeared in the *Journal of Higher Education* earlier in the same year as Gladwell's *New Yorker* essay: "The Channeling of Student Competition in Higher Education: Comparing Canada and the U.S." Young Canadians *do* compete with their peers for more promising college opportunities, Davies and Hammack noted, but they differ with their American counterparts in where and when, and thus how, they do this. "Rather than striving to enter prestigious institutions," they wrote, "Canadian students compete to enter lucrative fields of study such as business and engineering." This means that, instead of "the high school–based strategies adopted by aspiring U.S. youth," academic competition in Canada "is mostly absorbed by the postsecondary system itself, as students enter local universities in general arts and science programs and then compete for admission to more lucrative fields."[5]

Another factor that makes the lead-up to college very different, and much less stressful, for Canadian parents and children stems from an accident of institutional design. To the extent that Canadian colleges can be ranked by prestige, and to the extent that anyone cares about these rankings, the country's most prestigious college is probably University of Toronto. But where America's most prestigious college, Harvard, has about 5,000 undergrads, University of Toronto has 65,000. Compared to Canada's well-known universities, America's other prestigious private universities have similarly tiny undergraduate bodies. Duke's undergrads number about 6,000, Stanford's 7,000, Yale's 6,000, Princeton's 6,000, while, in Canada, the University of British Columbia has over 60,000, McGill 35,000, and Queens 27,000. If you move down to America's elite liberal arts colleges, the numbers get downright microscopic — Williams with 2,000, Amherst 1,800, Swarthmore 1,600, Reed a mere 1,400.

For high-achieving students, college attendance in the United States has much greater and more specific social meaning, our leafy little schools stacked upon each other in fine layers of status and prestige, compared to Canada with its big schools, their dull valence as status signifiers.[6] If you're one of the five hundred kids who slipped through the tiny keyhole into Williams College in

a given year, the purple "W" sticker on your mom's Prius carries way more distinction for you and her than whatever would
identify a young Canadian as being one of the fifteen thousand
who rolled through the roomy tunnel that leads to the University of British Columbia.

This points to the unhappy irony I mentioned above. Somehow, the broader choice of better-defined colleges in America,
instead of giving parents an easy feeling about their kids' admissions prospects, has become the institutional basis for an
exhausting, nerve-racking, bankrupting struggle over tiny margins of status and prestige. And instead of conferring consumer
power on American families, as we'll see in Chapter 7, this
struggle transfers immense disciplinary power to the admissions
departments of desirable colleges.

American parents pondering this comparison with Canada,
I submit, ought to be extremely jealous. What it shows is that
in Canada, striving for college opportunity means a lot less, in
terms of status and perceived advantage, and to the extent that
it happens, it mostly happens *in college*. America's arms-race
logic doesn't govern the high school and middle school years
of college-bound Canadian kids. This difference, experiencing
your children's middle and high school years as ones of general
growth and not compelled striving against other parents and
other children seems estimable from what you might call a family values perspective.

I use that familiar conservative phrase — "family values" —
advisedly. I anticipate a general conservative reflex against my
vaguely socialist invoking of Canada. Isn't it just like the wimpy
Canadians to want to escape a little healthy *competition*? And
surely the lazy Canadians pay some aggregate costs in dynamism

and productivity from their failure to stage a bitter achievement struggle among their teenagers. Surely America enjoys more muscular per capita output than it would if it adopted the Canadians' hippieish way of allocating and growing human capital in its teenage years.

The egalitarian structure of Canadian college education also, apparently, cuts against other values that conservatives in America often advocate, such as institutional pluralism and freedom of consumer choice. Davies and Hammack describe a sort of overt institutional sameness, in which Canadian universities, quite unlike their American counterparts, operate within a narrow range of both prestige and price. In Canada it matters what you study, but for most students it makes little difference, in either price or status, where you study it.[7]

For the typical American conservative, this—the idea of government power suppressing choice and variety among colleges, in a market dominated by government institutions— would stick somewhat painfully in the craw. But, again from a conservative perspective, consider what comes with our particular American regime of postsecondary education, our greater range of choice of overtly ranked colleges and universities. It's not just the competitive worry and busyness that afflicts us and our children and darkens the public perception of family life, that emboldens critics of marriage and family who are quick, generally too quick,[8] to pounce on studies saying these things make people less happy. It's also the way family time and family life have been hijacked by what is the most basic sort of collective action problem, a self-fueling cycle of fearful striving. Even small-government types have at least a theoretical interest in solving this type of problem.

And it's also at whose behest and prompting, to whose benefit and empowerment, we and our children engage in this competitive struggle, perform its prescribed functions. I'm referring
to the outsized social power, in America, of college administrators. The legacy of Wilbur Bender, Harvard's admissions director from 1952 to 1960, is instructive here. It's hard not to view
Bender as something like the Robert Moses or Dick Cheney of
American college education, someone who, working from an
undistinguished position with undefined powers, exerted a huge
influence that made the world a worse place. Admissions offices
throughout America, in other words, now follow the Bender
example.

As admissions head, Bender had to satisfy the constituencies
to which Harvard traditionally catered: Harvard alums with kids
applying, whose money Harvard wanted, and rich people with
kids applying, whose money Harvard also wanted. He also had to
balance these interests against the need to preserve the school's
reputation as an academic powerhouse. Harvard already eased
its high admissions standards in these cases, which people still
complain about today. But Bender expanded his administrative
mission by seeking not only to placate Harvard's alumni and maximize its financial endowment but also to heighten its *impact on
the world*. He would try to identify certain *types*—charismatic
young men who seemed destined to make a difference in the
world of affairs—and give an admissions boost to these kids. Not
incidentally, highlighting these vaguely WASPy and jockish character traits allowed Bender to place a soft quota on Jewish enrollment, which, for many Harvard stakeholders, had grown too fast.
In his *New Yorker* essay Gladwell calls this the "best-graduates
approach"—as opposed to a "best-students approach." That is,

Bender sought not just to select the brainiest high school students, who a year later would prove to be excellent Harvard students, but to divine which of his seventeen-year-old applicants would glorify his school by launching into the world five years later as high-impact Harvard *graduates.*

Gladwell justly criticizes Bender's efforts against Jews and "pansies," but Bender's mixed approach doesn't really bother him—judicious thumbs on the scale for rich kids, legacies, and future go-getters, and so on. I admire Gladwell's blasé attitude toward these practices, which rankle so many observers. He's entirely correct to scorn "the assumption that some great moral principle is at stake in the matter of whom schools like Harvard choose to let in." Getting worked up about this dubious principle is a weird American thing. Gladwell's Canadian. Canada doesn't have a Harvard.

He also credits Bender's best-graduates method with making a smart and useful distinction—familiar to statisticians and scientists—between *selection effects* and *treatment effects.* Bender realized that a Harvard *education* (treatment effect) may matter less for the school's goal of sending great leaders into the world, than a Harvard admissions process that identified these future leaders when they were still in high school (selection effect). Wouldn't this be a natural and healthy thing for a college, interested in its own social standing and institutional health, to focus on? From the college's perspective, yes.

From the family perspective, no. What Gladwell neglects is how the distinction between selection and treatment breaks down when—instead of lab rats or microbes—the thing being selected and/or treated is well-informed and self-aware people. When selection criteria become publicly known, while being attached to scarce and highly desirable outcomes for which aspirants can and must compete, they can start to have their own rather potent treatment effects. This is especially true when these criteria apply to Bender-style "character" standards. As colleges in general came to put more stress on character in their admissions standards, and as American families came to know this and to grasp its importance, the process of *choosing* certain administratively favorable sorts of teenagers became a machinery for *making* them.

Ambitious high schoolers still have to do as much as possible to boost their academic credentials, because, when push comes to shove, even Harvard will choose the kid with impressive inner force *and* super-high SATs and GPA over the apparent go-getter with lesser numbers. This explains why the test prep industry doubled in size between 1998 and 2012,[9] and why the role of Advanced Placement courses exploded in the same general time frame, from 566,720 students taking 899,463 AP exams in 1997 to 2,808,990 students taking 5,090,324 exams in 2018.[10]

But academic scores are only so malleable. However many hours of grinding study and weekend test prep kids do, their scores will tend to have a hard ceiling. Some kids, most kids, just aren't going to ace AP Calc or IB Physics. And even if your numbers are perfect, it turns out you're still competing against thousands of other kids with perfect numbers.

This is where Bender's "best-graduates" character standards become behavioral power for college administrators and a trap for families. It's all too easy, when colleges signal that they want to see the vigor of future leaders in their chosen students, for teenage applicants simply to *get vigorous*. Every middle schooler is a tabula rasa when it comes to resembling a future president or some other best graduate of a top college. There are all kinds of protopresidential traits that can be etched onto her persona starting now, whenever now is. Most obviously, she can run for student body president. To present herself as a future leader of business, she can start a business, even if she doesn't much like business. To signal a heightened suggestion of the inner force that, in turn, suggests a heightened probability of future impact in the global justice world of NGOs, she can start an NGO now, as a teenager. As we'll see in Chapter 7, private admissions coaches and college admissions officers actually suggest this.

A COUNSELOR FROM AN ELITE BAY AREA PREP SCHOOL MADE a funny aside to me about the parents at his school. "I can always tell when there's been one of those parties," he said. By which he meant one of those school-based parent parties. A PTA fundraiser probably. After those parties, parents would come to him in worse shape, and not because of the alcohol. The party talk was all about college. Airing their most recent college labors and worries to each other, as if therapeutically, they would get each other even more worked up.

We were talking over coffee a few months after the Laughlin-Huffman scandal, which, he said, had sent a jolt through his school's administration and board of directors. Shortly after the scandal hit the news the board brought him in for a talk. The first thing they wanted from him was assurance that no such hijinks—faked scores, shady deals with college coaches—were happening at their school. On this, he could assure them, the school was clean. The second worry the scandal raised was more

generic, only peripherally related to the celebrity crimes they'd
been reading about. The board wanted to know if their school
was . . . somehow . . . *slipping*? In its tawdry fashion the scandal
showed just how hard everyone's charging now, how seriously
parents of a certain station are taking the matter of college placement, and the board wanted assurance that this expensive and
highly ranked high school was charging hard too. These board
members were all alumni of the school, and they remembered
going to college pretty much where they'd wanted to, back when
they applied. But now there was all this news of rejection. Students at this rarefied school were piling up college rejections
in ways that didn't happen back in the day. Again their dutiful
counselor was able to reassure them: Oh yes, we're working hard
all right. He presented them with data showing that the school
and its students were actually working way, way harder at getting into college than those board members had, and, on at least
one measure, were much more impressive in their admissions
achievements. Back in the mid- to late eighties, only a fifth of
the school's graduates attended colleges with acceptance rates
under 20 percent. Now, over two-thirds do. Back then, just over a
third of the school's graduates attended colleges with acceptance
rates under 40 percent. Now almost all of them do.

It may be hard to sympathize with people who occupy the
very apex of this competitive system I'm describing, people
sitting in board meetings of expensive prep schools worrying
about keeping their clear edge over the rest of us. But it doesn't
matter if they're sympathetic characters or not. What matters is
what their predicament means. Their competitive adaptation
feeds into the fear psychology I've repeatedly mentioned, whose
most potent drive is not some positive desire, the pursuit of a

wonderful outcome, but instead a terrible aversion, a wincing recoil from the mental image of a terrible outcome, a greatest bad—what Thomas Hobbes called the *summum malum.*

For better-off parents the *summum malum* is all too easy to see, as it pertains to their children's future. Historian David Labaree describes this sociological quirk of the competitive system. "Parents who have [climbed] the educational hierarchy in order to [climb] the occupational hierarchy," he writes, "know full well what it takes to make the grade." But they bring another, somewhat paradoxical, trait to the competition that increases their advantage, a sort of adaptive phobia: "When you're at the top of the social system, there is little opportunity to rise higher but plenty of opportunity to fall farther down."[11] That is, the well-off and well educated not only have more weapons in the college battle. They have better motivation: their social vertigo makes them more organically desperate.

These observations track with time-use data cited by economists Garey and Valerie Ramey in their influential paper "The Rug Rat Race." Better-off and better-educated American parents, especially moms, began parenting more intensively, for more hours per week, beginning in the early 1990s. Educated American mothers, who were much more likely to be in the workforce than their own mothers were, were also spending much more time guiding and educating their kids than their own mothers had spent on them.

The Rameys argue that the main cause of this change in the United States was the perception that college admission was growing more competitive, and carried higher stakes now— with the rise of the "knowledge economy" and the decline of high-paying manufacturing jobs. Canadian parents faced the same changed economy as American parents did, the Rameys argue, but what they didn't face was the busy landscape of neurotically status-ranked colleges that we have in America. Canadian parents don't, shortly after bringing a new kid into the world, start wondering and worrying *which college* that kid might *get into*, and start optimizing the kid's skills and listable activities so that he'll matriculate at the most prestigious one possible eighteen years later.

In summarizing their argument, and perhaps trying to turn their article title into a catchphrase, the Rameys write, "This expenditure of childcare time in dissipative rivalry may be dubbed the 'rug rat race.'"[12] The phrase "rug rat race" has in fact become shorthand for the link between "helicopter parenting" and college-oriented competition among bourgeois dads and moms. But there's another phrase I find striking in the Rameys' summary, *dissipative rivalry*, which is another way of saying wasteful competition. This happens when competition becomes a self-fueling cycle, competition for its own sake, and it consumes more value than it generates.

Juliet and I are currently testing the limits of this critical understanding of competitive child-rearing as dissipative or wasteful. We do almost nothing that might be understood as overtly competitive or "enriching"—no math tutors, no piano or language lessons, no competitive sports or other admissions-oriented activities. This is partly because we have three kids and that stuff's expensive. But we haven't even done the free stuff. We know several couples who keep bilingual households, and we could have done that too. Juliet is fluent in Spanish, and her Mexican background gives her adequate pretext, these days, to make a bigger deal of speaking Spanish than she does. (Her dad was born in Mexico, but she learned her Spanish in school, and college, and Spain.) Our beloved longtime babysitter is Salvadoran. For my part, I'd have *loved* to pick up another language just by talking Spanish to my wife and kids and Nana Lucia.

But, even when our oldest was an infant, before we'd quite grasped the thing we were opting out of, Juliet recoiled against these competitive rigors, even when they involved speaking a language she loved. Speaking Spanish at home, when she was a native English speaker, just seemed too corny for her, too forced. These efforts carried a sense of some larger enterprise we just didn't want be part of. Taking them up seemed like inviting some moral or psychic pathogen into our home. Maybe future economists can do a careful multivariate study of what our defection from this competition ended up costing our kids.

In any case, as the Rameys show, worry about tighter admissions to preferred colleges seems to have driven, or at least contributed to, this more wearisome style of child-rearing. But it's unlikely that, starting in 1994, whole cohorts of parents carefully read the statistics and learned that relative returns to the investment in a college degree were growing at alarming rates, or that the demand curve for slots at preferred colleges was bending skyward. (Economists sometimes discuss ambient background incentives that move in the medium of culture as if they were conscious foreground considerations, informed by data printed out on family spreadsheets: "Marginal returns to an elite college degree have grown 4.8 percent, Marge. We need to get Tyler up to speed on starting an NGO now, while he's still in middle school.") It's probably better to view bourgeois parenting as a sort of cultural ecosystem and information about the rising importance of college as what ecologists and climatologists call an "external forcing mechanism." Not all parents had to learn of these dire trends for the new norms they inspired to spread widely and quickly within shared parental cultures. Indeed, most parents probably learned the anxious effort first, mimetically, as simply the way we Americans raise children now, and perhaps absorbed a vague competitive animus from seeing this effortful parenting around them, and only later learned what there was to be anxious about, the scarce and valuable thing they were competing over.

THE ADMISSIONS TOUR BEGAN WITH A FILM, GLOSSILY PRO-duced, filled with inspiring student interviews and soaring aerial shots of campus, which, from the sky, seemed a sort of tidy village against the steep and shapely coastal hills. I was the only solo person in the screening room. Everyone else was in a family group, teenager and parent or parents, with a handful of younger siblings and grandparents swelling some of these groups. I'd lied in the online reservation form. I said I had a ninth-grade daughter interested in Stanford, when, at the time, I had sixth-grade daughter and a fourth-grade daughter and a first-grade son, and I tried never to say the word "Stanford" anywhere they might hear it. I felt pretty conspicuous, sitting there alone, tapping a pen onto a little notepad. I figured I must look like a guy doing research on the other people in the room.

The rest of the tour was so impressive that it was, finally, given we were touring a college and not Versailles or a golf resort in an oil kingdom, kind of appalling. Our tour guide, a rising senior, was ostensibly a political science major but his real specialty seemed to be improv theater. He was fluently, casually funny and knowledgeable—he reminded me of the guy on PBS who plays piano and sings jokey songs about the electoral college. I've never been as comfortable doing anything as he was leading that campus tour. I could understand his easy confidence. His job was convincing high schoolers and their parents that Stanford is a desirable college, which by the criteria generally applied, I have to admit, it is.

The campus is just old enough for its original buildings to have the culturally suggestive (American Southwest) and quaintly periodized (1890ish) architectural styling crucial for any respectable college. But perhaps most imposing is how this core traditional style is augmented by the hypermodern aura of its newer buildings—the Gates Computer Science Building, the Hewlett Teaching Center, the Packard Electrical Engineering Building. Stanford, in other words, has everything—romantic past and idyllic present and lucratively computerized future. It can ring all the college-appeal notes, in cleaner tones, with sharper, more confident claps of the hammer, than any other school in America. At Stanford your child—should she be among the one in twenty-five applicants granted acceptance—will study subjects both traditional and cutting-edge, uselessly arty and oh-so-profitable, with the best professors and the most honed and polished classmates, alongside top-class college athletes whose big-time games she'll reach religious ecstasies attending. She'll enjoy the gleaming recreational facilities and expertly curated food and housing options, under the bluest undergraduate skies, before the happiest undergraduate vistas in America.

An important thing to keep in mind, while being wowed and beguiled by Stanford's admissions tour, is that you're participating in a strange war. An admissions tour is part of the broader campaign that every college is constantly waging to distinguish itself from, to make itself look more desirable than, as many other colleges as possible. Stanford comes into this contest with a couple huge advantages either accidental or vestigial. The weather is generally perfect in Palo Alto, for example, and the physical setting is hard to beat. And the only thing the school has to do to keep its glorious association with the most powerful commercial and technological force of the late modern world is not move away from Silicon Valley.

Most colleges have a harder time. For the many less selective private colleges, shrinking cohorts of high school graduates mean that the catastrophe they barely avoided in the 1980s will befall them in the 2020s. Small colleges are already closing. Many more are predicted to fail. But even if you're one of the lucky selective schools, you have a dozen or two, or maybe a hundred schools in your general competitive tier to set yourself against. And there's very little movement in the hierarchy. Once sorted into a status range, colleges tend strongly to stay in that range—which puts their frantic war efforts in a sad light. On a most basic level, they're all fighting and fighting to stay pretty much where they've always been. (And when there is movement in the status rankings, it typically has nothing to do with the colleges' own efforts and everything to do with unpredictable fads that seize trend-sensitive high schoolers. The major recent example of this is the skyrocketing appeal of big-city campuses, which followed the same forces that transformed and gentrified cities beginning in the 1990s, and saw a thrilling rise in application numbers for urban schools such as Tufts, NYU, and, indeed, Lori Loughlin's dream school USC.)

Another thing that makes the competition among colleges so strange is how little of substance it's actually *about*. As sociologists Paul DiMaggio and Walter Powell have written, colleges and universities follow a lawlike tendency known as "institutional isomorphism." As with disparate institutions in other fields of both for- and nonprofit sectors, most colleges and universities secure and protect their legitimacy not by distinguishing themselves from their competitors but by imitating them, displaying how soundly they reproduce the basic model that all the other colleges are also following, voicing the same themes, drawing faculty and staff with the same credentials, from the same sources.[13] In this, they're not unlike us parents, constantly looking around, building their inner model of how to be through fretful comparisons with their peers, constantly wondering if they're enough like everyone else. Even a place like Stanford, or its much older rival Harvard, is distinguished by measures of amplitude and intensity, magnificence within the given criteria, and not some fruitful deviation from them. The paradoxical quest of the college president, gilding his brand in this market while observing its isomorphic requirements, is to prove his school is better than its competitors by showing how closely it resembles them.

TO UNDERSTAND JUST HOW MUCH THEIR COMPETITION WITH each other requires a concomitant principle of neurotic imitation, consider college athletics. Now, college budgets are bloody fields of battle. There's never enough money for all the needy constituencies, from scientists wanting research money to poor kids wanting scholarships. And for all but the few schools with the biggest, most TV-enriched football and basketball programs, college sports are a huge money suck. They add budget stress to college administrators, and they make college more expensive for students and their families. In the concessions to scholastic mediocrity they require, they create conflict and propaganda trouble for fancy admissions departments, not to mention feelings of queasiness and compromise among faculty.

Also, importantly, American-style college sports are nonsensical. They're an absurdist feature on the academic landscape, like a circus tent in a nature preserve, slot machines in a hospital ward. What, exactly, are they doing there? And on top of their thematic dissonance with the idea and purpose of college, major sports events seriously degrade classroom attendance and concentration, time spent learning and studying and discussing academic things. In other words, as I can attest as a former student and instructor and professor at Division I colleges that glorified their sports teams, intercollegiate sports work directly against the main mission of their institutions.

So simply in the interest of thematic coherence, of not tending and paying for expensive and nonsensical and academically backward things at their academic institutions, college presidents would be well motivated to axe all their intercollegiate sports, zero out their athletic budgets. This could be a declaration of sensible priorities: Education first! Fiscal restraint! And you can bet that many of them dream of doing this, especially in budget season, but they can't because it would make their schools look weird. A total absence of sports teams suggests institutional crisis. You just assume sports were lopped off in some emergency surgery, and do people want to send their kids to a school that has a surgical scar where there's supposed to be an athletic department? The schools need the teams, mysteriously. Admissions officers who grumble about the scarce places they're giving to low-score "recruited athletes" will also brag about the school's stellar sports teams in the admissions literature. Those percentile-challenged athletes have a crucial importance for the college's image that admissions, especially, has a dire interest in burnishing. Maybe nobody goes to the soccer games, but soccer players in action, donning the college colors, always make for the most vivid photographs in the pamphlets.

This need for perpetual marketing amid constraints of institutional mimicry explains the postmodern character of college branding campaigns. How do you shine forth as blessedly unique from your competitors while retaining your comprehensive sameness with those competitors? You hire consultants to come up with empty phrases that say who you really are, now, supposedly. Our institutions of higher learning, devoted to piercing the layers of shared illusion and mere opinion and leading us common citizens to the underlying nub of truth, which we're otherwise resistant to facing, and on which everything rests, identify themselves with catchphrases they hired consultants to invent for them.

Schools at all levels of prestige use outside image consultants, but the example of a less prestigious school is my favorite. A good friend of mine was in his first tenure-track job at this school when its president informed his faculty that the university would soon be airing a new motto: "The Leader in Global Education." (It was the early 2000s. "Globalism" was a trendy theme at the time and seemed a positive, or at least irresistible, force.) After unveiling this catchphrase, according to my friend, the university's president met with faculty and asked them to help him flesh out this term, "global education," because up until then the school had put no particular emphasis on this field it was suddenly the leader in. In other words, he was asking his faculty to tell him what he meant by his own slogan. He'd adopted his school's new catchphrase with a pure lack of reference to any existing traits of the institution to which this phrase would apply. Indeed, they'd have to come up with one or two "global education" things now, largely cosmetic, to get their reality to resemble their catchphrase.

But the primary way in which colleges compete with each other, given the narrow boundaries imposed by their need to also imitate each other, is through their admissions offices. This is where we have to face something that most people, even most commentators on the problem of college admissions, tend to avoid. I will put it in quasi-Marxist language: applicants and their families, on one hand, and colleges in their admissions function, on the other, are separate classes, and the relation between these classes is one of fundamental conflict. The admissions department, if you're a parent turning your efforts to getting your kid into college, is your class enemy.

It's not a conspiracy, nor is it that admissions departments somehow attract bad people. It is simply a matter of incentives. The incentives of the current system spur colleges to invent and follow practices that make applicants and their families far more anxious, more unhappy, more pessimistic about their prospects than is necessary, because it is in the colleges' interests to do this. The status contest they're caught in with each other means that it's useful for colleges to jerk their applicants around. Your family's fear about college, in other words, empowers the admissions department. It's in their interest to generate more of it.

There's always been some competition among colleges *for* applicants, but the application glut that arose in the 1990s meant these colleges could also compete against each other *using* these applicants. Around this time, they began to tout their selectivity by publicizing their record-high numbers of applicants, and their record-low admissions rates. But what's good PR for colleges is bad news for applicants and their families. Nothing gets the dread going for academic strivers and their anxious parents like reading that Junior's "reach" school admits only one-twelfth of its applicants, and the school he'd considered his "safety" admits only a quarter.

The clash of interests between schools and families becomes even clearer when you consider that, for a lot of colleges, a portion of those rejections resulted from the tactic known as "recruit-to-deny." That is, armed with the test scores they bought from the College Board, schools send recruiting materials and letters of interest to students they know they won't admit, seeking to enhance their prestige by increasing the raw number of applicants they reject, hoping to push their acceptance rate downward until it's as close as possible to Stanford's incredible 4 percent.

Colleges' admissions numbers are more misleading even than this. Not only are these numbers cynically and cruelly inflated by the individual schools, via their recruit-to-deny side hustle. They also simply reflect the redundant applying that high schoolers increasingly do, precisely because of the scary story they absorb in their admissions research about those high rejection rates. From 1990 to 2012, according to a report by PBS, "the percentage of students applying to seven or more colleges increased from 9 to 28."[14] By 2015 that percentage number had already shot up to 36.[15] So the lower admission rates of selective schools are partly a function of background increases in the applicant population, but mostly a function of more competitive pre-college behavior within a larger part of that population. This change in the applicants' behavior, though, is inextricable from tactics the colleges themselves use to burnish their own standing—that is, upping the fear of rejection that haunts the applicant process.

Another, even clearer example of how colleges, in their admissions and marketing functions, work from interests structurally hostile to those of applicants and their families comes from George Washington University. When Stephen Joel Trachtenberg was president of GWU, he discovered a perhaps surprising method for juicing his application numbers and driving up his school's ranking: increasing tuition.[16] How could increasing the price for something make demand for it go *up*? What makes the college market different, such that it defies the basic economic law of supply and demand? Trachtenberg's answer was that college education belongs to a different kind of market, the market in which "luxury goods" such as Rolex watches and high-priced yachts are sold and bought.

In illustrating how such markets work, Trachtenberg explicitly concedes DiMaggio and Powell's claims about institutional isomorphism, the fundamental sameness of colleges. In conversation with Kevin Carey of the nonprofit New America, Trachtenberg compared the college market to the market in overpriced vodka. Vodka all tastes the same, he said, so the way you distinguish good from bad vodka is price. You know it's a good vodka by how expensive it is. Same with colleges. Armed with this insight, Trachtenberg made a bet that he could make George Washington appear more prestigious and attract more applications by—curious as it sounds—drastically increasing tuition. And it worked. Trachtenberg raised tuition until GW was the most expensive college in America, and, apparently as a result, applications jumped from six thousand to twenty thousand, and the average SAT score of the school's incoming class rose two hundred points. The school thus went from being "an inexpensive commuter school" with no status worth ranking to fifty-sixth place in *America's Best Colleges*—"just outside of the 'first tier.'"[17]

But the real lessons of Trachtenberg's vodka example are a little more interesting than he allows, in ways that illustrate the predicament of American parents. I can think of scenarios—say, gangsters gathering in a club—where overpriced vodka figures as something much more exigent than the word "luxury" suggests. You might call this thing "status," or you might call it not wanting to get shot for being a punk. So-called luxury goods, in other words, tend to figure in status markets defined by acute personal insecurity and fear, where status is a currency that keeps one from experiencing real or at least social death—outcomes people are willing to pay a great deal to avoid, much more, sometimes, than they can afford. Sometimes this sort of status expresses itself in people spending themselves into poverty on "luxury goods" because the alternative is seeing themselves erased from their social worlds. And sometimes the status one struggles to preserve doesn't seem like status at all. It's just the fearful readiness to sacrifice for your children in anxious times.

What Trachtenberg was selling as a college president, then, was more the surcease of fear than it was luxury for its own sake. To the extent that price increases themselves heighten this fear, make the competitive game seem more intense, they heighten the willingness of families to make this sacrifice, pay the raised prices. This was Trachtenberg's winning bet, though there's a not-so-triumphant coda to the GW tuition story. The school, upstart that it was, could not keep up with the tuition increases of older, more pedigreed schools, and, by 2015, it had plummeted to merely the forty-sixth most expensive college in America.[18]

Now, a likely objection at this point is that the tuition prices bandied about in gloomy discussions of college costs are *sticker* prices, merely nominal or official prices. For many students, the *actual* prices paid will be much lower. This is true, but it merely highlights another little tyranny at work in the American system. For many students, the sticker price is not the actual price because schools offer a variety of cost-relief packages, which are scaled to families' assessed ability to pay. This means that the eye-popping tuition, for a family that doesn't have three hundred grand to get their kid a college degree, begets a new institutional relationship. Parents ask, "How much is this college thing going to cost me, then, if not your incomprehensible sticker price?" The college's answer is: "How much do you got?"

Colleges' astronomical sticker prices, in other words, signal that their more specific plan is to max you out *as an individual*. They will learn your limit and match your cost burdens exactly to it. Merely telling them how much money you have isn't enough, though. If you're seeking relief from the massive nominal cost of your kid's college education, from the college's own funds, its financial aid office can look into the value of your house, your investments, your retirement accounts, and many other assets as they determine whether you *really* need this relief. You tell them, and then they investigate your finances to see if you're lying. Are you hiding money somewhere? If so, their forensic accountants are likely to find it. As I was told by a college-financing consultant, whose expertise came from working in the financial aid offices of selective West Coast colleges, the schools' ability to identify financial deception far exceeds parents' skills at perpetrating it.

This is not to deny that poor kids really do get affordably educated thanks to more affluent kids paying those sublime sticker prices. It is, though, to point out how the American system of higher education empowers administrators to claim an investigatory interest in the resources and inner lives of specific families seeking price relief. And remember, the price you might need relief in paying was set at its astronomical level in part to give the school some room in which to find your individual pain point, and so to impose the sort of individualized financial inquest to which you find yourself exposed in this moment. The price structure of American college education, in other words, presupposes an underlying machinery of individualized "relief," and so a concomitant machinery of intimate financial investigation.

The fact that families relate to college financial aid offices as to the Internal Revenue Service—prostrating themselves before financial detectives, nervously wondering if they'll survive the audit—shows the quasi-sovereign leverage over families that colleges have attained in our competitive system. That families not only submit to this level of forensic probing but express gratitude for the relative bargains they win in exchange for their compliance suggests that, under certain conditions of fearful striving, the norms of institutional citizenship can take a slavish turn, while gatekeeping institutions can grow imperious in their presumptions.

MY FAVORITE ILLUSTRATION OF HOW COLLEGES, IN THE INtertwined functions of admissions and institutional branding I describe above, pursue interests hostile to those of applicants and their families is seemingly minor, perhaps, but in its own way it's even more vivid and telling than some of the others I've mentioned, because it's so personal. As such it points toward the discussion that occupies the following chapter, on the probing methods of "holistic" admissions—of which the admissions essay is an increasingly central part, and so a growing source of stressful confusion for the college applicant.

Many colleges post examples of "essays that worked" within the admissions section of their websites. The apparent function of these example essays is to guide and reassure students faced with this mysterious writing challenge. Most of these posted essays exhibit the pathologies of personalized admissions I'll discuss in the following chapter, but the essays Hamilton College posted from its class of 2018 deserve special mention for how they illustrate my present point about class interests, colleges' structural hostility to families.[19]

The leading essay on Hamilton's page of helpful examples begins, "On the day my first novel was rejected, I was baking pies." I laughed through my nose when I read this. I thought: *This* is supposed to be helpful? *This* is supposed to reassure the anxious teenage applicant that he too can tackle the college essay? Well but anyway, I thought, at least it's a *rejected* novel, a merely *aspiring* author. Hamilton's just advertising one of those gig-economy virtues they're all talking about now, grit or resilience or whatever. Think of how insidious, how passive-aggressive, how *hostile* it would be if Hamilton really were offering an application essay by a published teenage novelist as a guiding example of one that "worked."

I read on. After a first full paragraph about pie making, the next paragraph includes the phrase "acquisition meeting," and a reference to multiple "senior editors" who'd already been interested in this "manuscript"—now, so far, in the essay's narrative present, rejected. The next paragraph begins with a reference to an "agent." This successful Hamilton applicant, the teenaged reader would be forced to realize, already had a *literary agent* when she composed her college essay. This agent, the essay goes on, was the only one who hadn't spurned the young writer upon learning her age as the author of at least one completed novel, possibly salable: fifteen. So this successful applicant was delivering completed novels into the publishing mill as a fifteen-year-old. Right. From here, there's an unexpected climax to the story, a sort of *mortis ex machina* that follows certain genre tendencies of the college essay but alters nothing in the publication plot, which is that a boy the writer barely knew died in a car crash. The coda, however, is entirely expected, which is that after the funeral for the half-known boy the successful applicant revised her novel, and "It sold in three days." The End.

When I read the title of the second essay, "The World from Seven Feet Up," my quick assumption was: the kid's a stilt walker, perhaps a performing clown. I found this humanizing, precisely because of the weirdness of clowns. I imagined a prospective

applicant having the same response, thinking: "Maybe my
hobby isn't so weird after all. Maybe I *can* write about my love
of taxidermy. Maybe I *can* describe my collection of stuffed pos-
sums." The kids reading this page aren't published novelists,
after all, but they are themselves, like this clown fellow, and the
admissions people say they just want you to be yourself in your
essay. They just want to get to know the real you. They also,
the kids know, want you to exhibit some defining quirk, to be,
instead of "well rounded" like in the old days, more queerly
shaped — "well lopsided," in the admissions parlance.

But, it turns out, this essay writer isn't some quirky stilt
walker, a young clown braving the clown stigma. He's a seven
footer. He's seven feet tall. Like the girl who already had a novel
published, a novel she wrote when she was fifteen, he's an extreme outlier, imposingly well lopsided. He's someone you, in
being merely yourself, could never be. "Some of our successful
applicants are teenage publishing sensations," Hamilton admissions is helpfully noting. "Others are seven feet tall."

On one hand, I don't believe the people in the Hamilton
admissions office really *want* to heighten the dread already in
the hearts of their applicants, but, on the other hand, they obviously can't help themselves. The young novelist's essay is the
real giveaway, because, precisely by the standards applied in the
world of selective admissions, it has some problems. The coy
buildup to the final bragging revelation is a little mortifying —
just the sort of thing admissions people mock when the big payoff glorifies them less. And the car-crash interlude is not just
irrelevant but outrageously, almost cynically so. (Admissions
officers often deride essays where kids seem to use poor people
as narrative props, but apparently it's okay to use dead people.)

Deep down, though, the college administrators who posted this essay are in the same position as the young novelist who wrote it. Despite her teenage book deal, she's fighting it out on the gusty steppe with her whole Hunger Games cohort. Like her, the admissions office of a "national liberal arts college" that's well regarded but not top ranked can't afford not to brag, even if it means taunting prospective applicants in a space ostensibly set aside for helping them.

chapter seven

Individually Selected

The Soft Tyranny of Holistic Admissions

T'S A CATHOLIC HIGH SCHOOL SO THEY STARTED THE SESSION with a prayer, which was led by the school's head counselor, my wife Juliet's boss and a friend of mine, who was on the stage of the big auditorium to introduce the main speaker, the associate dean for West Coast admissions of an East Coast liberal arts college. The prayer was customized to the occasion—College Night—in a way that struck me, even though I was raised Catholic and remember some of the Church's liturgical occasions having a quaintly specific emphasis. (A blessing of throats against the threat of rogue fish bones comes to mind.) The counselor at the mic asked God to bless and give strength to those present as they entered "the process." In the moment, trimming the phrase "the college admissions process" to just "the process" seemed somehow more descriptive, at a spiritual level, an addition-by-subtraction sort of thing. As such, it made the idea of praying before you enter this process seem even better.

The scheduled speaker, the West Coast dean of the East Coast college, was brought in to demystify the stressful process for the parents and kids there assembled. And he was indeed a reassuring presence—a strapping, jockish Latino man in his thirties who'd graduated not from the little college that employed him back east but from UC Berkeley, just up the freeway. And he was from the Bay Area himself, a local. He'd have fit right in at this big, multiethnic school well known for its sports teams. His main focus, the thing he wanted to highlight by way of trying to take some of the stress and mystery out of the process, was that students and parents had the power to make it a "very individualized process." He said he liked to use the "analogy of a sports car." Everybody's ideal sports car is different, he said, and it's the same with colleges.

I don't want to latch on to the darker, perhaps unintentional aspects of the sports car analogy—the suggestions of indulgence and expense, of "luxury goods." I want, rather, to focus on what the speaker was explicitly getting at, the idea that choosing a college is a deeply personal thing, idiosyncratic even, a matter of "feel" and—a word much used in the administrative discourse of college admissions—"fit."

The private college admissions business leans heavily on this conceit. Private admissions counselors tend to focus on the softer, more personal and qualitative parts of the college application—the admissions essay, especially, as well as the portfolio of nonacademic activities that admissions people like to see. By insisting that college admissions is really a matter of custom "fit" between student and school, people involved in the process mean to make that process sound more human, more intuitive, more *you*. They mean to be reassuring. "I know the process can seem like a big rat race," they're saying. "But rest assured. There are real human persons on the other end, reading your application from a holistic perspective. They sincerely want to get to know the real you."

In fact, this personalization of the admissions process is really a symptom of how sick it has become. As I've noted throughout this book, families and colleges are stuck in a collective-action problem, a feedback loop of "wasteful competition" in which anxious striving begets more anxious striving. One of the results of this process is that admissions offices are both obliged and empowered to take a deep look into the applicant's personality and moral worth. That is, at selective colleges, the traditional methods for ranking applicants have been overwhelmed by the size of their applicant pools, which seem to grow in both their human abundance and their intensity of qualifying merits every year. So admissions departments introduce and emphasize more subtle personal measures to help tell these highly similar kids apart. Of course these personal measures are murky things to judge, and they're easily gamed by frightened and ambitious and savvy applicants, and so the result is a sham of precision, standards of selection that are malleable and inscrutable — but which, nonetheless, admissions offices treat as supremely important and which students must therefore customize their young selves to satisfy.

It would seem natural to address this issue from the critical perspective of parents, in that it's parents and their children whose lives this process unsettles and hijacks, but it's oddly uncommon. Indeed, public commentary on college admissions, even when it's bemoaning the process, seldom blames the process, much less its personnel. To the extent that human actors are singled out for censure in the many books and articles on the admissions process, it's almost always *parents*—the celebrity cheaters, the wealthy dad making bossy phone calls to the admissions dean, the paranoid, pestering mom who's lost all sense of boundaries. To many observers, it seems, out-of-control parents are corrupting an otherwise healthy system.

Entitled and pathetic parents do make good reading, but even the abhorrent ones are reacting to incentives that come from the colleges themselves. Indeed, the unseemly bullying and wheedling of these extreme parents are merely extra-blatant expressions of an outlook—by turns obsequious and Machiavellian—that admissions standards and procedures encourage and reward. The incentives that drive the process leave us in our current unhappy predicament, in which everyone seems to acknowledge that college admissions has gone wildly out of whack, but the only people truly situated to make it better—the admissions officers of prestigious colleges and universities—keep introducing new ways to make it worse.

ADMISSIONS DEPARTMENTS ARE JUDGES IN A FIERCE COMPETITION. The harshness of this competition registers with everyone, but one thing that offsets this perception of harshness is the idea that it has a softer side. The modern admissions office is concerned not just with grades and SATs. It's interested in the applicant as a *whole person*, a unique individual. Virtually all selective colleges practice "holistic admissions," and admissions personnel of most other colleges speak the language of holistic admissions even when their application numbers make it less useful as a practice. But these supposedly softer and more human methods are really an optical, administrative response to a constantly growing problem of legibility and selection. With more applications from more kids, who are better prepared and more savvy about the process than college applicants ever were before, colleges have to squint really hard just to see among all these solid applicants, to discern meaningful differences between one contender for admission and another with virtually the same qualifications. Rather than search for ways to simplify their processes, admissions departments have made their selection protocols more elaborate in ways that, from an academic standpoint, seem unnecessary if not gratuitous. That is, a given selective college receives an abundance of applications from kids who satisfy any reasonable expectation of academic success at that or any similar school. For many colleges, applicants with these numbers would have outright flattered them, back in the day. They're hemming and hawing over kids they'd have ardently courted a couple decades ago. Given this, you might think that the colleges would yield to a certain randomness in their means of selection. If all these overachieving kids would be admitted by historical standards, and they should be able to do just fine, academically, then why get all nitpicky about which of them to admit? Why take on all the extra work?

Admissions officers will sometimes concede the basic point behind these questions. Juliet's boss conveyed a revealing tidbit to me from an Ivy League admissions dean, who told her that his office could simply replace the class they admitted with the next most competitive group of applicants, and the next several after that, and it would make no difference. Perhaps the hearsay quality of this confession renders it suspicious, but the head of admissions at Tufts University has made a similar, if not more revealing, confession, on the record. In 2015 he noted that 74 percent of the nearly twenty thousand applicants to Tufts were "deemed qualified for admission" while "42 percent were recommended for acceptance." The school's actual acceptance rate that year was 16 percent.[1]

It seems as if a sane approach to this glut of qualified applicants would be for a school's admissions office to take the names of all those they know will do fine there, spread them over a corkboard, and start throwing some darts, or, at the very least, buy one of those raffle drums, stuff the names of the qualified applicants into it, and start spinning and picking. Indeed, the most straightforward and compelling proposal to reform the admissions process—offered at different times by Barry Schwartz of Berkeley and Dalton Conley of Princeton—involves this very approach. Schwartz and Conley have both suggested that the best way to take the stress and pain out of selective admissions would be for schools to set a cutoff for academically viable applicants, and then make it a lottery from there. This would lower the social meaning and personal stakes of admissions decisions by conceding how arbitrary they really are.[2]

The colleges haven't done this, of course. Instead they've enlarged their view farther and farther beyond strictly academic qualifications, to peer deeper into the character of their applicants. They practice, as I noted, "holistic admissions." According to most accounts, admissions offices began systematically stressing qualitative line items such as extracurricular activities as the competitive behavior of applicants intensified in the 1980s, and the number of applicants and their applications lurched upward in the 1990s. These offices initially favored the "well-rounded" applicant. At the time, and indeed for much of the preceding eighty years of admissions practices, "well rounded" generally meant "not just a brainiac." So kids who were both smart *and* athletic or civically active would be given a tie-breaking advantage over those who were just smart. (Often, of course, "well rounded" also meant other things, such as "not Jewish" or "less likely to be homosexual.")

More recently, though, the idea of the well-rounded applicant has fallen into not just disfavor, among admissions people, but outright scorn. Now, instead of "well-rounded" generalist strivers, admissions offices favor the passionate specialist, otherwise known as the "well-lopsided" applicant. Admissions consultant Katherine Price describes the current preferences of admissions people: "It's better to be really involved in a small number of activities that show your leadership potential by holding board positions or maybe even being a president of a club or organization. Rather than doing a lot of different activities, here and there, colleges want to see that you're really passionate about something."[3]

Why would schools shift their emphasis from busy well-roundedness to passionate and committed well-lopsidedness? How did padding your résumé with many extracurriculars go from the right way to win over admissions officers to something that— as we'll see below—they openly mock? A pair of institutional reasons suggest themselves. First, the résumé padding grew too obvious, and the blatancy of it came to be a legitimation problem. Admissions departments were clearly being gamed. Word was getting out, and they were starting to look bad, stewards of a mechanistic process that turned kids into grinds and admissions people into obvious dupes.

Second, and more fundamentally, the optical problem it initially solved it began to exacerbate. In an era when fewer applicants were strategically attuned to the process, well-rounded applicants—those both academically qualified and busy with extracurriculars—were more exceptional. They stood out more and so became easier to see and choose. But when ambitious high schoolers came to know that standing out required more than just grades and scores, that a well-roundedness of playing and joining was strategic, and then sought to outdo each other through their sheer number of clubs and teams, all these well-rounded, résumé-padding candidates came to look alike.

Changing the rules to a more individualizing scheme solved both problems. Without actually reducing the stress and time investment of extracurriculars (because they now had to exhibit singular magnitudes of commitment and leadership), it gave the admissions process a huge legitimation victory. That is, it colored an intensifying selection process in the softer tones of "passion" and "individuality" and veiled it in a therapeutic conceit of applicants coming to understand and reveal their "true selves" through their passionate activities and their vulnerable admissions essays. At the same time, the new approach helped solve the optical problem, goading and compelling applicants to make themselves even more legible to its machinery of observation and selection. This has had a further benefit, for the admissions offices, of deepening their formative reach into the lives of these applicants and their families, their disciplinary influence and moral power over America's high-achieving teenagers.

At the same time, their more individualizing methods have given admissions departments greater influence within their own schools. This is evident in a sort of corollary that often appears alongside the ideal of well-lopsidedness. Admissions departments are seeking well-lopsided *applicants*, you sometimes read, so that they can compose a well-rounded *class*—that is, a class filled with people whose individuality has been divined through evolving means of administrative observation, and who have thus been chosen, one by one, to populate this incoming class.

This dainty customizing of incoming classes points in ironic directions. Selective colleges are now fielding applications from all over the country, and a key consideration as they people their freshman classes is geographic as well as ethnic diversity. They want as many American states as possible represented on campus, preferably all of them, to go along with some maximum level of ethnic diversity. The prep school counselor I quote in Chapter 6 described to me how he and his students must assume this when they consider schools. Big, boring California has forty million people, while exotic Delaware has less than a million. So, as in senatorial matters, being from California counts against you in the federalist regime of selective admissions. Of course this federalism is supposed to serve a broader cosmopolitanism, the idea that students learn best when they're surrounded by as much human difference (understood as the numerical maximum of established administrative categories) as possible. But this means that, in their careful, individualizing methods of choosing applicants for their representative value, in both ethnic and geographic terms, schools from all over the country will end up with student bodies that closely resemble one another in these terms. Bespoke admissions at the level of the individual student creates a standardized model at the level of the student body as a whole. A San Francisco kid escapes the gravitational pull of coastal California, matriculates at a selective liberal arts school in the Southeast, and there he finds pretty much the same distribution of types and accents and experiences as he would have if he'd gone to Occidental or Stanford. In any case, this merely expresses to a finer degree the isomorphic tendencies that colleges are already following, the driving urge to realize the same ideal. The regional college's fondest aspiration is to shed its regional accent and become a national college.

At the same time, these administrative prerogatives have inspired the notion that a college campus is, rather than a public sphere in which adults accept the existential risk that comes from alien thoughts and challenging facts, an exquisitely made *community*, in which finer normative expectations befitting the heightened intimacy of communal membership are enforced, both informally and administratively. It was, after all, knitted together with such a careful hand by admissions. This cozy communal idea seems to work against the cosmopolitan human geography that admissions people strive to create, in which differing sensibilities might be expected to jostle against each other in some fertile tension. But you can see how, on today's fully administered college campus, the cosmopolitan diversity of persons would generate a constant thrum of worry among campus executives. Risk-averse deans would, understandably, wish to control and channel the small outbreaks of conflict and misunderstanding that arise when energetic young people from different backgrounds come together, and when, given the administrative conceits behind the whole arrangement, each clash of persons resounds as a problematic clash of backgrounds. So, with everything that's at stake, you can see why administrators might prefer the more exacting rules of comportment, the lower thresholds for moral disturbance and deviation, implied in the word "community."

One consequence of these more personalized admissions practices is that the assessment of extracurricular activities and the reading of admissions essays and personal statements have come into tighter alignment. They are generally viewed together, in other words, as kindred parts of a single representation. Because admissions offices now strive to see and distinguish individuals, the personal testimony of the college essay, which is almost always a personal essay (or several of them), has come to be viewed as equaling, if not surpassing, extracurriculars as a means of seeing into the selves of applicants, even as these extracurriculars are expected to exhibit deeper, more passionate, more revealingly personal commitment. Indeed, the more selective the college, the greater importance its admissions people claim to give the admissions essay. For that reason, in the discussion that follows, I will treat them more or less interchangeably.

I say the process "sees into" and "divines" and "discovers" the individual selves of applicants, but that's not quite accurate. In such a high-stakes environment, with such suggestible and unformed subjects, colleges have created for themselves a sort of Heisenberg uncertainty dilemma: what they're observing changes in being observed. Eager, anxious, ambitious kids, hearing of the latest behavioral and character traits favored by admissions people, will do their best to affect or adopt those traits. As I noted above, this savviness and suggestibility are why the process no longer celebrates well-rounded applicants. It had created too many of them, and they'd made themselves much too uniformly round.

If you take this observation dilemma seriously, then the current buzzword of holistic admissions might strike you as odd. That buzzword is *authentic*. The words "authentic" and "authenticity" pop up everywhere in today's college admissions talk, often in jarring, self-contradictory, barely idiomatic formulations that, in their own way, show just how emphatic admissions people wish to sound about authenticity. John Boyer, dean of admissions at the University of Chicago, enthuses about the school's new test-optional application in these terms: "We are delighted to now also provide an admission process that makes UChicago even more accessible by enabling students to present their best, most authentic selves."[4] Jess Lord, dean of admissions at Haverford College, goes deeper: "Everybody's imperfect [and] those that portray that aspect of themselves [in their essays] are that much more authentic."[5] As I write, Hampshire College's admissions website features, as a sort of headline, a single two-word phrase: "Authentic Admissions." On one hand, you can see how the problem of wised-up applicants padding their résumés led admissions officers to worry over the problem of authenticity. But claiming to judge character in making your selections, and then changing your signaled idea of what good character looks like in the middle of the game, so that now it's totally different from what you said it was before, makes the whole character thing seem kind of arbitrary.

Indeed the derision that admissions readers (quite regularly) direct at their clumsier applicants often comes from these applicants' simple failure to know what admissions regime they're living in, to know which buzzword is the current buzzword. A Yale admissions officer was quoted at a 2012 College Board Forum saying, "We react negatively to anything that sounds forty-two and packaged."[6] I imagine that sounding forty-two and packaged was much closer to the mark in prior decades, much less likely to earn a derisive snort from an associate director of admissions back when Ivys were looking for the well-rounded applicant. But it's the twenty-first century now! Get with the program! Top-tier schools are looking for the applicant who "sounds" authentic.

This highlights a deeper problem with the new authenticity standard. *Sounding* something is not the same thing as *being* something, and I don't think it makes me a deconstructionist to say the only thing a college applicant can do, as to any character trait, is to "sound" it, to give the untestable semiotic suggestion of it, via the different bits of her application. Things look even more unreliable when you understand that the applicant *knows what her audience is looking for*, and her audience *has something she wants very badly*. At that point the personal trait—"passion" or "leadership" or whatever—starts to seem less like a personal trait and more like a condition for parole.

But this whole exercise goes from unreliable to absurd when the trait kids are straining to exhibit to the parole board is *authenticity*. Leave aside that the admissions department of a college is in no position to discern if the outer persona they're reading disparate signs of in an application authentically matches an inner person they're utterly unfamiliar with. It's more nonsensical than that. The people who made applying to college an elaborate performance, a nervous and yearslong exercise in self-construction, have now decided that this elaborate performance will be judged on the authenticity scale, that the end result of the mandatory fabrication must be "the real you." The tacit directive in all this—"Be authentic for us or we won't admit you"—puts kids in a tough position. Once you start thinking about *being authentic* as a conscious task, a mandate from an outside authority, you might be forgiven for having a panic attack. While it's bad that kids have to suffer this logical and psychological torment, it's also bad that admissions departments actually think that the anxiously curated renderings that appear in those applications can in any way be called "authentic." It's like someone watching Meryl Streep in her Oscar-winning role as Margaret Thatcher and thinking: now *that* is the real Meryl Streep.

Of course, for the clumsier applicants, the ones whose self-presentations cause admissions deans to "react negatively," their failures aren't ones of authenticity. They are, rather, failures of discernment, of judgment. In one of his many credulous columns bemoaning the college admissions process in the lead-up to his book on the topic, Frank Bruni of the *New York Times* shared some embarrassing stories fed to him by a former Yale admissions officer named Michael Motto. Bruni writes of one application by which Motto "found himself more and more impressed." "Then"—Bruni says, building in a dramatic pause—"he got to the essay." The essay was about how, during an involved conversation with an admired teacher, the applicant, instead of killing the conversational moment by running to the bathroom, chose to piss herself. Now, if this doesn't show admissions people's declared preference for commitment, I don't know what does. Motto relates the even ickier case of an applicant who "wrote about his genitalia, and how he was under-endowed." This applicant, Motto says, eyes rolling, "was going for something about masculinity and manhood, and how he had to get over certain things."[7]

Bruni and Motto cite these stories as evidence that "the process" has gone out of control, but what they're willing to confront of that process remains anodyne and abstract. "The process," to them, seems to consist entirely of weird and bad stories about applicants and parents. Neither of them thinks to connect the mortifying excesses they cite to the people who orchestrate that process and set its performative standards, the specific incitements that come from admissions personnel like Michael Motto. After all, nervous applicants are assured that "Being a little vulnerable can give great insight into your character" by Joie Jager-Hyman, who gained her special insights as an admissions consultant from her time as an admissions reader at Dartmouth.[8] And after all, one thing Dean Lord of Penn admissions wants applicants to know is that "everybody's imperfect," and that "those that portray that aspect of themselves are that much more authentic." Just as pissing yourself to keep a conversation going with a teacher signals robust commitment of a schoolish sort, a kid advised to "stand out" as "authentic" via "being a little vulnerable" about his "imperfections" is pretty well within the stated parameters when he submits a morbid essay about his little penis. Indeed, Ed Boland, another veteran of Yale admissions, recalls a girl whose essay on how she was a "serial farter" helped her *win admission* to Yale. While the boy with a little penis was "going for something about masculinity" in his essay, the serial farter, in Boland's words, was going for something about "gender and socialization."[9] (The girl's peers, boys, presumably, just assumed the farter was another boy.) The level of political edification in each essay seems pretty much equal, and the political gist of each is likewise highly similar. The difference would seem to be that a cringing small-penis confession is just way more queasy-making for the reader than an essay where a savvy teenage girl celebrates her harmless feminist farting.

What distinguishes an applicant pleasing to the admissions reader from the displeasing one, then, is almost certainly not authenticity. It is, rather, being better informed about how important it is to *sound* authentic rather than "packaged" or boastful, and, most likely, who had better advice and help in creating the right authenticity effect—cultured parents, costly admissions coaches, able and informed college counselors. My wife is a high school counselor, I like to think a very good one. I know at close secondhand how collaborative the essay-writing and application-building rigors are. The more competitive the student and the more selective her roster of college choices (and so the more likely these colleges are to emphasize the personal parts of the application), the more likely it is that this application will have passed before several sets of editorial eyes. Still, when they talk about the process, admissions readers often express irritation about essays that look "overcoached," by which they generally mean braggy essays filled with lofty themes and ten-dollar words. From reading these telltale signs they discern the troubling help, they claim, of paid essay coaches.

But these things, as admissions personnel must know, more likely show the *absence* of such help. One of the things essay coaches are paid for is surely their ability to hide their own influence. One former essay coach, Lacy Crawford, wrote a whole admissions-process novel, which tells the story of a lovably flawed yet skilled and careful essay coach named Anne, whose efforts

are devoted almost entirely to the patient, painstaking, sometimes agonized and heroic conjuring of a "true voice" from her
clients—a voice that sounds authentically like them and nothing like her, which would have been entirely inaccessible to
them if not for her.[10] The things Anne tells her clients to strike
from their essays and the things admissions people say they now
dislike in admissions essays—because they supposedly show
that the kid had an essay coach—are the exact same things.

This is totally predictable. Admissions coaches get paid to
see the world through the eyes of admissions readers. Indeed,
the higher-paid ones often have experience in admissions offices themselves. So, from the shared standpoint of the admissions coach and the admissions reader, the boy with the little
penis committed a misjudgment at once gross and exquisitely
subtle. Lacy Crawford's Anne would have told him that, for an
authentic essay in his true voice that stood out as vulnerable in
the *right* way, he needed to recalibrate his self-abasement. He
needed to come up with an imperfection that sounds authentic in a better way. That he submitted the grim essay he did
speaks less to how much he deserved to attend Yale (whatever
that means) than that he declined, for obvious reasons, to show
it to an essay coach.

This points to another dark aspect of all this personalizing, with its imposed subtleties of performance and discernment—the barely hidden class bias. Admissions personnel are
generally eager to add their voices to the chorus bewailing the
socioeconomic bias in standardized testing, but they're largely
incurious about the class bias in their own softer measures. In
practice, that is, what ends up resembling "authenticity" to admissions readers is an uncannily WASPy mix of dispensations

better understood as *discretion*, or, perhaps, *good taste*. After all, what admissions readers really dislike are the braggarts, and isn't bragging a vice of the classless, the parvenus and arrivistes? (I will leave unelaborated the class assumptions of the admissions coach I quote at the beginning of this chapter, who casually advises that high school students should get themselves placed on boards of directors of organizations.)

All this personalization, these authentic essays and passionate extracurriculars, ostensibly arose as aids in the selection process, finer and truer measures beyond mere numbers. They provide a deeper look into the real person, whether he or she deserves entry, whether he or she, by these subtler measures, might really belong here. At the same time, they become the object of so much effort and focus by applicants, their parents, and their essay coaches because they offer another promise of control. Kids may run up against hard limits on test scores and math grades, but they can still refine the self they present in their essays and extracurriculars, they can still crank up the passion to another level, because the schools say they think those things are important, too. The kind of person you are is important, too, they say.

But it's obvious that the latter undermines the former. The promise of human control mocks the conceit of improved administrative insight and precision. With such (perceived) high stakes, with so much anxiety and ambition fueling behavior, this human control will inevitably manifest itself as artifice, and then further artifice to hide the prior artifice. At some point amid these nervous iterations, the applicant is very likely to hire an outside expert. If you're evaluating essays based on whether they give you "insight" into a "real person behind the application," and you also know that perhaps a majority of your applicants are using paid essay coaches, and pretty much all of them are getting ample help from other sources as they strain to craft their essays according to what they think you want, then either you're engaged in an elaborate sort of self-deception, or you're not looking for what you claim to be looking for.

IN A SENSIBLE ESSAY ON THE COLLEGE ESSAY, NEW YORK *Times* writer Trip Gabriel notes that colleges' lurid focus on the essay, in which an authentic self is supposed to emerge into virgin clarity for the admissions reader, flies in the face of a stubborn reality: kids that age probably don't *have* a stable self.[11] At that age, a kid's personality is in flux. A teenage self is typically several things. To call it an "identity" that can be presented through authentic extracurriculars and a revealing personal essay is to commit not just an error but a self-contradiction. If kids can't know their real selves because those selves do not, strictly speaking, exist, how can admissions readers discern them?

Gabriel asks how fair this is, to put so much weight on this one criterion, uncanny (or expensively coached) as it is in its production, arbitrary as it is in its assessment, when the self it's supposed to exhibit in authentic clarity exists only as a rough composite, if not a scrambled collage. It's a good question, but there are others. What, for example, do admissions people think essay writing *is*? An essay is a construct, a finely calibrated act. The "authentic voice" they claim to be seeking, so as to have a truer look at the kid behind the numbers, is, if it's a good essay, a deeply self-conscious performance, inauthentic by definition.

As to the question of whether this or any other aspect of selective college admissions is fair, I can barely bring myself to judge. Unfairness—*moral* undeservingness—is everywhere in the process, even, or especially, in what some would call its fairest forms. Is it fair that some people have better brains for taking SATs and AP Calc? Does that aptitude translate into deservingness of the awesome privilege of Harvard admission and all the life benefits said to follow from this? Perhaps it's justifiable in specific ways, in light of specific higher ends that are served by the existence of institutions like Harvard. And if Harvard is somehow necessary for these higher ends, then are other things like legacy preferences, which seem unfair but which help Harvard thrive as an institution, justifiable, in some limited way? It seems unfair that rich kids who happen to have the right mom or dad get a boost in admissions, but then those shining merit cases didn't get their 160 IQs from treating lepers, and, if they actually did treat lepers, there's a good chance they did it for tactical reasons linked to their college applications—which sort of undermines the character claims the leper treating is rendered to support. (To be truly, authentically virtuous, the treating of lepers should go unmentioned in a college application.)

It seems that what we mean by fair, when it comes to things like college admissions, is that standards should not serve venal motives or destructive ends, rather than that they should serve some positive ideal of fairness as moral worth or deservingness. Is handing out government jobs according to scores on the Civil Service Exam fair? You probably wouldn't have to burrow too far down to find forces of moral randomness that might give you pause, make you wonder about the fairness of it all—the unearned advantages of some test takers, the unfair disadvantages of others.

But we don't have civil service exams to reach abstract fairness or moral perfection. We have them to prevent specific forms of patronage and corruption. The "fairness" they establish consists in their prevention of specific distortions of the federal employment process, for example a person in a position to influence the process using that influence to enrich or empower himself. Likewise, in elite college admissions, even the most egalitarian of us have to bite the bullet, cede most of the spoils to kids who won the amoral brain lottery, and maybe another chunk to those Richie Riches whose Harvard dads write the checks that help the school poach professors from its underendowed rivals.

Or maybe not, in the case of legacy admissions, because it involves people with privileged access to the process exploiting that access for personal gain. We take legacy admissions to be a more patent form of unfairness because it comes closer to the patronage example above (and also it's often just rich people hoarding more advantages for themselves). Still, like Malcolm Gladwell, I have a hard time getting outraged about legacy or money-influenced admissions. A kid who gets rejected from one elite school because Jared Kushner took his place is probably headed to another elite school. And to fixate on this as some kind of moral problem is to treat elite schools as a sort of moral commodity to which admission is an abstract right and from which rejection is a transcendent moral injury. This just puffs them up even more, raises the perceived stakes of admission. To put it another way, the general belief that Harvard seats are 25 percent filled with dim-bulb Jared Kushners does just a little to degrade the Harvard mystique, and to deflate the background

stakes we grant to the process as a whole, which is unequivo-
cally a good thing.

And to fixate on such deviations as obvious forms of injus-
tice is to give the normal admissions process a compliment it
does not deserve—because you know who has even more direct and more intimate access to the process, and who abuses
the power that comes from that access? The people who run
the process. There's a far more pressing question than legacy
admissions or other supposed adulterations of the process: the
unearned power that the people who run college admissions
departments exert over the lives and psyches, the values and beliefs, the self-conceptions and well-being of individual teenagers, entire cohorts of college-bound children, the entire cultures
of American childhood and child-rearing. Accidentally, thanks
to the historical and demographic and technological processes
I describe in Chapter 6, which transformed American college
education into an overheated market in status chasing and fear
management, massive social power lodged itself in the admissions departments of selective colleges and universities. Admissions personnel sit at a choke point in the flow of opportunity
in American society. Like the precinct boss in the days before
corruption laws, they control access to a scarce and desirable
good. And, like the precinct boss, they use this access to empower themselves. Perhaps a better, more aptly systemic parallel
is the monopoly power enjoyed by internet giants like Google
and Amazon, or investment banks that occupy bottlenecks in
the worldwide flow of money. In both these cases, the favored
institutions use their lucky positioning to extract "rents"—like
the archetypal rentiers, landowning nobles who lived off the
rents payed by the peasants who worked their inherited lands.

Instead of money rents, the admissions process generates what you might call "moral rents." What "holistic" admissions amounts to is not some neutral investigation into the true selves of those applicants. It couldn't be, given both the matter and the methods of investigation. It is, rather, a transaction, the possible offer of a certain matricular *quo*, pending the agreeable performance of a certain moral *quid*.

A defender of holistic admissions might respond that these personalized selection measures are pedagogically valuable, that they make for a richer classroom and campus. But this emphasis on these analytically absurd but morally powerful methods tracks a little too closely with the growing numerical leverage of these bureaucracies for this defense to be persuasive. That is, historically, admissions departments have used this moral influence to the precise degree that they've had it, and their ambition continues to grow in step with their leverage. Jeremiah Quinlan, Yale's undergraduate admissions dean, recently put it this way, regarding the "inputs" of the application process—the academic data and confessional insights students provide. "We want better inputs," he said. The traditional inputs "predict[ed] success academically. Now, we have the ability to get to know a student better, from a different type of submission."[12] The question nobody thinks to raise, much less answer, is: *Why?* Why is this latter ability important? Is Dean Quinlan saying that the kids who got into Yale back when the process had weaker leverage for extracting moral rents were somehow worse kids? At least one former Yale professor would claim the opposite is true.[13] And Dean Quinlan's blitheness in yearning for better inputs means something very different when we see admissions as the disciplinary process, the moral transaction, that it really is, rather than some naive discovery of true selves via neutral "inputs." The inputs flow both ways, in other words. As admissions departments request and extract more inputs from their applicants, they give themselves greater and deeper influence on the malleable teenage selves of those applicants.

NOTHING MORE CLEARLY REVEALS THE SPIRIT OF MORAL rent-seeking that animates the admissions process than a prominent recent move to reform that process—a report from the Harvard School of Education called *Turning the Tide*, released in 2016 and cosigned by eighty-five influential figures in the admissions world, mostly admissions deans from both highly selective and less selective private colleges and state universities.[14] The authors of *Turning the Tide* concede that college admissions offices sit at the opportunity chokepoint I describe, and that their position gives them prodigious leverage to extract moral rents in exchange for passage into their institutions. Their main complaint about this arrangement is that admissions offices do not use this leverage as much as they could, that the moral rents they charge are not high enough. "The college admissions process," they write in the report's executive summary, "is powerfully positioned to . . . help young people become more generous and humane."[15] The main report expands on this, making special reference to the moral failures of parents, as against the rich moralizing potential of admissions offices: "Some colleges have sought diligently to communicate the importance of the commitment [to the common good] in the admission process, but too often these messages are overwhelmed by messages from the larger culture and from parents that narrowly emphasize academic performance and personal success."[16] According to *Turning the Tide*, then, it's not really the admissions process that needs reforming. It's applicants and their families.

So the same college administrators who recruit underqualified applicants so they can reject them and otherwise pad their application numbers to make their institutions look better, and who sometimes simply lie with their data to improve their rankings, should step in to help raise America's children so they'll be "more generous and humane," more concerned with the "common good."

As a practical blueprint, *Turning the Tide* codifies a set of lingering anxieties and regrets that have germinated within the process for years, and its recommendations mainly intensify existing responses to these troubles. As I noted above, admissions offices have already sought to minimize the résumé padding in extracurricular activities that they used to encourage and reward, and this dovetails with the greater focus on college essays as soul portals and moral tests. *Turning the Tide*, then, prescribes as its reform what admissions deans were already doing—taking vague unease with their selection tools as license to extend the reach of those tools, to deepen both the psychological interest in and the moral claims their process makes upon suggestible teenage selves, the subtle concessions and compliance it extracts from them, and the moral demotion it seeks to impose on their parents.

What makes *Turning the Tide* a reform or advance, rather than just a reiteration, is its ambition and specificity. Among the themes of lingering regret that sound from within the process is that the stress on extracurricular activities is biased against poor kids. Some kids, in other words, spend time in soup kitchens not to win commitment points for their college applications but because they're hoping to get some soup. Under the heading "Recommendations for assessing ethical engagement and contributions to others across race, culture and class," *Turning the Tide* takes on this problem. Now, the most parsimonious, least invasive way of remedying the class bias in college admissions would seem to be for schools to admit more poor kids, to use poverty as some kind of grade and test-score multiplier.

But the recommendations in *Turning the Tide* are more holistic than that. "The admissions process," it suggests, "should clearly send the message to students, parents and other caregivers that not only community engagement and service, but also students' family contributions, such as caring for younger siblings, taking on major household duties or working outside the home to provide needed income are highly valued in the admissions process."[17] But the heading for this recommendation refers to "*assessing* ethical engagement and contributions to others." When family contributions become part of the application portfolio, admissions officers won't just be notating these family contributions, adding them up and saying, "Well done, young family man." They will be *assessing* them. The associate dean of admissions, perhaps having just overseen a new mailing of deceptively encouraging pamphlets to underqualified high school juniors, will want to know if a teenager is *truly* ethically engaged within her own home, or just saying she is. The following scenario is all too easy to imagine for anyone who's researched this topic: an admissions toss-up, in which the dean or the committee will be making the tough call as to which of two kids' contributions to the respective home lives of their impoverished families is, well, better.

According to another recommendation, admissions should begin "Assessing Students' Daily Awareness of and Contributions to Others."[18] Again, it is a subtle mystery how an admissions office would discern a distant applicant's daily awareness of anything, let alone of "others," and let alone *assess* this awareness. Another *Turning the Tide* recommendation concerns "Service that Develops Gratitude and a Sense of Responsibility for the Future."[19] This perhaps foretells a later, more ambitious stage of college admissions, one in which the process and its human facilitators don't just observe teenage dispositions and evaluate their attractiveness and authenticity, but prescribe new states, specific emotional outputs. The process already prodigiously generates new states, of course, altering the inner and outer lives of malleable high schoolers, molding them into more agreeable forms—but it does this passive-aggressively, for the most part, via the subtle transmission of new signals about new criteria. Here, however, the report's authors drop the passive-aggressiveness and explicitly suggest that applicants' striving for college admission should make them feel and be a specific way: grateful.

This is getting a little complicated and intimate. The "reformers'" big idea is to take a process defined by unwonted nosiness and presumption and make it way nosier and more presumptuous. To propose evaluating and ranking how applicants act inside their own homes, interact with and contribute to their own families? To envision discerning and judging an abstract internal state such as their "daily awareness" of other people? To recommend as a prescribed emotional output that applicants *be grateful?*

Among the other regrets about the process that the authors seek to address with these ambitious reforms is that the process as it currently runs is easily "gamed" by savvy applicants, the well-off and well coached, mainly.[20] In a way it's gratifying to see them admit this, since it's such an obvious feature of the process. But reforming the process by making the moral performance it requires more elaborate merely sets out new things to game. Everything that deepens and softens and complicates admissions gives a new edge to those who are well coached, without seeming to be, on how to play their part in its assorted moral transactions.

It's hard to say how consequential *Turning the Tide* will be in the long run. On one hand, its broader view of how far into kids' and families' lives an admissions office has a legitimate right to extend its sculpting touch is widely shared and applied already. On the other hand, the naked clarity of its moral ambitions, and the prestigious Harvard imprimatur it gives to these ambitions, will surely carry its own force in the admissions world. In its boldness and arrogance, it will surely inspire others in that world to say: "No. We're still not doing enough to improve other people's children."

The other major reform from within the admissions world, the Coalition Application, expresses the same assumption as *Turning the Tide* about the legitimate reach of the process— that is, that there is no limit to how far the admissions process should reach into the lives of applicants and their families. The Coalition App is an online application originally designed by and for a group of eighty of the most selective colleges in America, including every member of the Ivy League, known together as the Coalition for Access, Affordability, and Success. It now comprises 140 schools.

The Coalition App is intended to replace the Common Application for the schools that adopt it, and the declared mission behind it is to apply technology to improving access to the process. Now, as I describe in Chapter 6, the Common App helped create the admissions panic we now have by making it easier for kids to apply to a huge number of schools, which pushed acceptance rates into the single digits for many schools, which deepened kids' incentive to do even more admissions striving while applying to even more schools. But at least the Common App observes the traditional application deadlines, meaning high school students can do all their paperwork in the first few months of their senior year. The great innovation of the Coalition App, on the other hand, is that it takes the form of an online account that students can open when they reach *ninth grade*. After they open their Coalition App account, they can start right away with assembling a "portfolio" of their high school efforts, uploading papers and image files and other documents both curricular and extracurricular, into their personal master file, called a "locker."

Of course, in the present environment, "can" start in ninth will mean "must" start in ninth grade for a large number of anxious kids and parents. Veronica Hauad, deputy dean of admissions at the University of Chicago (one of the founding schools of the Coalition) explains some of the thinking behind encouraging students to start so early. "The application process shouldn't be this frenzied process in the fall of your senior year, which is already busy." To illustrate, she addresses a hypothetical high school student. "Let's think long term," she says, "about my identity and what my application will look like."[21]

Here is a flagrant example of how admissions reformers address discrete problems with their process by proposing huge expansions of it. (Senior-year deadlines making for a frantic fall semester? Let's fix that by making the process take up six more semesters and three more summers.) It's likewise a nice statement of the existential conceits of admissions personnel in prestigious colleges and universities. Two very different things get blithely bundled together in their minds—the profound matter of who a young person is becoming, and the administrative preference that the young person be more legible within a process of selection and rejection. "My identity and my application," she says, as if these two things are part of the same ethical process of becoming a person.

I would say that admissions officers are merely indifferent to how the latter might influence the former, how involvement in a mere selection process might distort the formation of teenage selves under certain high-stakes conditions, but the authors of *Turning the Tide*, whose cosigners include the Coalition itself, have already declared this as an explicit goal. Such candor about their formative intent may anger you, or it may reassure you, depending on your perspective, but it certainly ruins the pretense that the selection process is concerned with the discovery of authentic selves, rather than the disciplinary molding of preferred selves.

And yet the reformers persist in describing their human enterprise in the language of authenticity, the aspiration for clean therapeutic insight into *true* selves. When the Coalition App was first being announced in 2015, its champions were facing resistance from high school counselors concerned that it meant a takeover of kids' entire high school education by the college admissions process. John F. Latting, vice provost for undergraduate enrollment and dean of admissions at Emory University, was frustrated at this resistance, the failure of these counselors to appreciate the gravity of his enterprise, the purity of its ambitions. These counselors, after all, are dealing with mere people. Dean Latting is reading applications. "I can go down the components of an application and I am concerned about every single one of them as showing the true voice of an applicant," he said. "Literally, every single one."[22]

It's important to reiterate what the end point is to all this agonizing. What exactly does Dean James G. Nondorf of UChicago admissions mean when he says, "Deciding you want to go to one of our kinds of schools, you have to be doing things all through your high school years"? What does his UChicago colleague Dean Hauad mean when she recommends that applicants take care to fashion what their "identity . . . looks like"? They're not talking about kids cultivating their curiosities or their intellects, for the good inherent in those things, or even for the sake of becoming good college *students*. They're talking about "their application," as Dean Hauad puts it. They're not talking about how these applicants will appear to the professors they'll encounter over the ensuing four years. They're talking about how these students will appear to *them*, the admissions department. Students should treat their full four years of high school as a prelude to that one moment of being seen and evaluated by the selection bureaucrats of the colleges they apply to. The ambient, self-stoking fear that drives the process, and its underlying demographic facts, has given these bureaucrats the leverage to make this existential bargain seem mandatory, inescapable. And everything admissions offices do to refine the process, make it more personal, more elaborate, more explicit as a moral test, also raises the personal stakes for the kids caught up in it. No wonder these kids make such a big deal about those decision-day emails. No wonder, when they get ones that contain such phrases as "we regret" and "are unable," some of them kill themselves.

As the formal name of the Coalition suggests, the Coalition App is intended to improve "access" to more prestigious and selective colleges for poor and minority high school students. It's unclear whether it really will improve underprivileged students' access to college. Indeed, it's another illustration of how admissions deans address the social problems that bear upon the admissions process by making the process more complex, more ambitious, more invasive.

What is undeniable is that the Coalition App extends and intensifies the process's access to students, its disciplinary influence upon them, precisely by making the process less bounded and mandatory seeming, more fluid and quasi-voluntary—in other words, by turning it into a set of choices students nominally make themselves, but which they know they must make in a certain way. Simply opening a "locker" and having it to think about, a digital void to fill up, will alter a ninth grader's self-conception. A new channel of his agency has been summoned to busyness by a new tool. Possessor of this too, he will come to see himself—perhaps primarily, given the stakes—as its user.

So many parental anxieties and adaptations and stratagems, in America, owe to the obscure and looming presence of the college admissions process that it's worthwhile to consider, briefly, what a real reform of the process would look like. A real reform of this process would be one that makes the process simpler and less time-consuming, less mysterious and morally presumptuous. A powerful reform that would both simplify the process and lessen its moral reach and leverage is the one I mentioned above, working a lottery aspect into admissions. Admissions bureaucrats with thousands more applicants than they can accept soon reach a level of arbitrariness in their selection criteria, where they themselves admit that the students they're looking at have basically the same qualifications. At this point they launch a separate soul investigation that makes little sense academically but allows them to stage a powerful, utterly undeserved disciplinary claim on the inner lives of their applicants, which is the abiding scandal of college admissions.

They should, rather, renounce their soul procedures and concede that their successful applicants are lottery picked from a pool of equally qualified contenders. This would remove the engineered mystery and inflated personal stakes of the process, which now encourages teenagers to game out certain desired personality traits and then feel like ethical failures when, despite the self-exhibit they so passionately curated to accompany their manifest academic qualifications, they are rejected. Lotteries would reveal the personalizing admissions requirements—the essays and extracurriculars—as the administrative make-work and moral rent-seeking they are. More generally, they would dispel the haze of spiritualized meaning that surrounds the crude bureaucratic event of a kid being selected into one damn college or not.

A further improvement to college admissions—even before eliminating legacy preferences, on which I am fairly agnostic—would be to eliminate athletic scholarships and detach admissions from athletics. Scholarships and admissions preferences for "recruited athletes," especially in no-attendance boutique sports like crew and lacrosse and field hockey, are a perverse bonus for affluent families who can afford the years of training and travel that lead up to a recruiting visit from a college coach. And they are another way in which, in its institutional design, American higher education seeds American family life, in its earliest years, with potent incentives for pointless, yearslong, zero-sum competition, family against family. (I'd like to see the corrupt and moronic industry of big-money college sports eliminated too, but I'm trying to be parsimonious and practical here.)

Colleges are unlikely to ditch their athletic systems or adopt application lotteries, but, even so, describing such improvements trains a nice counterfactual light on the rotten things they would hypothetically improve. Seeing the admissions process in this light might give parents a better sense of what its procedures are really asking of them and their children, and why.

One measure colleges should be slow and careful in doing is eliminating standardized tests from their admissions requirements. Debates on the SAT and ACT rest on highly technical controversies of test design and psychometry that, frankly, I'm not qualified to referee or resolve. I will only say that a signal promise of such tests is worth keeping alive—identifying academic potential that institutionalized schooling has so far left hidden. To many ears, the term "underachiever" used to carry a note of praise and admiration, for the defiance of those high schoolers who managed to maintain low grades despite their

high scores. They had better things to do than homework—
playing and listening to and reading about music, playing sports,
driving around, getting into harmless trouble with their friends.
The underachievers were busy being kids while there was still
time, while they were still kids. Admissions readers at the selective schools now scorn the underachiever. Kids whose grades
are less competitive than their scores are an insult to the admissions process. Clearly, they don't have the ethically sound
view of their identity as a secondary offshoot of their college
application. The more general cost of ditching the SAT and
ACT should be obvious from the discussion that occupies this
chapter. It would raise the importance of the softer measures
admissions offices now emphasize, where assessing academically meaningless traits of personality and character becomes
a corrective process of influencing and prescribing those traits.
This is why many in the admissions world agitate against the
tests. It's another example of admissions offices addressing the
troubles generated by their process by gathering more power
for themselves, and making the process more complicated
and invasive, more stressful and mysterious, for applicants and
their families.

ADMISSIONS OFFICERS HAVE COME TO SEE THE PROCESS
they oversee and administer in therapeutic terms. That is, a
young person presents to admissions a knowledge problem, and
this knowledge problem has a psychotherapeutic, indeed psy-
choanalytic structure. Admissions personnel take themselves to
be engaged in a sort of Freudian melodrama. They present the college application as a set of therapeutic prompts, gentle invitations

for the applicant to free herself from repression and self-deceit and move toward authentic self-expression and self-knowledge. But, as in psychoanalysis, this process is haunted by uncertainty. There's always the risk that the applicant's personal confessions hide new evasions, new obstructions that block insight, prevent the healing appearance of the young self's uncorrupted truth. In the Freudian example—per a familiar comic portrait—the psychoanalyst tackles the problems of unreliable confession and uncertain clinical knowledge by having the patient's weekly sessions continue endlessly. Admissions deans, professing similar ambitions, have more limited methods. But instead of abandoning their quest for authentic insight into their young applicants, they treat the knowledge problem that makes this quest absurd as an ongoing crisis, which they must invent ever-new measures to solve. As Vice Provost for Undergraduate Enrollment Latting of Emory University lamented, "I can go down the components of an application and I am concerned about every single one of them as showing the true voice of an applicant. Literally, every single one."

If you recall that, twenty or thirty years ago, admissions departments weren't even *mentioning* authenticity, were not treating the therapeutic search for true voices and true selves as the goal of their investigations, and if you devote a moment's thought to the absurdity of this search, you will be tempted to laugh at Vice Provost Latting's hysterical protest against imperfect knowledge. But, laughable as this and other admissions testimony is, on its merits, I would like to present a good reason not to laugh. Setting up a yearslong, quasi-therapeutic process in which you goad young people to lay bare their vulnerable selves to you, when this process is actually a high-value transaction in which you use your massive leverage to mold those selves to your liking, is actually a terrible thing to do. It's not funny at all. In this process the discovery of true underlying selves is absurd and impossible, but the *making* of new selves, through the rewards and punishments you can deliver from your side of the deal, is a real possibility. Sometimes, as we've seen, admissions people will admit they have this formative leverage over young selves. But they fail to show the humility that should attend this admission, the clinician's awareness that to use this power is to abuse it. Instead, they have declared their desire to have more power. They wish to ply their soul leverage more directly. The name they give their updated plans for realizing these ambitions is "reform."

Reaction to such "reform" efforts has been depressing. Purported critics of the admissions process such as the *New York Times*'s Frank Bruni have gone along with the new plans to make college admissions even more invasive than it was already. The Coalition App sounds like some user-friendly art project, Harvard's *Turning the Tide* says a few nice things about social justice and "meaningful" extracurriculars, and that's good enough for the *New York Times*'s intrepid columnist. Equally depressing is the indifference of college faculty. Elite colleges are filled with humanities and social science professors who claim inspiration from the great social theorist Michel Foucault, who described the intimate, burrowing power that moves and works through therapeutic methods, especially when these methods are plied by authoritative institutions. And yet this power issues in prodigious measure, via these methods, from the authorities who choose the students who sit before them every day. Their schools are populated using the exact methods Foucault described, and yet, from them, one hears no Foucault-style complaints about the intimate and invasive moral training, the extended course of therapeutic discipline, through which their students are freshly passed.

The institutional power in question is notable, and troubling, because it is a both a concrete feature of the lives of individual American families and a serious shaping force in American society as a whole. Parents and children around the country find themselves asking "How high?" when emissaries from the college admissions process say "Jump!" They see little choice but to meet the demands that this process generates. Their kids' futures might be at stake. Besides, these demands are coming from colleges, "educators." But the admissions department isn't an educational body. It's an administrative one. Its mission isn't teaching. It's seeing and selecting. And, crucially, it doesn't keep its behavioral preferences and methods of seeing to itself. It sends them out as signals to teachers, counselors, admissions coaches, children, and parents. From there these signals drift into the larger culture, where they have formed themselves into a vague assumption, largely unquestioned, that a central ethical duty of American teenagers is to make themselves legible to a bureaucratic process and morally agreeable to its vain and blinkered personnel.

Conclusion

I N EARLY 2016 I WROTE AN ARTICLE ABOUT THE COLLEGE admissions process for the online *New Yorker*—the article, in fact, that inspired this book. The day it came out a friend, a psychotherapist whose patients are mainly stressed-out teenage girls, posted it on her Facebook page. I was gratified to see my friend giving her expert's thumbs-up to my article, but, this being Facebook, I was also able to look in as her "friends" who weren't my "friends" expressed a few thumbs-down sentiments, about both my writing and my unethical parenting. It was the odd experience, familiar to writers in the age of social media, of watching people talk about you like you're not there, until I *was* there, defending myself. I won't go into the details, except to say that my reaction was intemperate as usual, and one criticism that irked me was that I hadn't offered any solutions or advice.

This was true—I hadn't—though I didn't think a 1,600-word article carried a strong duty to offer solutions to a problem I was just coming to understand myself. Had I given advice, it would have been bad advice, most likely. But the thing is, four years later, I'm still shy about offering practical advice. This might be a problem in a book about family and parenting. Such books usually brim with advice. And it seems vaguely hostile or cruel to aggravate parental anxiety—if mainly by just saying "parental anxiety" a bunch of times—without pushing some convincing placebos to treat it.

One issue is that advice in parenting books is usually pitched to parents themselves. Do a little of this. Try not to do too much of that. But a key trait of the predicament I'm describing is that tackling it at the individual level is potentially costly, at this level. Indeed, our tendency to imagine and exaggerate and thereby actually heighten the costs of our predicament out of fear *is* the predicament. The problem is a collective-action one—individuals acting from a fearful mental picture of what other individuals are doing about a future they see as fearful too, which, perversely, tends to push the real world toward the imagined scenario they're afraid of. People in the early stages of a pandemic, worried about toilet paper shortages, will be more likely to hoard toilet paper, which basically assures that more of them will be left without toilet paper than if they'd all had some convincing assurance about toilet paper supplies.

You may be able to relax and—from aversion, or principle, or laziness—opt out of the competitive hassles I'm describing. But even if you can tell yourself that your chill attitude about the future won't leave your kids with a lesser share of that future, you can't *entirely* deny that the overwrought, overcompetitive, anxious, strategically miserable methods of some parents will be helpful on the basic measures. Some kids will surely end up with more prestigious degrees and higher incomes because their parents framed the question of advantage as a zero-sum game and played that game with maniacal purpose. Some kids will be more soundly situated in adulthood because their parents performed all the best neurotic overcompensations when they were children, armed them with all the right Hunger Games weaponry.

You have to accept that in some cases, the hard-core methods probably work, in their way. Some extra advantage does follow for some of the children of some of the parents who use those methods. But you might take comfort in thinking that, if you're not already on this path, you probably couldn't steer onto it now. You probably couldn't use those methods effectively, anyway, couldn't see them through. You're just not that kind of person.

And you might also take solace in certain findings from the field of economics that say you don't need to take this path—especially a famous pair of studies by Stacy Dale and the late Alan Krueger, who chaired President Obama's Council of Economic Advisers. Dale and Krueger performed a large study in 1999 that upended the common assumption that attending a more selective college increases people's incomes. Then, after much predictable controversy over their findings within the field of economics, they published a 2011 follow-up that confirmed their original research. Yes, graduates of more selective colleges have higher average incomes than graduates of less selective colleges, but, Dale and Krueger argued, the difference reflects selection rather than treatment effects. Selective colleges don't turn kids into bigger earners. They choose the kids who are more likely to be bigger earners. Dale and Krueger found that a better predictor of earnings is not what college someone attended but what college that person *got into*. The expected income of a person who got into the University of Pennsylvania (Ivy League) but attended Penn State (Big Ten) would be closer to that of an average Penn than an average Penn State graduate. Indeed, those who *applied to* more selective colleges but didn't get in had incomes closer, on average, to the selective schools that rejected them than to the less selective schools from which they graduated.

The point of this is not that you should have your academically average kid send in a hopeless application to Harvard because that will boost her future earnings into the Harvard range. It doesn't work that way. The point, as I see it, is that her success has less to do with external markers of competitive fitness than with the fairly stubborn matter of her personality and character. This message nudges us to trade in some measure of belief in our parental agency for a degree of acceptance and faith, a loving resignation before the sublime fact that your child is who she is. She's not an engine to which you can keep affixing custom parts to achieve ever-greater performance. She is a unique person with a given nature, which it's your job as a parent to help her cultivate. The Dale and Krueger studies help us believe it's this cultivated nature she's bringing into the world of money and work, and this nature, rather than the slightly more prestigious gates she squeezes through in the preceding years, that will determine her career success.[1]

Of course this is economics, and no finding is final in economics. Other studies have found some income premium from attending "better" colleges that can't be written off as a mere selection effect. But I focus on the Dale and Krueger studies because they tip the balance, slightly, in our view of child-rearing. They weaken the perceived necessity of doing the truly compromising thing, as this book understands that thing. If getting into the best possible college is not *that* important, then children and parents, wondering just how crucial the crucible of college admissions is, can address its disciplinary tasks, and all the prior adaptations in their children's lives, in a less agreeable, more rebellious spirit.

But if parents have to *choose* to believe the reassuring scenario, when the structure of incentives wants them to believe the scary one, then merely advising them to relax won't really work, on a general level. It just leaves us back where we started, stuck inside the feedback loop of parental worry. This is my frustration with books that scold parents for their overprotective fussing and teenagers for their sheeplike orientation to success. Just outside the narrow purview of these books are powerful structural and institutional forces that render the scolding approach slightly ridiculous. If the future looks scary, then parents are going to parent in ways that manage risk, that protect their kids from the Hobbesian nightmare—the greatest bad, the failed life of the child they love with a bottomless love. Many of them are going to hover like helicopters. If, thanks to this fear, people come to believe a successful life requires passage through a super-selective college, and if such colleges use the leverage this gives them to require sheepish levels of agreeableness in their successful applicants, then agreeable, sheepish college students are what you're going to get.

And these various pressures are likely to grow. As I write this conclusion, in late March of 2020, the country and the world are dealing with a novel coronavirus called COVID-19. Governments are trying to figure out how long they must continue their various shutdown measures. Pretty much everyone expects the economic fallout from these measures to be severe and long-lasting. Some predict that the economy we have in the wake of this pandemic simply will not be the one we had before the unfamiliar virus burned through the world we knew before it. In this case, as the usual passages to middle-class lives grow narrower, the competitive striving and behavioral bidding of aspirant families will likely intensify. It's all too easy to see the institution of college admissions enjoying greater power in this more desperate environment, turning itself into something even more vampiric than it was already.

The direct, demographic stresses will likely grow from two directions. First, in the near term, many high school graduates will simply defer going to college for the 2020–2021 school year, and perhaps the next year, rather than paying the inflated tuition for freshman seminars conducted as Zoom meetings. This means that the following years—assuming that the pandemic eases enough for colleges to resume normal business in 2021 or 2022—will see a huge backlog of college-bound high school graduates. Admissions pressures will be much, much higher during these and the ensuing few years, as the system disgorges its buildup of applicants and students. On top of this, the overall supply of admissions slots will contract as colleges, deprived of their yearly operating revenue, start to fail. Many schools were financially weak already, and the weakest were faltering and closing even before the pandemic hit. Many more will close over the next few years. We might even see some elite, name-brand colleges going under—their envied rank in *America's Best Colleges* simply surrendered, like one of the nicer huts in a medieval village, to a lesser rival who survived the plague.

If they act as they did in the face of the 1990–2019 application crunch, surviving admissions offices will respond to these heightened pressures by making their softer criteria, their "holistic" methods, even more invasive. Comprehending the increased leverage they possess in these darker scenarios of opportunity, they will use this leverage to impose on their teenage applicants an even more exacting model of how to be a person. This model will be, from any serious ethical standpoint, shallow and ridiculous, because it will have been formed to serve optical functions, by people whose job is to make administrative distinctions among highly similar teenagers, not to know or teach or even think about how to be a person. Admissions deans, refusing to concede the extreme randomness and arbitrariness of their procedures, will invent ever newer application "inputs" for applicants to exhibit as moral and behavioral outputs, and the entering classes of desirable colleges will consist of the most deeply conformed and normalized young strivers ever selected.

But it's possible the pandemic will turn into an even deeper crisis, a real reckoning for not just the admissions process but all the stages of competition that precede it. Perhaps the pressures themselves will cause a broad defection from the competitive system. Perhaps enough parents and their college-bound children will recoil from the new logic of battle, now more obviously dog-eat-dog than it already was. Perhaps families, with the rat race temporarily halted, will refuse to reenter it because the slowed-down life they've been living together has been surprisingly rich and loving. Perhaps influential figures in the admissions world will overreach, and their formative urges and methods, apparent to observers like me, will become repugnant to people who really matter—teenagers, parents, high school teachers forced to referee the various contests in this competition, high school counselors forced to act as clerks and underlings to admissions deans grown even hungrier for moral influence. Maybe other, wider and harsher disruptions will change the meaning of a bachelor's degree, for both prospective students and future employers. Maybe, in the moonscape economy the pandemic leaves us with, a college education will come to seem the indulgence it was a hundred years ago. Maybe the flight from college, like the feedback loops that have spun kids into college in recent decades, will be self-fueling. Fewer kids going to college, in other words, might mean fewer kids feeling the need to go to college. Perhaps these changes will weaken the degree inflation that has governed the labor market over the last several decades. Maybe after the pandemic a young person won't need a $150,000 bachelor's degree to get a job answering the phone at an insurance agency. Maybe prodigies of tech and engineering will take the dare made by Peter Thiel, the Silicon Valley investor who started a $100,000 fellowship for "young people who want to build things instead of sitting in a classroom."[2] But rather than applying for Peter Thiel's money, or in the event they apply but don't get it, maybe they'll just start skipping college and offering their raw teenage talent straight to employers, who, likewise freed from credentialing norms, will be willing to employ it.

For people lamenting both the spiraling cost of college and the patterns of pointless competition that take over the lives of American families, the tempting post-pandemic fantasies have been about disruption and destruction. These generally express pre-pandemic hopes and wishes. Until coronavirus, after all, the system of parental insecurity was so sprawling and self-reinforcing that practical change seemed impossible — the institutions that thrived on the ensuing competition being so well placed, and so effective at roiling parental fears while claiming to calm them. That this machinery might magically seize up and fall apart seemed the only thing to hope for. Indeed, in the article on admissions I wrote in 2016, my first impulse was to wish that, by the time my kids started high school, "the structure of academic competition . . . will have collapsed everywhere."[3]

Those who imagined deep change truly happening probably figured something internal would trigger the disruption — college costs, most likely, spurring some critical number to opt out — and the virtuous unraveling would happen from there. Few if any were imagining a pandemic as the cause. Surely nobody was hoping for one. But, either way, the fact that American society and American parents confront the predicament I describe as a quasi-natural force changeable only by spontaneous internal breakdowns or literal plagues bespeaks a political failure. Why, in other words, can't *we* change it?

That sounds like a rhetorical question — whose simple thrust is: "Of *course* we can change it!" — but, alas, it mostly isn't. It has a large literal side whose answer goes to the political and philosophical heart of this book. Why individual families find themselves stuck in their predicament is closely related to why this predicament is hard to change collectively, politically. Fragmentation and competition are deep traits of American society and politics. These things are not just incidental to our sprawling geography, with its many economic interests and religious groupings, its countless cultural veins and niches. They are also intentional within our political system, with its rivalrous branches of national government and its many competing sovereignties layered beneath the national level: state, county, township, city, town, village, business, home, consumer, citizen. It was considered wise, at our nation's founding, to set America's many elements not just alongside each other in a rich variety, but against each other in a perpetual stalemate of contrary, opposing, competing desires. This is not even, yet, to mention political economy, the fierce, restless, creative-destructive species of capitalism that has grown in America's well-aerated soil.

In other words, we face many stubborn obstacles, not just to addressing the problem of family lives overtaken by empty competition, but to recognizing ourselves as a "we" in the first place. In the American creed, the building of a shared sense of human fate and political agency, beyond the small and harmless scales of civil society, is considered a threat to liberty. And, even today, in certain influential political circles one associates with the phrase "family values," this philosophy of competition and fragmentation is taken as serving, above all, the cause of family life in its sovereignty and dignity. This view, I have tried to show in this book, is plausible only if you ignore the actual setting in which American families operate, the social forces that channel our competitive output through disciplinary procedures that, in turn, convert it into weary conformity. The sovereignty and dignity of American families are obviously not served by that kind of arrangement.

Acknowledgments

THIS BOOK WOULD NOT EXIST IF MICHAEL AGGER OF THE *New Yorker* online hadn't seen a few Twitter comments of mine about academic competition and college admissions and asked me to write a piece on these things, which hadn't occurred to me. This book would also not exist if my agent Tina Bennett hadn't read the piece and suggested I make it into a book, which also had not occurred to me. (The resulting book contains an ongoing critique of the paradigm of the empowered bourgeois enthralled with his own choice and agency, to which, it seems, its lucky, suggestible author represents some alternative model of self and action.) So, deep thanks to Michael, an uncannily good editor, and Tina, a brilliant agent. Deep thanks as well to John Kulka, my first editor at Basic Books. His early enthusiasm for this project was just the remedy for my early uncertainty about it.

Learning that your sympathetic editor is taking a new job just as you're starting the book he signed you to write is a nervous moment for a first-time author. This happened to me, when John left Basic Books for Library of America, but my new editor at Basic, Brian Distelberg, has been a joy to work with—a wise and friendly guide, a sharp reader, and a reassuring presence during both the early handoff from John and the unprecedented weirdness that befell the world just as the manuscript was being finished. Connor Guy, who was assigned to apply some discipline to my sentences, did his job with the perfect mix of thoroughness, discernment, and diplomacy. The book is far less wild and more readable for his efforts, if you can believe it.

Annette Lareau generously answered some out-of-nowhere queries from me, at something of a crisis moment. In my remembered history of this book, its calm and clear-eyed stage begins with the warm email conversation I had with Professor Lareau. Susan Holloway both answered my unsolicited questions and sent me work of her own that proved crucial to my understanding of the relationship between families and schools. Barry Schwartz read much of the manuscript and offered incisive criticism and invaluable encouragement at a crucial time.

In March 2017, the Institute for Advanced Studies in Culture at the University of Virginia invited me to lead a pair of roundtable discussions on this book's core themes and the more general topic of family life in America. It was a fantastic experience, and I thank Joe Davis for being such a generous and welcoming host. Thanks also to the excellent panelists who joined and grilled and energized me at IASC—Joe himself, James Poulos, Daniel Doneson, Rita Koganzon, Jackson

Lears, Elizabeth Lasch-Quinn, and Matt Crawford. I also need to thank Crawford for being my primary sounding board for the ideas that appear in this book, and most of the ideas that led up to it. My meeting him in 2001 was one of those lucky things that happen in a lucky life. I'd simply have many fewer and far dumber thoughts in my head if he and I hadn't become friends.

This book is dedicated to my parents, Mike and Ann Feeney. Their love and support and their profound moral example seemed only to grow and grow richer as we all got older. Sadly, the previous sentence was first written in the present tense, and it still applies in this tense to my wonderful dad, but my mom died while this book was being finished. I will retain the original present tense for the next sentence, though. My love and gratitude for them are inexpressible. Their constancy and devotion as parents accounts, I think, for my continuing closeness with my excellent brothers and sisters, Pete Feeney, Marc Feeney, Cara Drenth, Molly Feeney, and Michael Feeney—whom I also thank for innumerable reasons large and small, spiritual and practical. The work we shared and the time we spent together as our mother passed away were the most powerful testament to the enduring value and beauty of family I can imagine.

Special thanks go to Genevieve and Alfonso Arechiga, my mother- and father-in-law, for their logistical help and kid coverage as I wrote this book, and for welcoming me into their hilarious family, and for allowing their older daughter to set a path in life that would cross mine at the right moment.

Of course, then, my most awestruck and delighted thanks go to my wife, Juliet Arechiga, who made everything about this project easier, saner, and happier. My crossing paths with her was not just the luckiest event in my own life but one of the luckiest things that's ever happened to anyone, that I know of. Finally I must thank our children, Lucia, Mariana, and Dashiell, for turning my abstract belief in family as an important institution into a fond and fierce personal conviction, which is deepened every day by their hilarious and beautiful presence inside our shared world, our magic circle.

Notes

1. Timothy P. Carney, *Alienated America: Why Some Places Thrive While Others Collapse* (New York: Harper, 2019); Yuval Levin, *A Time to Build: From Family and Community to Congress and the Campus, How Recommitting to Our Institutions Can Revive the American Dream* (New York: Basic Books, 2020).

2. The central text for this line of analysis is Annette Lareau, *Unequal Childhoods: Class, Race, and Family Life* (Berkeley: University of California Press, 2003).

3. Marizio Doepke and Fabrizio Zilibotti, *Love, Money, and Parenting: How Economics Explains the Way We Raise Our Kids* (Princeton, NJ: Princeton University Press, 2019), 54–58.

4. See, especially, Stephen Levy, "Googlenomics: Cracking the Code of Internet Profits," in *In the Plex: How Google Thinks, Works, and Shapes Our Lives* (New York: Simon and Schuster, 2011), 69–120.

CHAPTER ONE: PARENTING IN PUBLIC

1. See, especially, Marizio Doepke and Fabrizio Zilibotti, *Love, Money, and Parenting: How Economics Explains the Way We Raise Our Kids* (Princeton, NJ: Princeton University Press, 2019), passim.

2. For testimony about the growing demands for kids' birthday parties, see Helaine Olen, "Spoiler Alert," *Slate*, January 22, 2015, accessed March 2020, https://slate.com/business/2015/01/kids-birthday-parties-keep-getting-more-extravagant-heres-how-we-let-it-happen.html; Lisa Hurley, "Event Pros See Growth in Children's Party Business," *Special Events*, May 5, 2015, accessed March 2020, www.specialevents.com/bar-bat-mitzvahschildrens-events/event-pros-see-growth-childrens-party-business; Chris Taylor, "How Parents Can Fight the Birthday-Industrial Complex," *Reuters*, January 20, 2016, accessed March 2020, www.reuters.com/article/us-money-parents-birthdayparties/how-parents-can-fight-the-birthday-industrial-complex-idUSKCN0UY27D.

3. The practice of handing out participation trophies, and indeed calling them "participation trophies," originated decades before the childhood years of our maligned "millennial generation." Such trophies were given out, though probably rarely, in the first two-thirds of the twentieth century, and they weren't typically given to the younger kids we think of as receiving them. Stefan Fatsis of *Slate* lists historical examples of the participation trophy awarded to high schoolers and even college students in the 1940s and 1950s, for various unexceptional achievements—playing fraternity sports, participating in 4-H competitions. But, consistent with my time line here, his examples of younger kids getting participation trophies for merely hanging around for a whole sports season, and this practice being more common, and of people finding it soft and weak and

condescending, begin in the early 1990s. Perhaps the earliest use of the expression "everyone gets a trophy"—in the derisive register familiar to us now—is a 1992 magazine essay by the unsentimental economics columnist Robert Samuelson. Stefan Fatsis, "We've Been Handing Out Participation Trophies for 100 Years," *Slate*, April 10, 2019, accessed October 2019, https://slate.com/culture/2019/04/participation-trophy-history-world-war-i.html; Robert Samuelson, "The Trophy Syndrome," *Newsweek*, December 20, 1992, accessed October 2019, www.newsweek.com/trophy-syndrome-195276.

4. For data about American parents spending time with their children starting in the early 1990s, see Doepke and Zilibotti, *Love, Money, and Parenting*, 54. See also Garey Ramey and Valerie Ramey, "Rug Rat Race" (Working Paper No. 15284, National Bureau of Economic Research, August 2009), accessed April 2019, www.nber.org/papers/w15284.pdf.

5. Ayelet Waldman, *Bad Mother* (New York: Doubleday, 2009), 5–8.

6. Susan Douglas and Meredith Michaels, *The Mommy Myth* (New York: The Free Press, 2004), 1.

7. Hanna Rosin, "Why Is This Attractive Woman Breast-Feeding This Giant Child?," *Slate*, May 10, 2012, accessed October 2019, slate.com/human-interest/2012/05/time-s-breast-feeding-cover.html.

8. Judith Warner, *Perfect Madness* (New York: Penguin, 2015), 116.

CHAPTER TWO: GETTING INTO PRESCHOOL

1. Greg J. Duncan and Katherine Magnuson, "Investing in Preschool Programs," *Journal of Economic Perspectives* 27, no. 2 (Spring 2013): 128, https://pubs.aeaweb.org/doi/pdfplus/10.1257/jep.27.2.109.

2. See "Invest in Early Childhood Development: Reduce Deficits, Strengthen the Economy," at Heckman's online project the Heckman Equation, accessed September 2019, https://heckman equation.org/resource/invest-in-early-childhood-development-reduce-deficits-strengthen-the-economy/.

3. Raj Chetty et al., "How Does Your Kindergarten Classroom Affect Your Earnings? Evidence from Project Start" (Working Paper No. 16381, National Bureau of Economic Research, September 2010, 37), accessed May 2020, www.nber.org/papers/w16381 .pdf.

4. Rachel Nania, "The Most Important Year in a Child's Life? Research Points to Preschool," WTOP.com, accessed September 2019, https://wtop.com/parenting/2017/09/the-most-important-year-in -a-childs-life-research-points-to-preschool/.

5. Helen Ladd, "Do Some Groups of Children Benefit More Than Others from Pre-Kindergarten Programs?," in *The Current State of Scientific Knowledge About Pre-Kindergarten Effects* (Washington, DC: Brookings Institution, 2017), 33, accessed September 2019, http://nieer.org/wp-content/uploads/2017/04/Brookings-Pre -Kindergrten-Effects.pdf.

6. Gretchen Morganson, "Wall Street and the Nursery School, a New York Story," *New York Times*, November 14, 2002, accessed September 2019, www.nytimes.com/2002/11/14 /business/wall-st-and-the-nursery-school-a-new-york-story.html. For the sake of simplicity I'm using "Citigroup" to refer to both Citigroup, the bank, and Salomon Smith Barney, the investment bank subsidiary of Citigroup for which Grubman performed his analyst work.

7. "Sins of the Father—Grubman Finds Tony Prep Schools Unkind to Kinder," *New York Post*, March 7, 2003, accessed September 2019, https://nypost.com/2003/03/07/sins-of-the-father-grubman -finds-tony-prep-schools-unkind-to-kinder/.

CHAPTER THREE: NOT PLAYING AROUND

1. Johan Huizinga, *Homo Ludens: A Study of the Play Element in Culture* (Boston: Beacon Press, 1971), 4.

2. Huizinga, *Homo Ludens*, 149–50.

3. Stuart L. Brown, *Play: How It Shapes the Brain, Opens the Imagination, and Invigorates the Soul* (New York: Avery, 2009), 19.

4. Huizinga, *Homo Ludens*, 12.

5. Huizinga wrote *Homo Ludens* in the 1930s, and its latter chapters include a bitter and prescient application of his ideas on play to the Nazi way in international relations. The permanent sports team may simply have been too suggestive of the army for him.

6. "About Montclair Soccer Club," Montclair Soccer Club, accessed April 2019, www.montclairsoccerclub.org/about.

7. "Club History," Marin FC, accessed April 2019, www.marinfc.com/club-history-and-mission.

8. Home page, Marin Juniors Volleyball Club, accessed April 2019, www.marinjuniors.com.

9. "Club Philosophy," Golden Bear Volleyball Club, accessed April 2019, www.goldenbearvolleyball.com/page/show/3704258-club-philosophy.

10. "Why Marin Juniors," Marin Juniors Volleyball Club, accessed April 2019, www.marinjuniors.com/whymj.

11. Home page, Marin Juniors Volleyball Club, accessed April 2019, www.marinjuniors.com.

12. Rick Eckstein, *How College Athletics Are Hurting Girls' Sports: The Pay-to-Play Pipeline* (New York: Rowman and Littlefield, 2017), 127.

13. "Competitive Youth Soccer," Spurs FC, accessed April 2019, www.spurssoccer.com/competitive-youth-soccer.

14. "MSC's Competitive Program: The Clippers," Montclair Soccer Club, accessed August 2020, www.montclairsoccerclub.org/competitive-teams/ competitive-teams.

15. "Mission, Values, and Philosophy," Walnut Creek Surf Soccer Club, accessed July 2019, www.wcsc.org/mission-values-and-philosophy/.

16. Jennifer Senior, *All Joy and No Fun: The Paradox of Modern Parenthood* (New York: Little Brown, 2014), 179.

17. Eckstein, *How College Athletics*, 6.

18. A similar explanatory focus characterizes other critical books on youth sports, such as Mark Hyman, *The Most Expensive Game in Town* (Boston: Beacon Press, 2012), and Jay J. Coakley, *Sports in Society* (New York: McGraw-Hill, 2011).

19. Michael Sokolove, "How a Soccer Star Is Made," *New York Times*, June 2, 2010, accessed April 2019, www.nytimes.com/2010 /06/06/magazine/06Soccer-t.html.

20. Sokolove, "How a Soccer Star Is Made."

21. "Join Sporting," Sporting St. Louis, accessed April 2019, www .sportingstl.com/join-sporting/.

22. The ad linked to the website of Strotheide Chiropractic of Chesterfield, Missouri, and Rock Island, Illinois, www.goodback.com/.

23. Tim Keown, "Where the 'Elite' Kids Shouldn't Meet," ESPN .com, April 24, 2011, accessed April 2019, www.espn.com/espn /commentary/story/_/page/keown-110823/elite-travel-baseball-basketball -teams-make-youth-sports-industrial-complex.

24. Eckstein, *How College Athletics*, 42.

25. Lareau, *Unequal Childhoods*, 140.

CHAPTER FOUR: PARENTS, KIDS, AND THE INTERNET

1. "What Happens When You Give Your Family Unlimited Screen Time?" *Good Morning America*, July 17, 2018, accessed November 2019, www.youtube.com/watch?v=KkiWS0fmnt0.

2. *Screenagers*, directed by Delaney Rustin (Seattle, WA: MyDoc Productions, 2016).

3. Günther Anders, "On Promethean Shame," in Christopher John Müller, *Prometheanism: Technology, Digital Culture, and Human Obsolescence* (London: Rowman and Littlefield, 2016), 30.

4. Anders, "On Promethean Shame," 38.

5. Anders, "On Promethean Shame," 43.

6. The apparent anachronism—1942 writings mentioning the hydrogen bomb (not developed until the 1950s)—results from the fact that this 1956 work, "On Promethean Shame," is citing Anders's 1942 journals.

7. Adam Gazzaley and Larry D. Rosen, *The Distracted Mind: Ancient Brains in a High-Tech World* (Cambridge, MA: The MIT Press, 2016), passim.

8. Gazzaley and Rosen, *The Distracted Mind*, 14–16.

9. Gazzaley and Rosen, *The Distracted Mind*, 140–148.

10. See Michel Foucault, "Nietzsche, Genealogy, History," in *The Foucault Reader*, ed. Paul Rabinow (New York: Pantheon, 1984), 76–100; Michel Foucault, *The History of Sexuality: Volume I: An Introduction* (New York: Vintage, 1980), 17–35.

11. Nir Eyal with Ryan Hoover, *Hooked: How to Build Habit-Forming Products* (New York: Penguin, 2014), 2.

12. Eyal with Hoover, *Hooked*, 8.

13. Eyal with Hoover, *Hooked*, 97.

14. Eyal with Hoover, *Hooked*, 8.

15. "Variable Rewards: Want to Hook Users? Drive Them Crazy," Nir & Far, accessed November 2019, www.nirandfar.com/want-to-hook-your-users-drive-them-crazy/.

CHAPTER FIVE: SCHOOLS AND FAMILIES

1. In the two years between the graduations of my oldest and second-oldest children, during which time I wrote these introductory paragraphs, the slideshow component of our grade school's graduation

was split off from the rest of the ceremony and given its own evening earlier in the final week of school.

2. Taylor Lorenz, "The Controversy Over Parents Who Eat Lunch with Their Children at School," *Atlantic*, December 1, 2018, accessed October 2019, www.theatlantic.com/education/archive/2018/12/should-parents-eat-lunch-their-children-school/577117/.

3. Harris Cooper, "Synthesis of Research on Homework," *Educational Leadership*, November 1989, 85–91; "Does Homework Improve Academic Achievement? A Synthesis of Research, 1987–2003," *Review of Educational Research*, Spring 2006, 1–62.

4. Janine Bempechat, "The Case for (Quality) Homework," *Education Next*, Winter 2019, accessed May 2020, www.educationnext.org/case-for-quality-homework-improves-learning-how-parents-can-help/.

5. "Homework: A Concern for the Whole Family—Helping Your Child With Homework," US Department of Education, accessed May 2020, www2.ed.gov/parents/academic/help/homework/part3.html.

6. No Child Left Behind Act, § 1118 (2002), accessed August 2020, www2.ed.gov/policy/elsec/leg/esea02/107-110.pdf.

7. California Department of Education, "Title I, Part A, Parent and Family Engagement," accessed August 2020, www.cde.ca.gov/sp/sw/t1/parentfamilyinvolve.asp.

8. Nermeen E. El Nokali, Heather J. Bachman, and Elizabeth Votruba-Drzal, "Parent Involvement and Children's Academic and Social Development in Elementary School," *Child Development* 81, no. 3 (May–June 2010): 988.

9. Xitao Fan and Michael Chen, "Parental Involvement and Students' Academic Achievement: A Meta-Analysis," *Educational Psychology Review* 13 (March 2001): 1.

10. Thurston Domina, "Leveling the Home Advantage: Assessing the Effectiveness of Parental Involvement in Elementary School," *Sociology of Education* 78 (July 2005): 245.

11. Xin Ma, Jianping Shen, Huilan Y. Krenn, Shanshan Hu, and Jing Yuan, "A Meta-Analysis of the Relationship Between Learning Outcomes and Parental Involvement During Early Childhood Education and Early Elementary Education," *Educational Psychology Review* 28 (December 2016): 771–801.

12. Williams H. Jeynes, "A Meta-Analysis: The Effects of Parental Involvement on Minority Children's Academic Achievement," *Education and Urban Society* 25, no. 2 (February 2003): 202.

13. Grace Chen, "Parental Involvement Is Key to Student Success," *Public School Review*, accessed November 2019, www.publicschoolreview.com/blog/parental-involvement-is-key-to-student-success.

14. Sira Park, Susan I. Stone, and Susan D. Holloway, "School-based Parental Involvement as a Predictor of Achievement and School Learning Environment: An Elementary School Analysis," *Children and Youth Services Review* 82 (2017), 195–206.

15. Park et al. "School-Based Parental Involvement," 202.

16. Park et al. "School-Based Parental Involvement," 203–204.

CHAPTER SIX: STRIVING TOGETHER

1. Soban Dep, "Felicity Huffman and Lori Loughlin: How College Admissions Scandal Ensnared Stars," *New York Times*, March 12, 2019, A16, accessed July 2019, www.nytimes.com/2019/03/12/arts/huffman-loughlin-college-scandal.html.

2. John Bound, Brad Hershbein, and Bridgett Terry Long, "Playing the Admissions Game: Student Reactions to Increasing College Competition," *Journal of Economic Perspectives* 33, no. 4 (Fall 2009): 119–146.

3. Caroline Hoxby, "The Changing Selectivity of American Colleges" (Working Paper No. 15446, National Bureau of Economic Research, October 2009).

4. Elizabeth Duffy and Idana Goldberg, *Crafting a Class* (Princeton, NJ: Princeton University Press, 1998), 65.

5. Scott Davies and Floyd M. Hammack, "The Channeling of Student Competition in Higher Education: Comparing Canada and the U.S.," *Journal of Higher Education* 76, no. 1 (2005), 96.

6. For a good discussion of the curious size difference between Canadian and American colleges and universities, see Joseph Heath, "The Bottleneck in U.S. Higher Education," *In Due Course*, June 22, 2014, accessed June 2020, http://induecourse.ca/the-bottleneck-in-u-s-higher-education/.

7. Davies and Hammack, "The Channeling of Student Competition," 96–97.

8. Kelsey Piper, "A new book says married women are miserable. Don't believe it," *Vox*, June 4, 2019, accessed June 2019, www.vox.com/future-perfect/2019/6/4/18650969/married-women-miserable-fake-paul-dolan-happiness.

9. Patrick Clark, "The Test Prep Industry Is Booming," *Bloomberg News*, October 8, 2014, accessed June 2019, www.bloomberg.com/news/articles/2014-10-08/sats-the-test-prep-business-is-booming.

10. College Board, "Annual AP Program Participation," accessed July 2019, https://secure-media.collegeboard.org/digitalServices/pdf/research/2018/2018-Annual-Participation.pdf.

11. David Labaree, *A Perfect Mess: The Unlikely Ascendancy of Higher Education in America* (Chicago: University of Chicago Press, 2017), 169.

12. Garey Ramey and Valerie Ramey, "The Rug Rat Race" (Working Paper No. 15284, National Bureau of Economic Research, August 2009), 18.

13. Paul J. DiMaggio and Walter W. Powell, "The Iron Cage Revisited: Institutional Isomorphism and Collective Rationality in Organizational Fields," *American Sociological Review* 48, no. 2 (April

1983): 147–160; Kevin Carey, *The End of College: Creating the Future of Learning and the University of Everywhere* (New York: Riverhead Books, 2015), 49. I owe a fuller hat tip to Carey's discussion of college competition.

14. "Why Colleges Aggressively Recruit Applicants Just to Turn Them Down," *PBS NewsHour*, January 12, 2015, accessed October 17, 2018, www.pbs.org/newshour/education/colleges-ratchet-recruiting -applicants-just-turn.

15. "2017 State of College Admission," National Association of College Admissions Counseling, 7, accessed July 2019, www .nacanet.org/globalassets/documents/publications/research/soca17fi-nal.pdf.

16. Full disclosure: I taught as an adjunct professor at George Washington University when Trachtenberg was the school's president. I had no contact with him at the time, nor any awareness of his marketing innovations.

17. Kevin Carey, "How to Raise a University's Profile: Pricing and Packaging," *New York Times*, February 6, 2015, accessed July 2019, www.nytimes.com/2015/02/08/education/edlife/how-to-raise-a -universitys-profile-pricing-and-packaging.html; Daniel Luzer, "The Prestige Racket," *Washington Monthly*, August 22, 2010, accessed July 2019, https://washingtonmonthly.com/2010/08/22/the-prestige-racket/.

18. Carey, "How to Raise a University's Profile."

19. Hamilton College Admissions, "Essays That Worked," accessed August 2018, www.hamilton.edu/admission/apply/college-essays -that-worked/2014-essays-that-worked.

CHAPTER SEVEN: INDIVIDUALLY SELECTED

1. Glenn Kessler, "End the College Application Inflation," *Washington Post*, April 18, 2015, accessed November 2018, www

.washingtonpost.com/opinions/no-more-application-inflation/2015
/04/17/9d0863ea-e202-11e4-905f-cc896d379a32_story.html.

2. Barry Schwartz, "Lotteries for College Admissions," *Atlantic*, July/August 2012, accessed June 2019, www.theatlantic.com /magazine/archive/2012/07/lotteries-for-college-admissions/309026/; Dalton Conley, "Enough fretting over college admissions. It's time for a lottery," *Washington Post*, August 13, 2018, accessed June 2019, www.washingtonpost.com/opinions/enough-fretting-over-college -admissions-its-time-for-a-lottery/2018/08/13/f65a072c-9a74-11e8-8d5e -c6c594024954_story.html.

3. Katherine Price, "Being Well-Rounded Is No Longer Necessary," Great College Advice, accessed February 2019, greatcollegeadvice .com/being-well-rounded-is-no-longer-necessary.

4. Danika Kmetz, "UChicago Launches Test-Optional Admissions Process with Expanded Financial Aid, Scholarship," *UChicago News*, June 14, 2018, accessed February 21, 2019, https://college.uchicago .edu/news/academic-stories/uchicago-launches-test-optional-admissions -process-expanded-financial-aid.

5. Justin Pope, "Colleges Seek 'Authenticity' in Hopefuls," *Washington Post*, August 22, 2007, accessed June 2019, www.washington post.com/wp-dyn/content/article/2007/08/22/AR2007082201571 .html.

6. Quoted by Carol Barash, "What Are College Admissions Officers Looking For?," NYT Parents in Action (from the 2012 College Board Forum), accessed June 2019, http://parentsinaction.org/college -admissions-officers-looking-application-essay/.

7. Frank Bruni, "Naked Confessions of the College-Bound," *New York Times*, June 14, 2014, accessed June 2019, www.nytimes.com /2014/06/15/opinion/sunday/frank-bruni-oversharing-in-admissions -essays.html.

8. Bruni, "Naked Confessions."

9. Ed Boland, "Former Yale Admissions Officer Reveals Secrets of Who Gets In," *New York Post*, February 7, 2016, accessed February 21, 2019, https://nypost.com/2016/02/07/former-yale-admissions -officer-reveals-secrets-of-who-gets-in/.

10. Lacy Crawford, *Early Decision* (New York: William Morrow, 2013).

11. Trip Gabriel, "The Almighty Essay," *New York Times*, January 7, 2011, accessed February 21, 2019, www.nytimes.com/2011/01/09 /education/09guidance-t.html.

12. Eric Hoover, "What Colleges Want in an Applicant (Everything)," *New York Times*, November 1, 2017, accessed November 5, 2018, www.nytimes.com/2017/11/01/education/edlife/what-college -admissions-wants.html.

13. William Deresiewicz, *Excellent Sheep: The Miseducation of the American Elite and the Way to a Meaningful Life* (New York: Free Press, 2014). For a more rigorous and more disturbing account encompassing the admissions process in general, see John Bound et al., "Playing the Admissions Game: Student Reactions to Increasing College Competition" (Working Paper No. 15272, National Bureau of Economic Research, August 2009), accessed October 2018, www .nber.org/papers/w15272.pdf. Bound and his coauthors cite several measures suggesting that increased competition for college admission actually hinders learning.

14. In their range of institutions, the signatories of *Turning the Tide* are an indication of how broadly shared the precepts and conceits and ambitions of holistic admissions are. Even admissions departments of highly *un*selective schools that don't have the luxury of rejecting large numbers of qualified students on the personal grounds of holistic admissions *aspire* to conduct their selection process in this way.

15. Making Caring Common, "Turning the Tide: Inspiring Concern for Others and the Common Good Through College Admissions

(Executive Summary)," accessed September 2018, https://static1
.squarespace.com/static/5b7c56e255b02c683659fe43/t/5bae62e2419
20257b85048e2/1538155239906/execsummary_turningthetide.pdf.

16. Making Caring Common, "Turning the Tide: Inspiring Concern for Others and the Common Good Through College Admissions (Main Report)," 8, accessed September 2018, https://static1.square space.com/static/5b7c56e255b02c683659fe43/t/5bae62a6b208fc9b61 a81ca9/1538155181693/report_turningthetide.pdf.

17. Making Caring Common, "Turning the Tide (Main Report)," 16.

18. Making Caring Common, "Turning the Tide (Main Report)," 17.

19. Making Caring Common, "Turning the Tide (Main Report)," 14.

20. Making Caring Common, "Turning the Tide (Executive Summary)," 3.

21. "How Can the College Application Process Be Improved?" KQED News, March 7, 2016, accessed November 9, 2018, www .kqed.org/mindshift/43692/how-can-the-college-admissions-process -be-improved.

22. Laura Pappano, "A New Coalition of Elite Colleges Tries to Reshape Admissions," *New York Times*, October 26, 2015, accessed November 25, 2018, www.nytimes.com/2015/11/01/education/edlife /can-a-new-coalition-of-elite-schools-reshape-college-admissions .html.

CONCLUSION

1. Stacy Berg Dale and Alan Krueger, "Estimating the Payoff to Attending a More Selective College: An Application of Selection on Observables and Unobservables" (Working Paper No. 7322, National Bureau of Economic Research, August 1999), accessed June 2020, www.nber.org/papers/w7322; "Estimating the Return to College Selectivity over the Career Using Administrative Earnings Data" (Work-

ing Paper No. 17159, National Bureau of Economic Research, June 2011), accessed June 2020, www.nber.org/papers/w17159.

2. Thiel Fellowship, accessed June 2020, thielfellowship.org.

3. Matt Feeney, "The Poisonous Reach of the College Admissions Process," *New Yorker* online, January 28, 2016, accessed June 2020, www.newyorker.com/culture/cultural-comment/the-poisonous -reach-of-the-college-admissions-process.

Index

LAURA ARECHIGA

MATT FEENEY holds a PhD in political philosophy from Duke University, and he has written for the *New Yorker, Slate, Pacific Standard, National Review,* and *Weekly Standard.* He lives with his wife and three children in Oakland, California.